TELLING ABOUT SOCIETY

HOWARD S. BECKER

Telling About Society

The University of Chicago Press : Chicago and London

Howard S. Becker, a sociologist and pianist who lives in San Francisco, is the author of *Writing for Social Scientists* and *Tricks of the Trade.*

The University of Chicago Press, Chicago 60637
The University of Chicago Press, Ltd., London
© 2007 by The University of Chicago
All rights reserved. Published 2007
Printed in the United States of America

16 15 14 13 12 11 10 09 08 07   1 2 3 4 5

ISBN-13: 978-0-226-04125-4   (cloth)
ISBN-13: 978-0-226-04126-1   (paper)
ISBN-10: 0-226-04125-5   (cloth)
ISBN-10: 0-226-04126-3   (paper)

LIBRARY OF CONGRESS CATALOGING-IN-PUBLICATION DATA
Becker, Howard Saul, 1928–
  Telling about society / Howard S. Becker.
    p.   cm.
  Includes bibliographical references and index.
  ISBN-13: 978-0-226-04125-4 (cloth : alk. paper)
  ISBN-10: 0-226-04125-5 (cloth : alk. paper)
  ISBN-13: 978-0-226-04126-1 (pbk. : alk. paper)
  ISBN-10: 0-226-04126-3 (pbk. : alk. paper)
  1. Sociology—Methodology. 2. Visual sociology. 3. Sociology in literature. 4. Arts and society.   I. Title.
  HM511.B43 2007
  301.01—dc22

                                                2006103504

♾ The paper used in this publication meets the minimum requirements of the American National Standard for Information Sciences—Permanence of Paper for Printed Library Materials, ANSI Z39.48-1992.

To the memory of Michèle de la Pradelle, Dwight Conquergood,
Alain Pessin, and Eliot Freidson, friends and scholars

Contents

Illustrations

Preface

This was never a conventional research project. The ideas grew out of my habitually random and haphazard reading, years of teaching, and just plain living while being pretty eclectic in my interests.

I've always been a theater- and moviegoer and a tireless reader of fiction. I always thought I was learning interesting stuff about society when I did that, applying a rule I had formulated early in life, "If it's fun, it must be worth doing." So I was already primed with a good stock of examples to think about. I had seen Shaw's play *Mrs. Warren's Profession* and enjoyed its dissection of the "social problem" of prostitution, and so I had it in my mind when I started looking for examples. I had read Dickens and Jane Austen and had them as examples of how novelists presented social analysis.

In 1970 I learned, as part of my preparation for working in the sociology of the arts, to make photographs, taking classes at the San Francisco Art Institute and getting involved in the photographic world there and in Chicago. Documentary photographers worried with me about how to present the social analyses they wanted to make, as did the students I soon acquired, and I began to see how their problems resembled the ones social scientists (including myself) faced in telling what they had to tell.

I have never been good at reading the official literature of officially designated disciplines and fields and never thought social science had a monopoly on knowing what goes on in society. I found as many good ideas in fiction, drama, film, and photography as I did in what I was "supposed" to be reading. And the ideas that came to me as I looked at documentary photographic projects or film migrated to my thinking about conventional social science as well.

I did do some serious reading in the polemical literature every field generates about problems of method. That literature contains much of what you might gather if you interviewed participants in those debates. The problems they raise are ones that confront practitioners in those fields, and the extended published discussions were immensely useful. Of course, when I had the chance to talk to people about problems of representation in their specific line of work, I jumped at it, but I didn't do any systematic interviewing or data gathering.

Teaching affected the development of my thinking in two very specific cases. When I taught sociology at Northwestern, I had the good fortune to cross paths with the late Dwight Conquergood, who taught in the Department of Performance Studies in the School of Speech. Dwight studied what he called the "performative aspect of society," the way social life can be seen as a series of performances. More to the point, he often presented the results of his research—on Southeast Asian refugees, on Chicago gang members—in the form of performances. This was something I had tried to do, without any real training and with no great success, with my colleagues Michal McCall and Lori Morris in a pair of sociological performances (Becker, McCall, and Morris 1989; Becker and McCall 1990) reporting on our collaborative research on theater communities in three cities. So when Dwight and I met, it was a short step to the idea of teaching a class called "Performing Social Science" together. His students came from his department and the larger Theater Department of the School of Speech; mine came mostly from sociology. They included graduate students and undergraduates. We taught the class in 1990 and 1991, and both times the main activity of the class consisted of performances by students (and, the second time, the teachers as well) of something that might be considered social science. Our definition was inclusive, so the pieces people did came from a variety of fields—history, sociology, literature, drama—and from the inventiveness of the students themselves. I'll occasionally refer to these events, which often embodied the organizational, scientific, and aesthetic concerns I'm interested in.

A class called "Telling About Society" that I taught twice, once at the University of California–Santa Barbara and a year later at the University of Washington, also gave me a lot to think about. The participants in this little adventure came from several departments and consisted almost entirely of graduate students. This meant that they were, inevitably, less adventurous than the undergraduates Conquergood and I had worked with at Northwestern, having more to lose and more pressing claims on their time and attention. On the other hand, they were more thoughtful about the ramifications of the topic, more willing to be critical and argumentative, and therefore more likely to provoke me to reopen questions I'd thought settled.

The class sessions took up different media each week: film, drama, statistical tables, and so on. I assigned readings or, just as often, presented the class with something to react to, some provocation to their stereotyped ideas of what constituted an appropriate way to report on society. I began the first meeting of the class, the first time I taught it, by describing Caryl Churchill's *Mad Forest* (1996), a play about a marriage between the children of two Romanian families that differ substantially in social class. The second act of the play illustrated exactly what the class might be about, since it is an artistic representation of the process social scientists sometimes called "elementary collective behavior" or "crowd formation." Chapter 12 tells how I made the students read the act aloud and then insisted to them that they had not only experienced an emotion but had also read the best analysis I knew of crowd formation. Many of them agreed. And I told them that set the problem of the class. What ways, other than the ones social scientists knew, can convey such information? I think many of the students would not have accepted that question as willingly if they had not had the theatrical experience they had just given themselves.

In succeeding weeks we saw Anna Deveare Smith's video *Fire in Crown Heights* (2001), in which she says the things many people from many social groups had said to her after that episode of violence in Brooklyn. We saw Frederick Wiseman's *Titicutt Follies* (1967), a documentary film about a Massachusetts hospital for the criminally insane. We looked at and discussed a collection I had made of sociological tables and charts, and I taught a minicourse I was ill-prepared to teach in mathematical models. I designed the seminar meetings with plenty of concrete examples to discuss, hoping to avoid what I thought would be sterile "theoretical" talk. My scheming worked pretty well, and the discussions were good enough that I usually spent the next day typing notes about our discussion and the thoughts it had stimulated.

In the class syllabus, I had told the students:

> The basic strategy of the course is comparative. What's to be compared are a wide variety of genres of representation: from films, novels, and plays, on the one hand, to tables, charts, graphs, and mathematical models, on the other, and whatever else we can think of in between. They'll be compared with respect to the way they solve the generic problems of representing social life. And that list of problems will in part be generated by seeing what kinds of problems are prominent in each genre. (This will make more sense as we do it; I can see how it might seem a little cryptic right now.)
>
> You can think of the subject matter we'll work with as a grid. Along one axis, kinds of media or genres, as in the list above. Along the other axis, problems that arise in making representations: the influence of budgets, the ethical obligations of makers of representations, ways of generalizing what one knows, degrees of polyvocality, etc. In principle, we could investigate every problem in every genre, fill in every box generated by that cross-classification, but that's not practical. So our "coverage" will be more than a little haphazard, influenced mainly by the materials we have easily available to talk about and by my own particular interests. But the list of what's to talk about can be extended to deal with other genres and problems, as the will of the people dictates.

And that attitude created the organizational problem of this book.

Robert Merton liked to find propositions that exemplified what they asserted, most successfully in his ideas about self-fulfilling prophecies. Putting this material together put me in just that position. How could I represent my analysis of representations?

I had two kinds of material to work with: ideas about communities organized around making and using particular kinds of representations, like films or novels or statistical tables; and examples, extended discussions of reports on society exemplifying what had been done in some of these fields. Much of my thinking had been stimulated by thinking about successful works of social representation, particularly beyond the disciplinary fences of social science, and I wanted my results to embody and emphasize that.

Cross-tabulating kinds of media (films, plays, tables, models, and all the rest) by kinds of analytic problems (what is the division of labor between makers and users of representations, for instance) would generate a very large collection of combinations to write about. That kind of classificatory structure underlies what I've done, but I didn't want to feel obligated to fill in all those descriptive and analytic boxes. Nor did I think that such an encyclopedic approach would be useful for my purpose, which I began to see as opening my own eyes, and those of others in the fields I was interested in (which by now went beyond social science), to a larger realm of representational possibilities.

I took a different approach, heavily influenced by my experience of and experiments with hypertext, in which many textual fragments can be read in a variety of orders, sometimes in any order the user chooses. The parts are dependent on one another but not so much that a given order is obligatory. In this spirit, the book has two parts: "Ideas" consists of short essays on general topics that become clearer when seen as aspects of representational worlds. "Examples" contains a number of appreciations and analyses of specific works or bodies of work, or kinds of representations that took on new meaning for me when I saw them in the light of the general ideas. Pieces in the two sections refer to one another, and I mean the whole to look more like a network of thoughts and examples than a linear argument. This approach perhaps best suits a computer, which makes it so easy for a reader to move from topic to topic, but here you have it in a printed book. Sorry about that.

So you can, and should, read the material in these two sections in any order that suits you, within and between sections. The parts are meant both to stand alone and to illuminate each other. The full meaning results from the way you knit the pieces together for your own purposes, whatever they are. If this works as I hope it will, social scientists and artists with documentary interests will both find something they can use.

Chicago, 1985—San Francisco, 2006

Acknowledgments

This project began in the 1980s, when my colleagues at Northwestern University (notably Andrew C. Gordon) and I received a grant from the now defunct System Development Foundation to study "Modes of Representation of Society." This vague title was meant to encompass our various interests in photography, statistical graphics, theater, and almost any other medium anyone had ever used to tell others what they thought they knew about society. A number of people worked with us over several years, but we never produced the enormous report such a pompous title called for. I wrote a paper (which appears here in somewhat altered form in some of the chapters), and some other people wrote things too; we all wrote a mountain of memos; in the end we went our separate ways, and that seemed to be the end of it, the lack of a big book apparently justifying the gloomy prediction of one of the foundation's board members that nothing would come of this grant.

Sometime in the mid to late 1990s, I got interested in these questions again, and I taught a seminar—"Telling About Society"—in the spring of 1997, when I was a visitor in the Sociology Department of the University of California–Santa Barbara, and the following year at the University of Washington. Both classes stimulated my thinking about the topic. I wrote myself long memos after every class, which, in various transformations, have found their way into this book. I can't remember which class stimulated which ideas, so in what follows I refer to "the seminar" when I want to tell about something that happened in one or the other of those classes. The students in both were an adventurous bunch who were willing to waste a quarter on something that had no apparent professional utility, and I thank all of them for their rambunctious and argumentative participation, chief among the things that led me to write all those memos.

I won't try to list all the people whose conversation and example have influenced me these many years; it's too hard to remember, I'm sure to leave people out, and they know or can guess who they are. Dianne Hagaman helped in all the ways anyone could imagine and also, what people who don't know her might not think of, with her tremendous expertise, born of years of loving study, in the field of Jane Austen and *Pride and Prejudice* (I wouldn't have dared chapter 14 without her help).

Over the years, I have written a number of pieces for presentation and publication here and there, and I have used some of them, mostly transformed quite a bit, in parts of this book. The following appear, in whole or in part, in various chapters:

"Telling About Society," in Howard S. Becker, *Doing Things Together* (Evanston, IL: Northwestern University Press, 1986), 121–36: chapter 1.

"Categories and Comparisons: How We Find Meaning in Photographs," *Visual Anthropology Review* 14 (1998–1999): 3–10: chapter 3.

"Aesthetics and Truth," in Howard S. Becker, *Doing Things Together* (Evanston, IL: Northwestern University Press, 1986), 293–301: chapter 7.

"Visual Sociology, Documentary Photography, and Photojournalism: It's (Almost) All a Matter of Context," *Visual Sociology* 10 (1995): 5–14: chapter 11.

"La politique de la présentation: Goffman et les institutions totales," in *Erving Goffman et les institutions totales,* edited by Charles Amourous and Alain Blanc, 59–77 (Paris: L'Harmattan, 2001); and, in English, as "The Politics of Presentation: Goffman and Total Institutions," *Symbolic Interaction* 26 (2003): 659–69: chapter 13.

"Sociologie, sociographie, Perec, and Passeron," in *Le Goût de l'enquête: Pour Jean-Claude Passeron*, edited by Jean-Louis Fabiani, 289–311 (Paris: L'Harmattan, 2001); a shorter version appears in English as "Georges Perec's Experiments in Social Description," *Ethnography* 2 (2001): 63–76: chapter 15.

"Calvino, sociologue Urbain," in Howard S. Becker, *Paroles et musique* (Paris: L'Harmattan, 2003), 73–89: chapter 16.

Part I : Ideas

1

Telling About Society

I have lived for many years in San Francisco, on the lower slope of Russian Hill or in the upper reaches of North Beach; how I describe it depends on whom I am trying to impress. I live near Fisherman's Wharf, on the route many people take from that tourist attraction to their motel downtown or on Lombard Street's motel row. Looking out my front window, I often see small groups of tourists standing, alternately looking at their maps and at the large hills that stand between them and where they want to be. It's clear what has happened. The map's straight line looked like a nice walk through a residential neighborhood, one that might show them how the natives live. Now they are thinking, as a young Briton I offered to help said to me, "I've got to get to my motel and I am *not* climbing that bloody hill!"

Why don't the maps those people consult alert them to the hills? Cartographers know how to indicate hills, so it is not a restriction of the medium that inconveniences walkers. But the maps are made for motorists, originally (though no longer) paid for by gasoline companies and tire manufacturers, and distributed through service stations (Paumgarten 2006, 92)—and drivers worry less than pedestrians do about hills.

Those maps, and the networks of people and organizations who make and use them, exemplify a more general problem. An ordinary street map of San Francisco is a conventionalized representation of that urban society: a visual description of its streets and landmarks and of their arrangement in space. Social scientists and ordinary citizens routinely use not only maps but also a great variety of other representations of social reality—a few random examples are documentary films, statistical tables, and the stories people tell one another to explain who they are and what they are doing. All of them, like the maps, give a picture that is only partial but nevertheless adequate for some purpose. All of them arise in organizational settings, which constrain what can be done and define the purposes the work will have to satisfy. This understanding suggests several interesting problems: How do the needs and practices of organizations shape our descriptions and analyses (call them representations) of social reality? How do the people who use those representations come to define them as adequate? Such questions have a bearing on traditional questions about knowing and telling in science but go beyond them to include problems more traditionally associated with the arts and with the experience and analysis of everyday life.

For many years, I've been involved with a variety of ways of telling about society, professionally and out of native curiosity. I'm a sociologist, so the ways of telling that come most immediately to my mind are the ones sociologists routinely use: ethnographic description, theoretical discourse, statistical tables (and such visual representations of numbers as bar charts), historical narrative, and so on. But many years ago I went to art school and became a photographer, and in the process I developed a strong and lasting interest in photographic representations of society, which documentary and other photographers have been making since the invention of the medium. That led quite naturally to thinking about film as still another way of telling about society. And not just documentary films but fiction films as well. I'd been an avid reader of fiction since I was a kid, and like most other readers of stories, I knew that they are not just made-up fantasies, that they often contain observations worth reading about how society is constructed and works. Why not dramatic representations of stories on the stage too? Having always been interested and involved in all these ways of telling about society, I decided to take advantage of the somewhat haphazard and random collection of examples that had deposited in my brain.

To do what? To see the problems anyone who tries to do the job of representing society has to solve, what kinds of solutions have been found and tried, and with what results. To see what the problems of different media have in common and how solutions that work for one kind of telling look when you try them on some other kind. To see what, for instance, statistical tables have in common with documentary photographic projects, what mathematical models have in common with avant-garde fiction. To see what solutions to the problem of description one field might import from another.

So I'm interested in novels, statistics, histories, ethnographies, photographs, films, and any other way people have tried to tell others what they know about their society or some other society that interests them. I'll call the products of all this activity in all these media "reports about society" or, sometimes, "representations of society." What problems and issues arise in making those reports, in whatever medium? I've constructed a list of those issues from the things people who do this kind of work talk and complain about to each other, using as a basic principle of discovery this idea: if it's a problem in one way of making representations, it's a problem in every way of doing so. But the people who work in one area may have solved that problem to their own satisfaction, so that they don't even think of it as a problem, while for other people it seems an insoluble dilemma. Which means that the latter can learn something from the former.

I've been inclusive in making these comparisons, encompassing (at least in principle) every medium and genre people use or have ever used. Of course, I haven't talked about everything. But I have tried to avoid the most obvious conventional biases and have considered, in addition to reputable scientific formats and those invented and used by professionals in recognized scientific disciplines, those used by artists and laypeople as well. A list will suggest this range of topics: from the social sciences, such modes of representation as mathematical models, statistical tables and graphs, maps, ethnographic prose, and historical narrative; from the arts, novels, films, still photographs, and drama; from the large shadowy area in between, life histories and other biographical and autobiographical materials, reportage (including the mixed genres of docudrama, documentary film, and fictionalized fact), and the storytelling, mapmaking, and other representational activities of laypeople (or people acting in a lay capacity, as even professionals do most of the time).

Who Tells?

We are all curious about the society we live in. We need to know, on the most routine basis and in the most ordinary way, how our society works. What rules govern the organizations we participate in? What routine patterns of behavior do others engage in? Knowing these things, we can organize our own behavior, learn what we want, how to get it, what it will cost, what opportunities of action various situations offer us.

Where do we learn this stuff? Most immediately, from our experience of daily living. We interact with all sorts of people and groups and organizations. We talk to people of all kinds in all kinds of situations. Of course, not *all* kinds: everyone's social experience of that face-to-face kind is limited by their social connections, their situation in society, their economic resources, their geographical location. You can get by with that limited knowledge, but in modern societies (probably in all societies) we need to know more than what we learn from personal experience. We need, or at least want, to know about other people and places, other situations, other times, other ways of life, other possibilities, other opportunities.

So we look for "representations of society," in which other people tell us about all those situations and places and times we don't know firsthand but would like to know about. With the additional information, we can make more complex plans and react in a more complex way to our own immediate life situations.

Simply put, a "representation of society" is something someone tells us about some aspect of social life. That definition covers a lot of territory. At one extreme lie the ordinary representations we make for one another, as lay folks, in the course of daily life. Take mapmaking. In many situations and for many purposes, this is a highly professionalized activity based on centuries of combined practical experience, mathematical reasoning, and scientific scholarship. But in many other situations, it's an ordinary activity we all do once in a while. I ask you to visit me sometime, but you don't know how to drive to where I live. I can give you verbal directions: "Coming from Berkeley, you take the first exit on the right off the Bay Bridge, turn left at the bottom of the ramp, go several blocks and turn left on to Sacramento, keep going until you hit Kearny, turn right and go up to Columbus . . ." I can suggest you consult a standard street map along with my directions, or I can just tell you that I live near the intersection of Lombard and Jones and let you use the map to find that spot. Or I can draw my own little map, personalized for you. I can show where you would start from—"your house"—and draw in the relevant streets, indicating where you should turn, how long each leg will be, what landmarks you will pass, and how you will know when you reach "my house." These days an Internet site will tell you all that, or you can let your GPS device do it for you.

Those are all representations of a portion of society, contained in a simple geographical relationship; a simpler and better way of saying it is that these are all ways of telling about society or some portion thereof. Some of the ways, the standard automobile map or the computer description, are made by highly trained professionals using a lot of specialized equipment and knowledge. The verbal description and the homemade map are made by people just like the people to whom they are given, people who have no more geographical knowledge or ability than any ordinarily competent adult. They all work, in different ways, to do the job of leading someone from one place to another.

My own professional colleagues—sociologists and other social scientists—like to talk as though they have a monopoly on creating such representations, as though the knowledge of society they produce is the only "real" knowledge about that subject. That's not true. And they like to make the equally silly claim that the ways they have of telling about society are the best ways to do that job or the only way it can be done properly, or that their ways of doing the job guard against all sorts of terrible mistakes we would otherwise make.

That kind of talk is just a standard professional power grab. Considering the ways that people who work in other fields—visual artists, novelists, playwrights, photographers, and filmmakers—as well as laypeople represent society will show analytic dimensions and possibilities that social science has often ignored that might otherwise be useful. I will concentrate on the representational work done by other kinds of workers, as well as that done by social scientists. Social scientists know how to do their job, and that's adequate for many purposes. But their ways aren't the only ways.

What are some of the other ways? We can categorize representational activities in many ways. We could talk about media—film vs. words vs. numbers, for instance. We might talk about the intent of the makers of the representations: science vs. art vs. reportage. Such a comprehensive review would serve many purposes well, but not my purpose of exploring generic problems of representation and the variety of solutions the world has so far produced. Looking at some major, highly organized ways of telling about society means attending to the distinctions among science, art, and reportage. Those are not so much distinct ways of doing something as they are ways of organizing what might be, from the point of view of materials and methods, pretty much the same activity. (Later, in chapter 11, I'll compare three ways of using still photographs to do those three kinds of work, seeing how the same photographs might be art, journalism, or social science.)

Telling about society usually involves an interpretive community, an organization of people who routinely make standardized representations of a particular kind ("makers") for others ("users") who routinely use them for standardized purposes. The makers and users have adapted what they do to what the others do, so that the organization of making and using is, at least for a while, a stable unity, a *world* (used in a technical sense I've developed elsewhere [Becker 1982] and will discuss more fully below).

Often enough, some people don't fit well into these organized worlds of makers and users. These experimenters and innovators don't do things as they are usually done, and therefore their works may not have many users. But their solutions to standard problems tell us a lot and open our eyes to possibilities more conventional practice doesn't see. Interpretive communities often borrow procedures and forms, using them to do something the originators in that other community never thought of or intended, producing mixtures of method and style to fit into changing conditions in the larger organizations they belong to.

This is all very abstract. Here's a more specific list of standard formats for telling about society, which have produced exemplary works of social representation worth inspecting carefully:

Fiction. Works of fiction, novels and stories, have often served as vehicles of social analysis. The sagas of families, classes, and professional groups by writers as dissimilar in aims and talent as Honoré de Balzac, Émile Zola, Thomas Mann, C. P. Snow, and Anthony Powell have always been understood to embody, and to depend on for their power and aesthetic virtues, complex descriptions of social life and its constituent processes. The works of Charles Dickens, taken singly and as a whole, have been understood (as he intended them to be) as a way of describing to a large public the organizations that produced the ills his society suffered from.

Drama. Similarly, the theater has often been a vehicle for the exploration of social life, most especially the description and analysis of social ills. George Bernard Shaw used the dramatic form to embody his understanding of how "social problems" came about and how deeply they penetrated the body politic. His *Mrs. Warren's Profession* explains the workings of the business of prostitution as it provided the livelihood of at least some of the British upper classes; and *Major Barbara* did the same for war and munitions making. Many playwrights have used drama for similar purposes (Henrik Ibsen, Arthur Miller, David Mamet).

To say that these works and authors deal in social analysis doesn't mean that that is "all" they do or that their works are "only" sociology in artistic disguise. Not at all. Their authors have purposes in mind beyond social analysis. But even the most formalist critic should realize that some part of the effect of many works of art depends on their "sociological" content and on the belief of readers and audiences that what these works tell them about society is, in some sense, "true."

Films. In the most obvious case, documentary film—Barbara Koppel's 1976 *Harlan County, U.S.A.* and Edgar Morin and Jean Rouch's 1961 *Chronique d'un été* are well known examples—has had as a primary object the description of society, often, but not necessarily overtly, in a reformist mode, aiming to show viewers what's wrong with current social arrangements. Fiction films also often mean to analyze and comment on the societies they present, many times those in which they are made. Examples range from Gillo Pontecorvo's pseudodocumentary *Battle of Algiers* (1966) to classic Hollywood fare like Elia Kazan's 1947 *Gentleman's Agreement*.

Photographs. Likewise, still photographers have, from the beginnings of the genre, often occupied themselves with social analysis. A well-defined genre of documentary photography has had a long and illustrious history. Some exemplary works of that genre include Brassaï's *The Secret Paris of the '30s* (1976), Walker Evans's *American Photographs* ([1938] 1975), and Robert Frank's *The Americans* ([1959] 1969).

So far I have talked about "artistic" modes of making representations of society. Other representations are more associated with "science."

Maps. Maps, associated with the discipline of geography (more specifically, cartography), are an efficient way of displaying large amounts of information about social units considered in their spatial dimension.

Tables. The invention of the statistical table in the eighteenth century made it possible to summarize vast numbers of specific observations in a compact and comparable format. These compact descriptions help governments and others organize purposeful social action. A governmental census is the classical form of such use. Scientists use tables to display data others can use to evaluate their theories. Twentieth-century social scientists became increasingly dependent on the tabular display of quantitative data gathered specifically for that purpose.

Mathematical models. Some social scientists have described social life by reducing it to abstract entities displayed as mathematical models. These models, intentionally removed from social reality, can convey basic relations characteristic of social life. They have been used to analyze such varied social phenomena as kinship systems and the world of commercial popular music.

Ethnography. A classic form of social description has been the ethnography, a detailed verbal description of the way of life, considered in its entirety, of some social unit, archetypally but not necessarily a small tribal group. The method came to be applied, and is widely applied now, to organizations of all kinds: schools, factories, urban neighborhoods, hospitals, and social movements.

Somewhere between the extremes of art and science lie history and biography, usually devoted to detailed and accurate accounts of past events but often equally given to evaluating large generalizations about matters the other social sciences deal with. (Remember that all of today's sociological reports will be raw material for historians of the future, as masterworks of sociology like the Lynds' studies of "Middletown" have turned from social analysis into historical document.)

Finally, there are the sports, mavericks, and innovators I spoke of earlier. Some makers of representations of society mix methods and genres, experiment with forms and languages, and provide analyses of social phenomena in places we don't expect them and in forms we don't recognize as either art or science or that we see as some unusual and unfamiliar mixture of genres. So Hans Haacke, who can be called a conceptual artist, uses uncomplicated devices to lead users to unexpected conclusions. Georges Perec and Italo Calvino, members of the French literary group OULIPO (Motte 1998) devoted to esoteric literary experiments, made the novel, in one form or another, a vehicle for subtle sociological thinking. And in David Antin's "talk pieces," stories that may or may not be fictions convey complex social analyses and ideas. Like all such experiments, the work of these artists forces us to reconsider procedures we usually take for granted, and I'll discuss their work at length later in the book.

Facts

I must make an important distinction, even though it is fallacious and misleading and every word involved is slippery and indeterminate. I don't think those faults make much difference for my purpose here. It's the distinction between "fact" and "idea" (or "interpretation"). One part of any report on society (of any of the kinds I've just outlined) is a description of how things are: how some kinds of things are, in some place, at some time. This is how many people there are in the United States, as counted in the year 2000 by the U.S. Bureau of the Census. This is how many of them are women and how many are men. This is the age distribution of that population—so many below five, so many aged five to ten, all the way up. This is the racial composition of that population. This is the distribution of their incomes. This is that income distribution in racial and gender subgroups of the population.

Those are facts about the U.S. population (and, of course, similar facts are more or less available for all the other countries in the world). They are descriptions of what a person who went looking for such numbers would find, the evidence that results from the operations demographers and statisticians have undertaken in accordance with the procedures of their craft.

In the same way, anthropologists tell us, for instance, how *these* people living in *this* society reckon kinship: they recognize these categories of familial relationship and think this is how people related in those ways should behave toward one another; these are, in the classical phrase, their mutual rights and obligations. Anthropologists support their analyses with accounts of the facts about how those people talk and behave, contained in the field notes that report their on-the-spot observations and interviews, just as demographers support descriptions of the U.S. population with the data produced by the census. In either case, the professionals begin with evidence gathered in ways their craft peers recognize as sufficient to warrant the factual status of the results.

Now for the caveats. Thomas Kuhn long ago persuaded me that facts are never just facts but are rather, as he said, "theory-laden" (1970). Every statement of a fact presupposes a theory that explains what entities are out there to describe, what characteristics they can have, which of those characteristics can be observed and which can only be inferred from characteristics that are observable, and so on.

Theories often seem so obvious as to be self-evident. Does anyone need to argue that you can tell a human being when you see one and distinguish such a being from some other kind of animal? Does it need arguing that these human beings can be characterized as male or female? Or as black, white, Asian, or of another racial variety?

In fact, scientists and laypeople argue about things like that all the time, as the continually shifting racial categories in censuses all over the world make clear. Characteristics like gender and race don't appear in nature in an obvious way. Every society has ways of telling boys from girls and distinguishing members of racial categories its members think are important from one another. But these categories rest on theories about the essential characteristics of humans, and the nature of the categories and the methods of assigning people to them vary between societies. So we can never take facts for granted. There are no pure facts, only "facts" that take on meaning from an underlying theory.

Moreover, facts are facts only when they are accepted as such by the people to whom those facts are relevant. Am I indulging in a pernicious kind of relativism, or malicious wordplay? Maybe, but I don't think we have to discuss whether there is an ultimate reality science will eventually reveal in order to recognize that reasonable people, including reasonable scientists, often disagree on what constitutes a fact, and when a fact really is a fact. Those disagreements arise because scientists often disagree on what constitutes adequate evidence for the existence of a fact. Bruno Latour (1987, 23–29) has demonstrated, well enough to suit me and many others, that, as he so neatly puts it, the fate of a scientific finding lies in the hands of those who take it up afterward. If they accept it as fact, it will be treated as fact. Does that mean that any damn thing can be a fact? No, because one of the "actants," to use Latour's inelegant expression, that must agree with the interpretation is the object about which the statements of fact are made. I can say the moon is made of green cheese, but the moon will have to cooperate, exhibiting those characteristics that other people will recognize as green cheese–like, or else my fact will become an unacceptable nonfact. Worse yet, my fact may not even be disputed; it may just be ignored, so that you might say it doesn't exist at all, at least not in the discourse of scientists who study the moon. There may be an ultimate reality, but we are all fallible human beings and may be wrong, so all facts are disputable in the real world we live in. That fact is at least as obdurate and hard to talk away as any other scientific fact.

Finally, facts are not accepted in general or by the world at large, they are accepted or rejected by the particular audiences their proponents present them to. Does this mean science is situational and its findings therefore not universally true? I'm not taking a position on such ultimate questions of epistemology, just recognizing what's obvious: when we make a report about society, we make it to somebody, and who those somebodies are affects how we present what we know and how users react to what we present to them. Audiences differ— this is important—in what they know and know how to do, in what they believe and will accept, on faith or with evidence of some kind. Different kinds of reports routinely go to different kinds of audiences: statistical tables to people more or less trained to read them, mathematical models to people with highly specialized training in the relevant disciplines, photographs to a wide variety of lay and professional audiences, and so on.

Instead of facts supported by evidence that makes them acceptable as fact, then, we have facts based on a theory, accepted by some people because they have been gathered in a way acceptable to some community of makers and users.

Interpretations

It's not easy to separate interpretations from facts. Every fact, in its social context, implies and invites interpretations. People move easily and without much thought from one to the other. The same facts will support many interpretations. To say, to take a provocative example, that racial groups differ in IQ scores might well be a fact—that is, demonstrated by the use of tests commonly used by psychologists who make a business of such measurement. But to interpret such a finding as a demonstration that such differences are genetic—inherited and thus not easily changed—is not a fact, it's an interpretation of the meaning of the reported fact. An alternate interpretation says the fact demonstrates that the IQ test is culture specific and can't be used to compare different populations.

Neither do the findings about race, gender, and income we can find in the U.S. Census speak for themselves. Someone speaks for them, interpreting their meaning. People argue more about interpretations than they do about facts. We can agree on the numbers describing the relations between gender, race, and income, but the same census data might be interpreted to show the existence of discrimination, the lessening of discrimination, the joint working of two disadvantaged conditions (being female, being black) on income, or many other possible stories.

A report about society, then, is an artifact consisting of statements of fact, based on evidence acceptable to some audience, and interpretations of those facts similarly acceptable to some audience.

2

Representations of Society as Organizational Products

People who gather facts about society and interpret them don't start from scratch every time they report. They use forms, methods, and ideas that some social group, large or small, already has available as a way of doing that job.

Reports on society (remember that *representation* and *report* refer to the same thing) make most sense when you see them in organizational context, as activities, as ways some people tell what they think they know to other people who want to know it, as organized activities shaped by the joint efforts of everyone involved. It's a confusing error to focus on nouns rather than verbs, on the objects rather than the activities, as though we were investigating tables or charts or ethnographies or movies. It makes more sense to see those artifacts as the frozen remains of collective action, brought to life whenever someone uses them—as people's making and reading charts or prose, making and seeing films. We should understand the expression *a film* as shorthand for the activity of "making a film" "or "seeing a film."

That's a distinction with a difference. Concentrating on the object misdirects our attention to the formal and technical capabilities of a medium: how many bits of information a television monitor with a particular degree of resolution can convey, or whether a purely visual medium can communicate such logical notions as causality. Concentrating on organized activity, on the other hand, shows that what a medium can do is always a function of the way organizational constraints affect its use. What photographs can convey depends in part on the budget of the photographic project, which limits how many photographs can be used and how they can be displayed, how much money will be spent making them (put another way, how much photographers' time will be paid for), and the amount and kind of attention viewers will put into interpreting them.

Seeing reports about society organizationally means bringing all aspects of the organizations in which they are made into the analysis: bureaucratic structures, budgets, professional codes, and audience characteristics and abilities all impinge on telling about society. Workers decide how to go about making representations by seeing what is possible, logical, feasible, and desirable, given the conditions under which they are making them and the people they are making them for.

It makes sense to speak, in rough analogy to the idea of an art world (Becker 1982), of worlds of makers and users of representations: the worlds of documentary film or statistical graphics, of mathematical modeling or anthropological monographs. These worlds consist of all the people and artifacts whose activities of making and using center on a particular kind of representation: all the cartographers, scientists, data gatherers, printers, designers, corporations, geography departments, pilots, ship captains, drivers, and pedestrians whose cooperation makes up a world of maps, for instance.

These worlds differ in the relative knowledge and power of makers and users. In highly professionalized worlds, professionals mostly make artifacts for use by other professionals: scientific researchers make their reports and inscriptions (Latour and Woolgar 1979; Latour 1983, 1986, 1987) for colleagues who know as much (or almost as much) about the work as they do. In the extreme case, makers and users are the same people—a situation almost realized in such esoteric worlds as mathematical modeling.

Members of more differentiated worlds usually share some basic knowledge, despite the differences in their actual work. That's why sociology students who will never do statistical work learn the latest versions of multivariate statistical analysis. Other professionals, however, do much of their work for lay users: cartographers make maps for motorists who know just enough about cartography to get to the next town, and filmmakers make movies for people who never heard of a jump cut. (Of course, these professionals usually worry about what their professional peers will think of their work as well.) Lay-people tell stories, make maps, and write down figures for each other too. What gets made, communicated, and understood varies among these typical kinds of settings.

This makes it useless to talk of media or forms in the abstract, although I already have and will continue to. Abstract terms like *film* or *statistical table* not only need active verbs like *making* or *seeing* to have meaning but are also shorthand for more contextually specific formulations like *tables made for the census* or *big-budget feature films made in Hollywood*. The organizational constraints of the census and Hollywood are best thought of as integral parts of the artifacts made in those places. So my focus differs from a more common and conventional one, which treats the artifact as the main thing and the activities through which it is produced and consumed as secondary.

The form and content of representations vary because social organizations vary. Social organization shapes not only what gets made but also what users want the representation to do, what job they think needs doing (like finding your way to your friend's house or knowing what the latest findings in your field are), and what standards they will use to judge it. Because the jobs that users call on representations to do depend so heavily on organizational definitions, I'm not concerned with what many people think is a major methodological problem (indeed *the* problem): given a particular representational job to be done, what is the best way to do it? If that were the question, you could set up a task—to communicate an array of numbers, for example—and then see which way of organizing a table or chart would communicate that information most honestly, adequately, and efficiently (as people compare computers by seeing how fast they can find prime numbers). I've avoided judgments about the adequacy of any mode of representation, not taking any of them as the yardstick against which all other methods should be judged. Nor have I adopted the slightly more relativistic position that, while the jobs to be done may differ, there is a best way of doing each kind of job. That isn't relativistic asceticism on my part either. It seems more useful, more likely to lead to new understanding of representations, to think of every way of representing social reality as *perfect*—for something. The question is, *what* something is it good for? The answer to that is organizational: since the organization of that area of social life has made one (or more) of the jobs the representation might do the one(s) that must be done, users and makers alike will judge every method according to its efficiency and reliability in producing the most satisfactory result, or maybe just a less unsatisfactory result than, other available possibilities.

Despite superficial differences between genres and media, the same fundamental problems occur in all of them. The influence of budgets, the role of professionalization, what knowledge audiences must have for a representation to be effective, what is ethically permissible in making a representation—all these are common to every form of representation making. How these problems are dealt with varies depending on organizational resources and purposes.

Such problems are debated in every field that makes representations. Novelists worry about the same ethical dilemmas sociologists and anthropologists do, and filmmakers share social scientists' concern about budgets. The literature of those debates, and informal observations and interviews in those fields, has given me a lot of data. I've also found work in the sociology of science, concerned with problems of representation and rhetoric, very helpful (see, for instance, Gusfield 1976; 1981, especially 83–108; Latour and Bastide 1986; Bazerman 1988; Clifford 1988; Geertz 1983).

Transformations

Scientists, as Latour describes them, continually transform their materials. They begin with an observation in the laboratory or field and turn that into writing in a notebook, the notes into a table, the table into a chart, the chart into a conclusion, the conclusion into the title of an article. At each step, the observation becomes more abstract, more divorced from the concreteness of its original setting. Latour shows, in a description of French soil scientists working in Brazil (Latour 1995), how these transformations occur: how a clod of dirt changes into a piece of scientific evidence when the scientist puts it in a box and makes it part of an array of similar, comparable clods from other parts of the parcel of land under study. This, Latour says, is what the work of science is: transforming objects so that they can be used to "show" or "demonstrate" what the scientist wants to persuade others of.

Scientists make these transformations in standardized ways, using standard instruments to do standard operations on standardized materials and report the results in standardized ways, designed to give users what they need to judge the ideas presented without burdening them with other material they don't need. What's needed is established by convention. You need everything that answers possible questions and nothing to do with what no one will question. We can look for similar operations in the making of every kind of representation of social life. What raw materials do the makers start with? What transformations do they put the materials through?

Latour says that the fate of a scientific argument or finding is always in the hands of later users; they decide whether it will be rejected or accepted and incorporated into the body of fact everyone in that science accepts (1987, 29). Which users make these important decisions is always a relevant question.

In some worlds the representation soon leaves the "inside" world of the makers, experts, and adepts and enters lay worlds, in which what users make of the object may vary considerably from what the makers intended. Makers try to control what users make of their representation, building constraints into it that limit the uses and interpretations viewers can make. But authors often have the bizarre experience of hearing readers explain that their work means something that they have gone to a lot of trouble to prevent it from meaning.

Here's a checklist of interesting questions to be asked about the transformations that materials undergo in the hands of makers and users in any representational world.

- What route does the object follow once it leaves the original makers?
- What do the people into whose hands it falls at each stage make of it?
- What do they need or want it for?
- What equipment do they have for interpreting it?

- What elements, built into the object, constrain viewing and interpretation?
- How do makers head off alternate interpretations?
- How do they prevent users from making this or that of it?
- Latour says a scientific fact is a statement that has withstood tests that tried to deny its existence (1987, 74–79, 87–90). Who applies what tests to representations of society?
- In what typical arenas of testing are representations presented (journals, theaters, etc.), and where do people who have an interest in seeing if they are true do the testing?

Making Representations

Any representation of social reality—a documentary film, a demographic study, a realistic novel—is necessarily partial, less than what you would experience and have available to interpret if you were in the actual setting it represents. That's, after all, why people make representations: to report only what users need in order to do whatever they want to do. An efficient representation tells you everything you need to know for your purposes, without wasting your time with what you don't need. Because everyone expects these artifacts to be trimmed down that way, makers and users of representations must perform several operations on the reality they experience to get to the final understanding they want to communicate. Social organization affects the making and use of representations by affecting how makers go through these operations.

SELECTION : Every medium, in any of its conventional uses, leaves out much, in fact most, of reality. Even media that seem more comprehensive than the obviously abstract words and numbers social scientists usually use leave practically everything out. Film (still or moving) and video leave out the third dimension, smells, and tactile sensations and are inevitably a small sample of the entire span of time during which the represented events took place (although Andy Warhol's film *Empire State* lasted the full eight hours of the event it portrayed—someone sleeping). Written representations usually, but not necessarily, leave out all the visual elements of experience (it still surprises readers when a novelist like W. G. Seybald [2001] incorporates photographs into his story). Every medium leaves out whatever happens after we stop our representational activities. It describes whatever-it-is up to now, and then it stops. Some sociologists point out that numerical representations leave out the human element, or emotions, or symbolically negotiated meaning—these scholars use the criterion of completeness to criticize work they don't like. But no one, neither users nor makers, ever regards incompleteness in itself as a crime. Instead, they recognize it as the way you do that sort of thing. Road maps, tremendously abstract and incomplete renderings of the geographic reality they represent, satisfy even the sternest critic of incomplete representations. They contain just what drivers need to get from one place to another (even if they do sometimes mislead pedestrians).

Since any representation always and necessarily leaves out elements of reality, the interesting and researchable questions are these: Which of the possible elements are included? Who finds that selection reasonable and acceptable? Who complains about it? What criteria do people apply when they make those judgments? Some criteria, to suggest the possibilities, are genre related ("if it doesn't include this [or does include that] it isn't really a novel [or photograph or ethnography or table or . . .]") or professional ("that's how *real* statisticians [or filmmakers or historians or . . .] always do it").

TRANSLATION : Think of translation as a function that maps one set of elements (the parts of reality that makers want to represent) onto another set of elements (the conventional ones available in the medium as it is currently used). Anthropologists turn their on-the-spot observations into field notes, from which they construct standardized ethnographic descriptions; survey researchers turn field interviews into numbers, out of which they create tables and charts; historians combine their index cards into narratives, character sketches, and analyses; filmmakers edit and splice raw footage into shots, scenes, and movies. Users of representations never deal with reality itself but rather with reality translated into the materials and conventional language of a particular craft.

Standard ways of making representations give makers a standard set of elements to use in constructing their artifacts, including materials and their capabilities: film with a particular light sensitivity, so many grains of light-sensitive material per square inch and thus a particular degree of resolution, which makes possible the representation of elements of a certain size but not smaller; conceptual elements, like the idea of plot or character in fiction; and conventional units of meaning, like the wipes, fades, and other transitional cinematic devices that indicate the passage of time.

Makers expect standard elements to have standard effects, so that consumers of representations made with those effects will respond in standard ways. And users expect the same thing in reverse: that makers will use standard elements they are familiar with and know how to respond to. Representations made when that condition obtains—when everything works exactly as it understood to by all the parties involved—are "perfect." Everything works just as everyone expects it will. But that condition never exists completely. Materials don't behave as advertised. Audiences don't understand what the maker thought they would. The available language can't, after all, express the maker's idea. What happens when these inevitably inadequate representations are presented to an audience that does not know what it should know? Often enough, most people, makers and users alike—and especially those whose opinion counts, because they are powerful and important—respond near enough to what the original makers intended that the result is "acceptable" to everyone involved.

The criteria defining acceptability vary. Take the issue of the "transparency" of the prose, tables, and pictures people use to report scientific results. Both the makers and users of scientific representations would like the verbal, numerical, and visual languages they use in their articles and reports to be neutral standard elements that add nothing to what is being reported. Like a clear glass window, they would allow results to be seen through them without being affected by being seen through anything. Kuhn, as I noted earlier, argued persuasively that no such "transparent" descriptive scientific language is possible, that all descriptions are "theory laden" (1970). More to the point, it is clear that even the width of bars in a bar chart and the size and style of type in a table, let alone the nouns and adjectives in an ethnography or historical narrative, affect our interpretation of what is reported. Wide bars in a chart make us feel that the quantities reported are larger than we might think if the bars were narrow. When we conventionally call users of illegal drugs "abusers" or "addicts," we communicate a lot more than a scientifically defined "fact." But all these methods of portraying social reality have been acceptable to scientific and lay audiences alike, whose members taught themselves to accept or ignore or discount for the unwanted effects of the communicative elements they accepted as standard.

Standard elements have the features already found in investigations of art worlds. They make efficient communication of ideas and facts possible by creating a shorthand known to everyone who needs the material. But they simultaneously constrain what a maker can do, because every set of translations makes saying some things easier while making saying other things more difficult. To take a contemporary example, social scientists conventionally represent race and gender discrimination in job promotions in a multiple-regression equation, a standard statistical technique whose results show what proportion of the variation in promotions among subgroups in a population is due to the independent effects of such separate variables as race, gender, education, and seniority. But as Charles Ragin, Susan Meyer, and Kriss Drass showed (1984), that way of representing discrimination does not answer the questions sociologists interested in general social processes ask or those that courts trying to decide whether laws against racial discrimination have been broken ask. The results of a multiple regression cannot tell you how the chances for promotion of a young white male differ from those of an older black female; they can tell you only the weight of a variable like age or gender in an equation, not at all the same thing. Ragin, Meyer, and Drass advocate making another statistical element standard: the Boolean algorithm (details can be found in the article just cited or in Becker 1998, 183–94), which represents discrimination as the differences in chances of promotion for a person with a particular combination of those attributes as compared to mean rates for a whole population. This *is* what social scientists and courts want to know. (Related and complementary arguments are made in Lieberson 1985.)

Some constraints on what a representation can tell us arise from the way representational activity is organized. Organizationally constrained budgets—time and attention as well as money—limit the potential of media and formats. Books and movies are as long as makers can afford to make them and as users will pay attention to. If makers had more money and users would sit still for it, every ethnography might contain every field note the anthropologist made and every step in the analytic process (which Clyde Kluckhohn [1945] thought the only proper way to publish life history materials). These elements can still be provided, but not at a price in time or money anyone will pay.

ARRANGEMENT : The elements of the situation, the facts a representation describes, having been chosen and translated, and the interpretations it makes of them must be arranged in some order so that users can grasp what is being said. The order given to elements is both *arbitrary*—you can always see another way to have done it—and *determined* by standard ways of doing things, just as the elements are. Arrangement makes narratives out of random elements. It communicates such notions as causality, so that viewers see the order of photographs on a gallery wall or in a book as meaningful, interpreting earlier pictures in the arrangement as the "conditions" that produced the "consequences" depicted in the later ones. When I tell a story (personal, historical, or sociological), listeners will hear the earlier elements as "explanations" of those that come later; a character's actions in one episode become evidence for a personality that reveals itself fully in later ones. Students of statistical tables and graphics are particularly sensitive to the effects of arrangement on interpretations.

No maker of representations of society can avoid this issue, since, as many studies have shown, users of representations see order and logic even in random arrangements of elements. People find logic in the arrangement of photographs whether the photographer intended it or not, and they respond to typefaces as "frivolous," "serious," or "scientific," independent of a text's content. Social scientists and methodologists have yet to treat this as a serious problem; what to do about it is one of the things that get passed on as professional lore. (Edward Tufte [1983, 1990], however, has devoted a lot of attention to the way graphical and typographical elements and arrangements affect the interpretation of statistical displays.)

INTERPRETATION : Representations exist fully only when someone is using them, reading or viewing or listening and thus completing the communication by interpreting the results and constructing for themselves a reality out of what the maker showed them. The road map exists when I use it to get to the next town, Dickens's novels when I read them and imagine Victorian England, a statistical table when I inspect it and evaluate the propositions it suggests. These things reach their full potential in use.

What users know how to do interpretively thus becomes a major constraint on what a representation can accomplish. Users must know and be capable of using the conventional elements and formats of the medium and genre. Makers can't take that knowledge and ability for granted. Historical studies (e.g., Cohen 1982) have shown that it was not until well into the nineteenth century that most inhabitants of the United States were "numerate," capable of understanding and using standard arithmetic operations. Anthropological studies show that what such literary critics as Roland Barthes and Susan Sontag insist is the universal appeal to our sense of reality embodied in still photographs and film is instead a learned skill. Professionalized fields expect users to become knowledgeable consumers of representations through training in graduate or professional school, although what is expected to be known varies from time to time. Sociology graduate departments expect their students to acquire a certain amount of statistical sophistication (for which read, in part, "ability to read formulas and tables"), but few expect their students to know much about mathematical models.

Users interpret representations by finding the answers to two kinds of questions in them. On the one hand, they want to know "the facts": what happened at the battle of Bull Run, where the slum communities of Los Angeles are located, what the median income of white-collar suburbs is, what the correlation is between race, income, and education in the United States in 1980, what it is "really like" to be an astronaut. The answers to questions like these, at every level of specificity, help people orient their actions. On the other hand, users want answers to moral questions: not just what the correlation between race, education, and income is but why the correlation is what it is, whose fault it is, and what ought to be done about it. They want to know whether the Civil War, and thus the battle of Bull Run, was "necessary" or could have been prevented, whether astronaut John Glenn was the kind of man who deserved to be president; and so on. On the most superficial inspection, almost any factual question about society displays a strong moral dimension, which accounts for the ferocious battles that often occur over what seem to be minor matters of technical interpretation. Arthur Jensen's statistical mistakes in the analysis of intelligence test results upset people who were not statisticians.

Users and Makers

We all act as both users and makers of representations, telling stories and listening to them, making causal analyses and reading them. As in any other service relationship, the interests of makers and users usually differ considerably, particularly when, as so often, the makers are professionals who make those representations full time for pay and the users are amateurs who use them occasionally, in a habitual and uninspected way (see the classic analysis of routine and emergency in Hughes 1984, 316–25). Representational worlds differ in which set of interests dominates.

In worlds dominated by makers, representations take the form of an *argument*, a presentation of just that material that makes the points the maker wants to get across and no more (current work on the rhetoric of scientific writing, mentioned earlier, makes this point). In a professionalized world of representation making, makers usually control the circumstances of the making, for all the reasons Hughes pointed out: what is out of the ordinary for most users of their results is what they do all day long. Even if others have substantial power, professionals know so much more about how to manipulate the process that they retain great control. Powerful users who support representation making over a long period of time typically learn enough to overcome that disability, but casual users seldom do. So professionally made representations embody the choices and interests of makers and, indirectly, of the people who can afford to hire them, and thus may well not show the hills a pedestrian would like to know about.

The members of user-dominated worlds, on the other hand, use representations as *files*, archives to be ransacked for answers to whatever questions any competent user might have in mind and for information to be put to whatever use the users would like. Think of the difference between the street map you buy at the store and the detailed, annotated map I draw to show *you* how to get to *my* house, a map that takes into account the time you have available for the trip, your possible interest in seeing a few interesting sights, and your aversion to heavy traffic. Lay representations are typically more localized and more responsive to user wishes than are those made by professionals. Similarly, amateur snapshots satisfy their makers' need for documents to show to a circle of intimates who know everyone in the pictures, while the photographs made by journalists, artists, and social scientists, oriented to the standards of professional communities, aim to please their professional colleagues and other highly knowledgeable viewers (Bourdieu 1990).

Some artifacts seem to be *essentially* files. A map, after all, seems to be a simple repository of geographic and other facts that users can consult for their own purposes. In fact, maps can be made in a great variety of ways, none of them a simple translation of reality, so that they are in some important sense arguments designed to persuade their users of something, perhaps just by taking that something for granted. Thus, some formerly voiceless peoples claim that the maps that dominate world thinking are "Eurocentric," the technical choices that shaped them leading to results that arbitrarily make Europe and North America look like the center of the world. Those maps might be said to embody the argument that Europe and North America are "more important" than those other places off on the edge of the map.

Yet arguments and files are not kinds of objects but rather kinds of uses, ways of doing something rather than things. We see this when we notice that users are not powerless and, in fact, often remake the products they are presented with to suit their own desires and needs.

Scholars in every field routinely ignore the arguments made by the scholarly papers they cite and instead merely rifle the literature for results that can be put to *their* purposes. In short, they use the literature not as the body of arguments its makers intended but rather as a file of results with which to answer questions the original authors never thought of. This kind of rebellious use of cultural products has been studied in other areas: the sociology of technology (Oudshoorn and Pinch 2003), the inventive uses of digital games and other internet phenomena (Karaganis forthcoming), and cultural studies. Constance Penley (1997) described a sizable group of straight, working-class women who had commandeered the characters of *Star Trek* for their own creative work: homosexual erotica involving the major characters (Captain Kirk and Mr. Spock were a favorite couple) and distributed via the Internet. In all these cases, users thoroughly remade what makers had intended to be a one-way communication into raw material for their own constructions made for their own purposes and uses. Users can always take things into their own hands this way.

So?

What I have said implies a relativistic view of knowledge, at least to this degree: The way we pose questions and the way we frame answers come in a great variety of flavors—the various examples I've cited attest to that—and there's no guaranteed best way of choosing between them, since they are all good for conveying something. The same reality can be described in many ways, since the descriptions can be answers to any of a multitude of questions. We can agree in principle that our procedures ought to let us get the same answer to the same question, but in fact we ask the same question only when the circumstances of social interaction and organization have produced consensus on what constitutes a "good question." That doesn't happen very often, only when the conditions of people's lives lead them to see certain problems as common, as requiring certain kinds of representations of social reality on a routine basis, and thus lead to the development of professions and crafts that make those representations for routine use.

So some questions get asked and answered while others, every bit as good, interesting, worthwhile, and even scientifically important, are ignored, at least until society changes enough that the people who need those answers come to command the resources that will let them get an answer. Until then, pedestrians are going to be surprised by San Francisco's hills.

3

Who Does What?

Representations are made in a world of cooperating makers and users. The work of making them is divided among several kinds of makers, and between makers and users. If a representation requires the four kinds of work specified earlier, who does each kind? What the makers don't do must be done by the users, if a representation is to be created and communicated more or less to the satisfaction of everyone involved. Once they establish a division of labor, how do the cooperating parties coordinate the different things they do?

Sometimes the maker does most of the work, leaving only a limited margin of autonomy to the user. When we see a film, the filmmaker has chosen and arranged everything, and our activity is restricted to seeing what we can make of what's been done and having an opinion about it and the matters it takes up. (Of course, changes in technology make it possible for us to see films in an order other than the one the maker intended, though not if we see it in a theater.) But even while allowing us an apparent freedom to interpret and judge what we see as we will, filmmakers use all the devices of their craft to channel our responses in the direction they want us to go. The authors of scientific articles, in Latour's description (1987, 21–62) of their activities, intend to keep readers under even stricter control. They anticipate questions and criticisms of their work and build answers and defenses into what they write so that the reader finds it impossible to counter their arguments. At least, they aim for that kind of control, though they often fail to achieve it and so become the target of criticism and, worse yet, see their results appropriated for uses they never intended and may not approve.

In other worlds of representation making, makers leave much of the work of arranging and interpreting to users. Some artists who make representations of social reality do that deliberately. Refusing to make the generalizations that seem to leap out of the material they present, they resolutely leave that job to users. Here too the freedom is sometimes more apparent than real, because the makers use the technical and conceptual tools of their trades to channel user activity and response.

Suppose that you have made the hard choices of what to include in the report (the story, the film, whatever a report is called in the medium you are working in) you want to make on the social phenomena you've investigated. You've got the "data," the raw material. You have swallowed a bitter pill and accepted that you can't incorporate everything you have collected and think and still achieve anything useful to you or the people you mean your report for. You accept that some, perhaps a great deal, of your hard-won knowledge and material will end up, as film people used to say, on the cutting-room floor. Now you have what remains after this winnowing, a pile of fragments: strips of film, pages of numbers, files full of field notes.

How can you arrange all this stuff, put it together so that it communicates what you want to communicate to the people you want to communicate it to (and, of course, communicate what they want you to communicate to them)? Writers of social science (and other scholarly) texts typically experience this as the problem of constructing an argument, saying what needs to be said in an order that presents your ideas so efficiently and clearly that readers or viewers will not mistake them for something you didn't mean and so that all criticisms and questions will be forestalled. Dissertation advisers and journal editors repeatedly tell authors to "get your argument straight." And that advice applies, beyond the logical arrangement of propositions and conclusions and ideas, to the presentation of your evidence, the material you have selected from your investigation's data. How do you arrange that material, whatever its form, so that it says what your formal argument says and makes your conclusions manifest, unmistakable, and inescapable to any reasonable reader or viewer?

The answers to questions like these take us directly to the question of the variety of ways that makers and users can divide the representational labor between them. I'll focus on two quite different examples: the conventional social science problem of presenting statistical data—numbers—in tabular form and the problem of arranging what are usually called documentary photographs in some sort of order for presentation on the wall of a gallery, in a slide show, or in a book.

The Statistical Problem

Let's begin with the statistical problem. I have done a census or a survey or an experiment and have counted a number of things. In a census, we count people and find out a number of things about each person we count: their age, sex, race, last grade of school completed, income during the previous year, and so on, depending on the design of the particular census. In an experiment, we create two or more groups, do things (the "experimental treatment") to one group and nothing to the other (the "control group"), and measure a variety of things we think will result from that "treatment." Surveys mimic the experiment, though the researcher cannot control who gets what experimental treatment applied to them, since what is taken to be a causal variable is something like age or sex or some aspect of previous experience that the researcher cannot manipulate but will "control for" statistically.

Doing any of these things produces a lot of numbers. The individual numbers don't mean or matter much. I don't care, and neither does anyone but the person's family and friends, what age this particular person is or how much money she made last year. If I add up all the incomes of people of a certain kind and find their mean, that may seem on the surface more interesting, but it actually isn't. The average income reported by people who live on this particular block in Chicago is $19,615. Twenty-seven percent of the people living on a particular block tell the census they are black (that's how the U.S. Census measures race), or thirty-six percent say they are over 65. So what? Those numbers, standing alone, still aren't interesting.

Why? Because we haven't yet asked the crucial further question: compared to what? The readers of census tables make sense of the numbers in them by comparing them with one another. They look at two numbers and ask: Are they the same, or is one bigger than the other? And if one is bigger, is the difference big enough to take seriously? To make that figure of $19,615 as the average income of a block's inhabitants meaningful, we have to compare it to another number. To what? To, perhaps, the $29,500 (or 50 percent more) that people who live on another block make. Armed with that comparison, we might conclude that the city is characterized by a geographical segregation of income groups. Or perhaps blacks or people who are over 65 make 25 percent less than people of other races or ages, so that we can conclude that there is racial or age discrimination in income. Now we think we know something. The difference between the two numbers, revealed by the comparison, conveys the important information.

It isn't only the difference between two coordinate groups (black vs. white, greater than 65 vs. less than 65). We might compare the group we studied to the larger group that contains it—the people on this block compared to the entire city—or with some external standard, the people of this racial group compared to the "poverty line."

The problem of arranging my statistical results, my numbers, is a problem of making the relevant comparisons visible. That's why the volumes of the U.S. Census don't provide any conclusions. Being files rather than arguments, they don't explicitly compare anything; they just provide the raw materials for comparisons, which is why so many people can make a living rearranging what is available free to us all in those census publications.

In fact, the census usually prints data in a tabular form that makes some comparisons easy, as in this cross-tabulation of income by age I've invented to illustrate the point. The rows of the table are labeled with age groups (0–15, 15–25, 25–35, etc.), and the columns with income groups ($10,000–15,000, $15,000–25,000, etc.). The cells of this grid of rows and columns contain numbers, the number of people characterized by that combination of age and income. This makes it easy to compare adjacent cells and learn that there are more people age 25–35 in the $15,000–$25,000 income bracket than people 35–50 (if that's the case) but that the income difference between the two age groups lessens as income increases. All we have to do is look from one cell to the cell next to it to see that, above $40,000, the numbers are the same in the adjacent cells. But we might want to compare non-adjacent cells—the income differences between people aged 15–25 and people over 65—and then we would have to copy the numbers we want to another piece of paper in order to place them side by side for comparison.

Hypothetical census table

Income (in $)	Age					
	0–15	15–25	25–35	35–50	50–65	65+
0–15,000						
15,000–25,000	400	300	200	100	75	60
25,000–40,000	350	275	225	125	70	55
40,000–60,000	250	250	250	150	50	50
60,000–90,000	50	125	200	200	40	30
90,000+	25	100	175	175	25	35

In statistical comparisons like these, what we are comparing appears in the labels of the rows and columns of a table. If we're interested in the relation between average income and age, we head the columns with the names of the age categories and the rows with categories of income. The reader takes on the analytic job of seeing that people over 65 make less, if that's the case, than people in other age categories.

Census tables are made by highly trained professionals for a large and varied audience of potential users. Those users don't have to create the categories of comparison: age and income, or gender, race, years of education, and all the other variables so easily available from the U.S. Census Web site or in its publications. The makers of the table have done that analytic work—creating the categories—already, just by labeling the headings of the rows and columns with those dimensions (typical headings for many census tables). Making these the headings of the rows and columns—the dimensions of the table—tells users to make comparisons like these: Do people aged 35–50 earn more than people 25–35? Or, with other variables represented in the rows and columns, do blacks get less schooling than whites? Do women earn less than men? The professionals who design tables worry about arranging the dimensions and numbers so that readers can easily make the important comparisons. (See the discussions in Tukey 1972 and Tufte 1983, 1990, and the historical discussion in Desrosières 1993.)

The Photographic Problem

That's how things work in a world of representation making in which professionals do a lot of the work for a large and heterogeneous group of users. Now consider similar problems as they arise in the world of documentary photography, which seems, on the surface, very different. And it is, but there are similarities that let us specify the actual differences more precisely. Doing that shows us another way of dividing the labor of arranging between makers and users.

Suppose that I have made a large number of photographs—a serious documentary photographer pursuing a big topic would make many thousands of exposures—and have selected the images I think best convey the ideas I have arrived at about that topic as I went about making them. And let's take a classic example of the genre, one of the most discussed and admired works of its kind, often held up as a model for aspiring documentary photographers: Walker Evans's *American Photographs* ([1938] 1975).

Evans created this book from photographs he made over a period of several years, all over the eastern United States, south and north (the farthest west he got was Baton Rouge): New York, Pennsylvania, Mississippi, Alabama, and so on. And not all in the United States— you have to interpret the title generously, since he made three of the pictures in Havana). He wasn't completely clear about what he was after when he made all these images. According to Alan Trachtenberg, a profound student of his work, Evans was trying to answer the questions the Great Depression had raised for a lot of American intellectuals: "What is special about the American people? What are their characteristic beliefs, their folk history, their heroes, their work patterns, and their leisure? . . . Evans's concept of America cannot easily be defined by enlisting him in any particular camp, but it can be said that his work belongs within the general pattern of . . . the search for an authentic American culture and one's own Americanness" (Trachtenberg 1989, 247).

We can find further evidence about Evans's intentions in a letter he wrote to a friend when he was at work making these pictures, listing what he was after:

> People, all classes, surrounded by bunches of the new down-and-out.
>
> Automobiles and the automobile landscape.
>
> Architecture, American urban taste. commerce, small scale, large scale, the city street atmosphere, the street smell, the hateful smell, women's clubs, fake culture, bad education, religion in decay.
>
> The movies.
>
> Evidence of what people of the city read, eat, see for amusement, do for relaxation and not get it.
>
> Sex.
>
> Advertising.
>
> A lot else, you see what I mean. (244)

His intuition, led by such concerns, produced the archive of images he drew from for the book. He finally chose one hundred pictures from that archive for his exhibit at the Museum of Modern Art. From those he took eighty-seven to be included in *American Photographs*.

Having made these choices, he now had to deal with what seems an apparently simple problem: in what order should the images appear in the book?

There's a preliminary, practical question. Not what order to put the images in to generate an effect you want, but what order of viewing you can get viewers to respect. You can't force people who come to an exhibit to see the photographs in a particular order, and you can easily observe that some viewers come through the entrance and immediately start working their way around to the right, while others, with equal conviction, turn left. And, maddeningly for the photographer, readers as often leaf through a photo book from the end as from the beginning. Does the order of the images in a photographic sequence matter? Photographers regard this apparently simple question as crucial and difficult.

Whatever the problems, photographers, along with exhibit designers and museum curators, want to make viewers see things in a specific arrangement that they hope will push viewers to make certain comparisons along certain dimensions, generating particular moods. They understand that a single image is ambiguous and does not easily and unequivocally reveal "what it is about." When photographers make pictures for such other purposes as news and advertising, they usually compose them so as to exclude all "extraneous" detail, everything except the "point" of the news story or the product feature to which they want to call attention. They choose the details that surround that point carefully, to emphasize the story's main ideas or enhance the product's appeal (Hagaman 1996, 11). Pictures made for scientific purposes similarly restrict their content to what the maker (usually the author of the scientific article) wants users to know and rigorously exclude anything extraneous to that purpose.

Documentary photographers like Evans don't reduce the contents of a photograph in so ruthlessly comprehensive a way. Looking for photographic truth, they let what's there be there. As a result, most pictures made as "documentary" purposely contain a large amount of detail, all sorts of stuff that was in the area when the image was made, even when that stuff does not support any simple interpretation of what's going on. The crucial work of interpretation is left to the user, with whatever control the maker attempts left implicit. Though the pictures are carefully composed, so that the detail is not just random noise, viewers can interpret them in many ways, depending on which details they emphasize and what they make of them.

An image that contains so much detail will always support more than one interpretation, and certainly more than the simple scripts that inform newspaper stories or advertisements. Which raises this question: since this division of labor leaves the interpretation to users, how will those users know what's important, what the idea is, what the photographer had in mind, what they are "supposed to get out of this picture"? How can photographers arrange the pictures so that what they had in mind will shape the interpretations of the people who see their work?

Ordinarily, a caption tells us what's important, points out what we should attend to, tells us what we can ignore, indicates how the connections that link the objects and people in the picture. Some documentary photographers help viewers along with extended captions. Dorothea Lange sometimes attached a lengthy explanation, as when she captioned the image (sometimes called "Tractored Out" and reproduced in many places, for instance, in Stryker and Wood 1973, 100) of a small farmhouse marooned in a plowed-up field—the result of the buying up of small Dust Bowl farms by large agricultural conglomerates, which didn't even bother to demolish the small owner's home—"Abandoned farmhouse on a large mechanized cotton farm" (see figure 3.1). Sometimes photographers embed their images in a text.

Danny Lyon's book about a motorcycle gang (Lyon 1968) mixes photographs of the gang in action with long interviews with its members. Other photographers— Evans was one—leave their images verbally unattended, except for the place and date of the image's making, and this has the result Trachtenberg describes:

> An uncaptioned sequence of pictures suggests a hidden author, one who keeps out of the reader's way—like Flaubert or Henry James— but maintains a consistent point of view, a physical and moral perspective. The analogy cannot be exact, for what choice does the editor of photographs really have? Except for its denotations, what it is a picture of, a photograph can arouse widely varying interpretations, and thus, unless an editor anchors the image in an unambiguous caption, its meaning is too open and indeterminate to provide a reliably secure point of view. (251)

The maker can, however, indicate the image's meaning, using what the film director Sergei Eisenstein called *montage*. Again, Trachtenberg:

> Any grouping of images within the book can be taken as an example of Evans' adaptation of the montage device, which can be restated as a dialectical process of thesis giving rise to counter-thesis, together producing as feeling and/or idea an unseen, unstated synthesis. Each picture discloses a link to the next, a hint or germ of an antithetical image to follow. The reader is expected to remember each image fully, in all its details and nuances, for the most inconspicuous details become significant in echoes and allusions further on. What the pictures say they say in and through the texture of relations which unfold—continuities, doublings, reversals, climaxes, and resolutions. (259)

3.1 Dorothea Lange: Tractored Out: Abandoned farmhouse on a large mechanized cotton farm.

That is, the image an image follows, the image it precedes, and those even farther away in the sequence of pictures the viewer sees—all those pictures condition our understanding of the picture we are looking at right now. In fact, every image influences our understanding of every other image. Nathan Lyons distinguishes a *series*, in which the order of the photographs is important, from a *sequence*, where it isn't. If what eventually matters are the resonances and echoes between the photographs, which attentive readers, as Trachtenberg says, have stored up in their heads, then the initial order in which we encounter them may not, after all, be so important to our ultimate understanding of the work. Whatever the order, on this view, all the images we have seen affect our understanding of any single image.

Comparison

How does that happen? How do we use the materials of a sequence of images to create our understanding of what they "mean," the ideas they convey beyond a mere listing of what's there?

We do it by comparison, just as the readers of statistical tables make sense of numbers by comparing them with one another. To be explicit, we look at two pictures together and see what they have in common, and we take that common feature to be maybe not everything the picture is about but, at least provisionally, one of the things it is about. Using the language Leonard Meyer (1956) and Barbara Herrnstein Smith (1968), respectively, used about music and poetry, we might say that we hypothesize that that common feature is what these pictures are about. We go on, of course, to test the hypothesis with succeeding pictures, as Meyer and Smith suggest we do in listening to music or reading poetry. We look at a third picture, seeing if it has the features our hypothesis about similarities suggests. When it doesn't have them exactly, but only partly, we revise our hypothesis, our idea of what the sequence is about. And so on, comparing each picture that follows, again and again, to the images that have come before, using the accumulated understanding of similarities to arrive at our understanding of what the whole sequence is about.

We don't, of course, just find similarities, any more than the statistician finds that all the numbers in a table are the same. The statistician sees which number is bigger. But photographs contain more detail than an unadorned number, so we have more comparisons to make and more complicated hypotheses to consider than whether two items are the same. We find differences as well as similarities, and we note those differences and see what we can make of them. Do they suggest a second theme? A variation on the first theme? Do we see a connection between the two themes?

Trachtenberg does just that with the first six images in *American Photographs*, explaining how the successive references to cameras and photographs and situations of photographing lead viewers to conclude, if their reading of similarities and differences coincides with Trachtenberg's, that the sequence is about photography and image making (it is useful to read what follows with Evans's book in hand, looking for the features and relationships Trachtenberg describes):

> The movement from the opening picture through the second to the third encapsulates the method of the book: from a conception of the

photograph as mere identification to a subversion of that idea in the second image (where "Studio" cues our response to the wit in the event: a single picture made of, and commenting upon, many small pictures), to a picture free of writing and full of ambiguity, of the two boys looking elsewhere. Their glances beyond the frame of the image tell us that the world is wider and more full of circumstance than any photograph can show, that photographs cannot properly "identify" because they leave out too much, that reading has its limits and must take the arbitrariness of the picture's frame into account: an admission of contingency absent from the "studio" images implied or shown in the preceding pictures. (264)

The subtlety of Trachtenberg's analysis shows what a sophisticated reader can make of a carefully arranged sequence of photographs. But note two things about a reading like this. One is that the reader must really be sophisticated, must know how to "read" photographs in a sophisticated way. The other makes itself evident in a comparison with the reading of statistical tables.

A sophisticated reader of photographs does consciously and carefully what any ordinary reader of photographs does unreflectively and carelessly. A conscious and careful reading differs from an "ordinary" reading, first of all, in its deliberate thoroughness. We can guess that all viewers of a photograph respond, whether they know it or not, to everything in the frame. They are all affected by the tonalities and composition, they register all the small details, but they don't know they are doing it. They take a quick look, add it all up, and say, "Oh, yeah, that's striking," or "That's sad," or "It really captures the essence of that thing." But they don't know what went into their summing up of what the photograph captured or just how they conducted their interpretive operations. How you conduct these summarizing operations makes a difference, just as how you calculate a statistical measure of central tendency makes a difference; a mean is not a median is not a mode.

A conscious and careful reading, on the other hand, takes time. The sophisticated viewer goes over every part of the picture, registering explicitly what's there, what point of view it represents (where the photographer put the camera in order to get that particular view, among the many that might have been chosen), the time of day, the things that were left out but perhaps hinted at by the framing of the image, and so on. The sophisticated viewer knows the photographer could have made, and perhaps did make, many other versions of the same material, in which all those choices were made differently, and so reads what's in the frame as the result of the photographer's deliberate choices, which combine to produce the final effect. A careful reader of photographs spends a long time on each image.

As a result, a sequence of photographs has the kind of meaning Trachtenberg teaches us to look for only when the reader puts that kind of time into the consideration of every photograph and of the relations of each of the photographs to all the others. A book like *American Photographs* thus requires as careful a reading as a complex poem of similar length (Trachtenberg compares Evans's book to T. S. Eliot's *The Waste Land*).

The second major difference between the statistical table and the photographic sequence, and the more important one here, is that the division of labor between users and makers differs in the two cases. The maker of a table does a lot of interpretive work for users that the maker of a photographic sequence requires users to do for themselves. In a table, remember, the rows and columns are labeled with the names of the categories, and their subdivisions, which we are to take account of. The statistician who prepared the table has done that analytic work for users, telling them, in those row and column headings, that age, sex, race, income, education, and other variables are what matter and that they are divisible into just the divisions recognized in the labels (25–35 years old, $15,000–$25,000, male or female). The grid constructed by putting two or more of these divided categories together (as I put age and income together earlier, creating what statisticians call a cross tabulation) lays out all the possible combinations. The entries in the resulting cells tell us how many cases of each combination there are: how many people who are between 25 and 35 years old make between $15,000 and $25,000 a year, and how many make between $60,000 and $90,000, and so on for every combination of age and income.

We can think of the sequence of photographs in *American Photo-*

graphs as something like the entries in such a table or grid, each image a piece of "data," a fact given to users to work with. When they compare the images in a photographic sequence, however, they don't have the kind of help given by the headings of the table's rows and columns. No one made a table or labeled the rows and columns for them. No one told them what the important dimensions for comparison are, at least not explicitly. And consequently, no one has described the range of possible combinations for them. The photographer leaves that work to the viewer, the first step of whose analytic job is to find out what the dimensions of comparison are, or might be, or could be. The next step is to work out from that what kinds of combinations of people and situations and their interaction the segment of society the photographer is telling us about contains. The result of their work is not the items to be found in the cells of the resulting table but the labels on the rows and columns themselves, the dimensions that the comparisons between the images tell us are important.

What kind of dimensions can we find in *American Photographs*, and what would the resulting table look like? What follows is one possibility, a sketchy, merely illustrative analysis that starts with two images Evans made of the experience of women in the streets of New York. Other interpretations than the one I've made are possible, which is one of the results that follows from this exercise.

In "A Girl on Fulton Street, New York, 1929" (39), we see a slim young white woman, turned away from us so that we see only her left side in profile (figure 3.2). She's wearing a dark coat with a large fur collar and holding a muff of the same fur, and she wears a black cloche over her bobbed hair. She has what you might want to call a "hard," even "angry" look; you might want to say she looks "wary." Or you might not. We can agree that she doesn't look relaxed or at ease. She's the only figure in the frame in sharp focus. Three men behind her, all wearing fedoras, are a little blurred, and the figures beyond them even more so. They're in a crowded downtown street lined with stores, some advertising signs, and a construction crane.

"42nd Street" (43), separated from the first image by "Interior of Negro Preacher's House, Florida, 1933," shows a black woman, older and heavier, well dressed in a coat with a fur collar, a string of pearls

3.2 Walker Evans: A Girl on Fulton Street, New York, 1929. Image © The Metropolitan Museum of Art.

around her neck, and a hat perhaps a little less stylish than the white woman's (figure 3.3). She stands near the stairs to the elevated train, down which a man is coming, and the street behind her is filled with traffic, signs, and the supports for the train tracks. The tones are darker than those in the Fulton Street picture. The woman's look is harder to describe: heavy-lidded, a little suspicious of the man who is making the photograph, a little wary too.

Considering these two pictures, you might provisionally conclude something about women's experience on these New York streets, and

3.3 Walker Evans: 42nd Street. Image © The Metropolitan Museum of Art.

perhaps something more general about the lives of women, as those are embodied in just such moments on the streets as Evans gives us. When we compare the two images, our intuitive grasp of how they seem alike tells us some of the dimensions of comparison. We might say that women in New York are ill at ease and wary when they are on the streets. And our next thought is that these two women are alike in that way, the likeness emphasized by the similarity of their hats and furs, even though they differ in age and race, but they are both very different from the country woman who appeared earlier in the book ("Alabama Cotton Tenant Farmer's Wife, 1936," 33) in her plain dress and hairdo, standing against the weathered boards of her house (figure 3.4). She doesn't look wary, but you couldn't say she looks at ease either; we might think she's a little bashful and embarrassed to have the photographer from New York making her picture with that big camera, that she might be wondering what he wants with a picture of her. That tells us that "wary" does not exhaust the possibilities; there are still more things to include in our thinking about women's lives.

We can go on to compare these women to the men we see—for instance, the dapper older black man wearing a white suit and a white

3.4 Walker Evans: Alabama Cotton Tenant Farmer's
Wife, 1936. Image © The Metropolitan Museum of Art.

straw hat with a black band standing in front of a newsstand filled
with Spanish-language magazines and newspapers, topped by a Coca-
Cola sign ("Citizen in Downtown Havana, 1932," 45). He seems so at
home, so unwary, so at ease, in another urban milieu, in another
country (figure 3.5).

The first outcome of such a photographic analysis, conducted by
the viewer with the materials the photographer provided, might be
that "Girl on Fulton Street" tells us that this white woman, and perhaps all white women or all white women of a certain age and class,
standing in the street in New York look like this, the "this" suggesting
perhaps a mood or an attitude toward being in public and on display.
When we see "42nd Street," we conclude, provisionally, that this black
woman standing in the New York street also looks like that, her own

3.5 Walker Evans: Citizen in Downtown Havana, 1932.
Image © The Metropolitan Museum of Art.

version of "like that." But we also compare the entries in what now
look like two adjacent cells in a grid, a table in the making. We decide
that the two have this look in common and that what they have in
common suggests something about the way women feel they must
conduct themselves in public in New York. We might decide, looking
hard, that the looks differ as well—that the black woman's gaze is per-

haps more guarded—in ways that may be traceable to the differing social situations of black and white women, or to the different situation
of women of different ages, or to the different situations of women of
different social classes. And we take those notions to other pictures in
the sequence, and perhaps decide that being a woman in New York
makes you hard in ways that living in Alabama don't, and vice versa.
And that adds another dimension to the table of possibilities. So the
viewer's work produces not just a list of possible combinations of life
situations but the grid of comparisons itself, the space defined by the
intersections of all these possibilities and their interconnections.

Let's be logical about what's going on. Every time we describe
someone as a "woman" or "white," or describe a situation as "urban,"
we automatically introduce other possible labels, which might be
symmetrical—"man"—but more likely will be a list of coordinate alternatives: "black," "Asian," "Native American," and so on. If one situation is "urban," that points to other degrees of population density:
"suburban" and "rural," maybe "exurban," perhaps others. The term
we use alerts us to the existence of a dimension along which there are
other positions than the one we've pointed to.

The imaginary table I've been referring to expresses the logical
analysis visually. It shows all the possible combinations of the descriptive dimensions we have used informally. Having included
"woman," because the two New Yorkers are women, we created, for
our analysis, the dimension of gender (so making room for the category "man"). Noting that the two women differ racially gave us race as
a dimension; we don't know all the subtypes we will use under that
heading yet. Seeing the women react "warily" to being observed on
the street in New York, we created a dimension of "reactions to being
observed in public." We have to add, remembering the Alabama farm
woman, the rural-urban continuum, with whatever stops along it we
think appropriate or necessary.

In this way, we do the work that census statisticians do for us when
they lay out a table. We name the rows and columns. When we combine them, labeling the columns with gender terms and the rows with
names of possible attitudes toward being observed in public (recognizing that we will surely add more rows as we see more kinds of re-

actions to being in public), we see a larger conceptual space than Evans pictured, but one that is implied (if you accept this analysis) by the images he put in his book. We have some help from the photographer, who composed the images so as to suggest some possibilities rather than others and then arranged them in a way that hints, through the comparisons I've been discussing, at what the dimensions and intersections of the table are or might be.

Having done all that, which sounds like more work than it is, we can go on to inspect other images, about which it hadn't occurred to us to raise such questions, to see what they add to our understanding of the specific cases pictured but also of the general ideas and categories suggested.

Now we can see some advantages the photographic method has over the tabular one used by statisticians. I was originally going to create the table that the preceding analysis of Evans's book might generate, but I gave up the idea when I realized what a mess that would make. Tabular forms are very helpful when you deal with a relatively few categories. You generate a manageable number of labels and cells. But every time you add a new dimension, you double the number of cells required. (You'll find a very clear discussion of the process in Danto 1964. He uses the example of judgments of artistic worth but also explains the logic of the analysis very clearly.) In the simplest case, two variables, each taking only two values, generates four cells. Example: age, divided into old and young, cross-tabulated with gender, divided into male and female. (As an exercise, you can draw these tables for yourself.) Each cell contains an important fact: how many people have just that combination of characteristics (in a slightly more complex version, what percentage of the people in that cell have a value of x on a third characteristic, like "rich" as opposed to "poor"). If you now add the population density variable, divided into rural and urban, you must divide each of the four age/gender cells into two, one for rural, one for urban, ending up with eight cells. Every additional subdivision—if you, for instance, added a category for suburban—increases the number of subheads in a row or column and the number of cells. (We'll return to the problems of displaying such information in a table in chapter 5.)

When you cross-tabulate four or five characteristics, the resulting table has so many cells that it's difficult—not impossible, but difficult—to find the two numbers the table is supposed to help you compare, and it has defeated its own purpose. A table with ten cross-tabulated variables, containing 1,024 cells, is so unwieldy you would have trouble publishing it, and if you managed that, users would have a hard time manipulating it physically, let alone making sense of its entries.

The documentary photograph works differently. It typically contains so much detail that an interested user can easily make a great many comparisons between any two such images, every comparison suggesting a dimension of variation and its possible subdivisions and adding to a list of questions to be asked in looking at succeeding images in the sequence. It contains, in embryo, all of these possibilities, the number mainly constrained by the user's ingenuity in exploring what's there. Not all the comparisons will produce ideas that can be sustained over the course of a long sequence, hypotheses about what the sequence is about that hold up when confronted with the succeeding images. But some, and not just a few, will do that. These ideas will not contradict each other. They will be complementary, suggesting more complex hypotheses that link the subthemes a viewer might construct.

All this work of constructing categories of comparison and their divisions, creating hypotheses and checking them, falls to the user. The maker furnishes the raw materials (in truth, not so raw as all that), artfully chosen and arranged to be sure, but after that it's up to the user to construct the analysis, with all its paraphernalia. That's a far different division of representational labor from the one that goes into the making and use of a census table.

The multitude of details in a documentary image gives viewers material with which to construct more than one comparison of the kind I've alluded to. You can make more than one table out of a lengthy sequence of detailed photographs. There are many comparisons to make, many dimensions to explore, many stories to tell. We might, for instance, focus not on the women standing in the street but on the streets themselves, the way they look, and what they tell us about life

3.6 Walker Evans: Main Street, Saratoga Springs, New York, 1931. Image © The Metropolitan Museum of Art.

in America. That means that we will now include in our comparison all the images of streets in which no people appear, such as the haunting image of automobiles parked head-in to the curb in the rain ("Main Street, Saratoga Springs, New York, 1931," 59). Which leads us to comparisons with other streets seen in other pictures, in Bethlehem, Pennsylvania (117), Fredericksburg, Virginia (153), and a variety of other towns, large and small (figures 3.6, 3.7, 3.8).

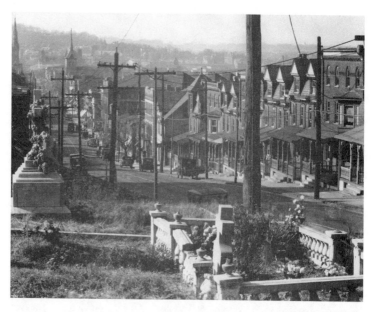

3.7 Walker Evans: Street and Graveyard in Bethlehem, Pennsylvania.

3.8 Walker Evans: Frame Houses in Virginia, 1936.

So a well-made photographic sequence supports a large number of comparisons and thus a large number of interpretations, which is why we can continue to attribute more and more meaning to what is, after all, a small number of images. And why it is difficult—in fact, impossible—to settle on a definitive interpretation of such a work, and why *American Photographs* repays repeated readings by giving you new interpretive possibilities. Evans did his part of the job. He made and selected the pictures, which contain the possibilities, and put them in a book. He left the rest for the user to do.

4

The Work Users Do

Some representations of social life require their users to do a lot of work. How many users have the knowledge and skills it takes to do that work? What happens if they can't or won't do it? How do the makers of representations deal with the differential ability and willingness of users to do the work their reports demand?

Construing

Some representations seem to give up their meaning easily. You take it in at a glance, like picking an orange off a tree in the backyard. Others require more work, more thinking about, more pondering of the implications. Let's use the word *construal* to refer to the message recipient's making something of it, interpreting it, giving meaning to it or taking meaning from it.

A user can take any representation of society in one of those two ways: as obvious, with the meaning so "just there" as to require only minimal and routine message handling, or as dense, requiring careful attention to all the details. "Obvious" and "dense" aren't natural characteristics of objects or events. Rather, they describe the way we decide to attend to those things.

We attend to representations in the ways we have learned. Representations seem obvious to users who already know all they need to know to take in their meaning, and dense, requiring more work, when the users haven't encountered anything quite like that before. We have all had some training, starting as small children, in construing such objects, but we haven't all had training and experience with all kinds of representations. These abilities are distributed differentially along all kinds of lines of social division.

We can read every photograph as either obvious or dense (I'll show how you can read the same photograph in different ways in chapter 10). Many photographs make use of conventions well known to so many kinds of people that just a few hints tell experienced users, people who ordinarily come in contact with them, the whole story, the way most of us can guess at the full text of signs we only see fragments of. In well-organized representational worlds, users know how to construe the representations they routinely run into. Take, as an example, sports feature photographs—not the action photographs made during the game or match or competition but the ones of the other activities surrounding the big game—which are organizationally constrained (Hagaman 1993) to be highly formulaic so as to be easily readable by experienced viewers. They deal with a small selection of situations, well known to the newspaper readers who routinely see them.

The most common images (I follow Hagaman's analysis closely here) deal with a player or team winning or losing. Every game that has a winner, of course, also has a loser. Which side the picture shows as the winner depends on which town the newspaper for which it is made serves. Photographs in Chicago papers treat the Cubs and Sox as "our team," whose wins we celebrate, while New York papers treat the Yankees and Mets as "ours." Readers don't have to figure that out; it's part of the equipment they bring to their interpretive activity. (Photographs made for the wire services, which service many newspapers in many cities, usually include a selection from which local editors can choose one appropriate to their hometown team.) When "our" team wins, we see the jubilant winners, individually or collectively, their arms up in the air, heads thrown back, mouths open, or hugging one another. When "our" team loses, we see a lone loser sitting on a bench, head down, shoulders sagging, perhaps with another player's consoling arm around the shoulder. These stereotypical poses appear in photographs of athletes of all kinds: amateurs and professionals, women and men, adults and children.

Well-socialized Americans (and, no doubt, more and more people everywhere) learn this language of gesture and posture as children and so take only a second to extract the intended meaning from a picture of an athlete with his arms reaching into the sky and a big smile on his face. What else could it mean? He won! In the same way, they know the language of losing. When they see someone sitting on a bench, alone, head down, they know, from the hundreds and thousands of such pictures they have seen before, that that player lost. What else? The meaning is not obvious because such gestures, presented in that visual language, are inherently obvious. It's obvious because users have learned the language the way all languages are learned, through constant repetition. They *know* how to read that image.

Photographers picture winners and losers in that easily construed way so that newspaper readers need give the images only a second or two while scanning the results of yesterday's games. The images give up their essential meaning quickly to those who know the code. Because users know the language and photographers know that they know it, such images are easily made, once the image makers master the language, so that they can meet the requirements of the editor who sent them to cover the game quickly and efficiently.

Easily read images—images made in a widely known visual language—show up beyond the sports pages. The standard topics of big-time, serious photojournalism—war, famine, assassinations—have a repertoire of similarly canonical pictures, which use highly conventional visual language easily interpreted by any well-socialized user. Famines dependably produce the small child with the swollen belly. Assassinations come in two forms. The photographer lucky enough to have been on the scene when the killing happened gets the assassin pointing the gun as the victim falls to the ground. Photographers who arrive later must content themselves with the victim lying on the ground in a pool of blood. And everyone who sees such a picture knows "what it means."

Making such an easily read image takes skill. The photographer has to fill the frame with the formulaic image, excluding details that would distract users from the formulaic clues or blurring those "extraneous" details (what editors sometimes refer to as "clutter") through selective focus (Hagaman 1993, 50–51, 59–63).

As we have seen in Walker Evans's work, other pictures, just as skillfully made, have the opposite intention: to include details whose meaning is not obvious, which do not use already well known conventional visual language, details that reward attentive study and thought. These images seem plain or uninteresting to people who don't look at them carefully. They don't use the commonly understood codes that tell users what they are about. Instead, they force users to pick out relevant materials consciously and work out their interconnections, see what can be made of them.

This is what makes artists who take up the work of social analysis so interesting. They don't want to present the formulaic and already known or use already well known language. They want to show the people who look at their pictures something they haven't seen before. When photographers do use visual language everyone knows, they want to make the viewer see new meanings in it.

The conceptual artist Hans Haacke exemplifies this point (Becker and Walton 1975). Haacke once described his work as the study of systems: natural systems, as in his early sealed plastic cube containing a small amount of moisture, whose alternate condensation and evaporation displayed the systemic character of those processes; and, in his later work, social systems, in pieces explicitly displaying the workings of political and economic power (Haacke 1975, especially 59–123).

His "Guggenheim Project" (Haacke 1975, 59–67), for example, consists of seven panels of type containing a lot of facts about the trustees of the Solomon R. Guggenheim Museum in New York City: who the trustees of the museum are, their family connections (they are almost all members of the Guggenheim family, though many have different surnames), what other boards (of companies and organizations) they sit on, and many facts about the crimes committed by those companies, especially their exploitation of indigenous workers in third world countries. The Guggenheim piece announces no conclusions and makes no generalizations; there is not a hint of Marxist or any other variety of political analysis—just the recitation of facts. Haacke does not point a finger at guilty parties or allege any conspiracies. Still less does he say that this bastion of modern art and progressive artistic thinking gets its support from wealth based on the exploitation of labor in countries less advanced than the United States.

But someone who inspects this work would have to be extraordinarily obtuse and willfully unseeing not to arrive at just that conclusion. Haacke takes advantage of ordinary readers' habitual methods of reasoning by using a well-known format, a simple listing of unquestioned facts: names, dates, places, official offices held. So you learn who the trustees of the museum are, that most of them belong to the same extended family, that they sit on the boards of several corporations, that these corporations engage in mining activities throughout the world. As you take in each "obvious" fact, you add it to what you already know, and . . . the conclusion that the museum is financed by the exploitation of oppressed laborers around the world is there for the taking.

But it isn't there just like that; you have to know how to take it. Since most users know that, the conclusion results from the work they do, arranging these simple and indisputable facts as syllogisms and drawing the conclusions those syllogisms, apparently inevitably and naturally, lead to. Haacke used the same technique to display, for example, the political (most importantly, Nazi) connections of a German industrialist who was chairman of the Friends of the Cologne Wallraf-Richartz-Museum, which had donated Edouard Manet's painting *Bunch of Asparagus* to the museum (Haacke 1975, 69–94).

I used the word *construe* to refer to this activity, through which users in interpretive communities (I'll come back to that expression shortly) easily and "naturally" extract and make sense of a representation's meaning. I did that to make clear that such work must be done before a representation gives up its meaning to a user. What is that work? *Construe* refers, in its primary meaning, to analyzing the grammar of a statement, to understanding the terms in which it is put and how they are connected to each other; the more extended meaning is "to discover and apply the meaning of; interpret." Let's take this seriously.

Users often skip this step and, in fact, may ignore the representational artifact so carefully constructed for them altogether. I don't mean the kind of casual look and quick read, the flipping through a book of photographs from the back that so irritates photographers. I mean the practice Lawrence McGill describes in his study of the reading practices of students taking a class in science, in which they were required to read many articles containing large numbers of numerical tables. He says:

> The students' orientation toward reading these articles is that they must "get through them" in order to meet the requirements of their classes. These students take pains to avoid the dross, that material extraneous to "the point" the article is trying to get across. Statistical tables, descriptions of methodology, and results are thought of as canned procedures appearing in virtually every research article (that is, these are the sections that read as though they were "written because they *had* to be"). Their purposes are known and understood, and students pay attention to them only if given a good reason. (McGill 1990, 135)

Since they seldom found such a good reason, they pretty much ignored the tables that constituted the heart of the articles they read, reasoning that those tables must say what the authors said they said or the editors would have rejected the article. They memorized the conclusions, which they thought were sure to be what the class examination would quiz them on, accepting on faith that the other stuff in fact supported those statements.

So users might not do the work left to them, might just not bother at all, not look at the photograph; they might go to sleep during the film, rush past the table, skip large sections of the novel. It happens.

But often enough, it *doesn't* happen, and even when it does, we might decide to ignore people who ignore what we have made for them. We'll keep our eyes on the alert for interested viewers who are willing to do the work necessary to disentangle the meaning from the package it comes in.

We can begin the analysis of the construal of representations by noting that all these representations serve as devices for summarizing data and ideas. Every version of social science analysis has to do the job of making less out of more, in the process making what has been gathered more intelligible and assimilable (this important topic gets chapter 6 all to itself). Latour (1987, especially 233–43) describes in detail how scientists summarize and reduce their data, removing more and more detail from what they report in order to make what's left more transportable and comparable. He calls this series of transformations a *cascade*.

What the reader has to do is sometimes called, in connection with written texts, "unpacking" the representation, that is, undoing the summarizing that has produced the artifact we are inspecting. We can begin our thinking here by taking up one set of examples, the collection of tables and charts I put together for my seminar on this topic. These demanding tables and charts required some interpretive work, some construal.

Some tables are simple enough but very detailed, giving a level of detail most readers today would consider excessive, requiring too much attention for what they deliver. It's quite possible that confronted with these tables that go beyond what's conventionally expected, readers would just, as some of McGill's interviewees did, skip them, trusting that they say what the author who presents them says they say.

Consider two tables in W. E. B. DuBois's study of Philadelphia's historic black area, the Seventh Ward, the smaller of which, occupying only half a page, is labeled "OCCUPATIONS—MALES, TEN TO TWENTY-ONE YEARS OF AGE. SEVENTH WARD, 1896"; the larger one, which takes up two and a half pages, is the same except for the age group, changed to "TWENTY-ONE AND OVER" (DuBois [1899] 1996, 105–7).

These tables give a very detailed breakdown of the occupations of black juveniles and adults, far more detailed than anyone needs now or, probably, than anyone needed in 1899. What purpose would anyone have for a breakdown of boys 'occupations by one-year age intervals? And for a contemporary reader, some of the occupational names no longer mean anything. Many students in my seminar had no idea what a "hostler" did, that being one of the many esoteric and no longer well known occupations Dubois counted. (I knew it had something to do with horses but had to consult a dictionary to learn the full definition: "a person who takes charge of horses, as at an inn; a stableman.") More to the point, why bother to list, in a table divided into age categories, occupations like china repairer or wicker worker, of which there were only one each? Still, it's all there for the taking, if you're in the mood to take it.

The table contains more information than any of us now think we need. Nevertheless, everyone in the seminar I confronted with this material knew how to read it. Many people, perhaps especially social science students, know how to do that. We all knew that the table was two-dimensional, that the dimensions were occupation and age, and that the numbers in the cells opposite the occupational titles and under the age headings told how many of each there were. The cell for "31–40 year old wicker-worker" had a "1" in it, meaning that there was one of those, just as the "28" in the cell for "21–30 year old barbers" meant there were twenty-eight men that old in that trade. And so on.

Many people find two-dimensional tables less obvious than these trained graduate students did. I discovered that when I had to teach a class of graduating college seniors majoring in sociology how to make sense of such an object (as I explained one in the last chapter), saying that the vertical dimension represented one element that had different values, the horizontal dimension a second variable that also had different values, and that the cells contained the number of cases (people) meeting both criteria.

The charts that often decorate social science reports serve as metaphors, two-dimensional representations of a complicated social reality. I'll analyze these metaphors in detail in chapter 10, just noting here that charts, no matter how simple they are, require construing and that what's to be made of them is never obvious. Looking at them, you have to consciously say to yourself, "Let's see, this line means this and that line means that; when you compare them, this line is longer than that one, so the quantity represented is greater." Or like some of the charts discussed later, they use symbols and formats created for the occasion, specific to these data and this analysis, so that the reader has to consciously identify the components and learn what they stand for and what, therefore, can be taken from the chart.

Plays, novels, films, and photographs generate different problems, particularly when the people who make them are artists. Artists usually think that their work speaks for itself, that they have already said everything there is to say about the topic, whatever it is, in the work itself, and that any lack of clarity means the viewer didn't do the work necessary to make the meaning clear. That could be put as "You didn't read carefully," or "You didn't look at the photograph carefully," or "You were asleep when the crucial event in the play took place." In general, they charge that the viewer didn't pay the kind of complete attention the work requires.

Who Knows How to Do What?
Interpretive Communities

If makers leave it to users to interpret the work, deriving its ramifications and consequences for themselves, its final meaning rests on what users know how to do with it, and with works like it. Knowledge of how to interpret what a user makes is not always—not usually, really—distributed uniformly through a community of makers and users of a given kind of representation.

Steven Shapin was interested in that problem as it arose at the beginning of the development of modern science. He wanted to know how Robert Boyle, the seventeenth-century English "experimental natural philosopher," communicated his findings in physical science to his colleagues and other interested parties. Shapin's analysis (1994) does not deal with telling about society, but it does explain how ways of telling depend on viewers' ways of understanding, and how, therefore, makers change how they tell their story when they want to reach a new audience. Shapin's analysis gives us a template for understanding how ways of telling about society might similarly change.

Speaking about Boyle's reluctance to put his findings in mathematical language and his preference for a verbal, though necessarily longer, way of reporting, Shapin says:

> Boyle understood mathematics to encompass an abstract, esoteric, and private form of culture. That was a major reason why he worried about its place within experimental natural philosophy. If experimental philosophy was to secure legitimacy and truth by implementing a public language, then the incorporation of mathematical culture might threaten a new privacy. In specifying that mathematics was written for mathematicians, Copernicus had only given prominent voice to widespread understandings of the place of mathematics in the

overall literate culture. As Kuhn has observed, it was only the nonex-
perimental mathematical sciences that were characterized, even in
antiquity, "by vocabularies and techniques inaccessible to laymen and
thus by bodies of literature directed exclusively to practitioners." Boyle
reportedly remarked upon the relative inaccessibility of mathematics.
To go on as mathematicians did was, in his view, to restrict the size of
the practicing community. Such restriction risked its very capacity to
produce physical truth. To be sure, mathematical culture possessed
very powerful means of securing *belief* in the truth of its propositions,
while the proportion of those *believers* whose assent was freely and
competently given was small. In contrast, members of a properly constituted experimental community freely gave their assent on the bases
of witness and the trustworthy testimony of other witnesses.

. . . Boyle sought to make historically specific experimental performances vivid in readers' minds and to make it morally warrantable
that these things had actually been done as, when, and where described. This type of narrative was also reckoned to be more *intelligible*
than alternative styles of communication. His *Hydrostatical Paradoxes*
specified that he *could have* reported findings in more stylized and
mathematical form, but had *chosen* not to do so: "Those who are not
used to read mathematical books, are wont to be so indisposed to apprehend things, that must be explicated by schemes [diagrams]; and I
have found the generality of learned men, and even of these new
philosophers, that are not skilled in mathematicks," so unacquainted
with hydrostatical theorems that a more expansive and inclusive exposition was indicated. Notions of this sort could not "be thoroughly
understood without such a clear explication of [these] theorems as, to
a person not versed in mathematical writings, could scarce be satis-
factorily delivered in a few words." Many words had to be used. It was,
Boyle confided, "out of choice, that I declin'd that close and concise
way of writing." He was writing not "to credit myself, but to instruct
others," and, for that reason, "I had rather geometricians should not
commend the shortness of my proofs, than that those other readers,
whom I chiefly designed to gratify, would not thoroughly apprehend
the meaning of them." (Shapin 1994, 336–37)

Boyle worried that an inappropriate mode of representation might
bring about an undesirable restriction of the potential audience. He
feared that readers would ignore unfamiliar language and styles of

reasoning, and some of the language of science developing in his time was esoteric in just that way, especially in its use of mathematical formulas, geometric diagrams, and the forms of reasoning to conclusions associated with them. I'll leave aside the question of whether such a restriction on who can read what an analyst of society can write is something that must be avoided or whether it is necessary to the development of scientific thought. That's an old and not particularly fruitful debate.

Let's instead appropriate the question for our concern about telling about society, exploring the less contentious sociological question of the different ways that the knowledge necessary for making and reading representations of social life is distributed. Who understands the work an analyst of society presents? At one extreme, some works about society present themselves, we could say, "to whom it may concern": to any competent member of the society who might be interested. At the other extreme, some works are presented to a very small and select group of people who alone can be expected to understand them and be able to interpret their arcane, not generally familiar, terminology and modes of reasoning. The two can be exemplified by, on the one hand, novels or photographs or films—and most especially the one among those that is aimed at the largest and most heterogeneous audience, the Hollywood film—and, on the other, the mathematical model.

The people who make Hollywood films mean them to be understood by anyone (with the dialogue dubbed in the appropriate languages) in the entire world. The language of film is, as a historical fact, now interpretable by anyone. There are probably no longer any people so isolated from Western marketing as to make such simple mistakes as thinking that an actor who had been killed in a film had really been killed and thus could appear in any future films only as a ghost, or wondering where actors went when they stepped out of the frame. (It has sometimes been said that tribal peoples with no exposure to Western cultural products have made such mistakes, but I can't find anyone who has said that in print. Let it stand, nevertheless, as a possibility.) No, everyone understands that those simple devices are just that, devices—and everyone understands much more com-

plex matters, such as the way techniques like fades and wipeouts indicate the passage of time or the movement of the film's action to a
different geographic location. Everyone understands, as well, the
meaning of the sequential cuts from one face to another that indicate
a dialogue is taking place between two people or that things are now
being seen from someone else's perspective.

Which doesn't mean that audience members "know" these technical devices in the self-conscious and manipulable way a filmmaker or
film aficionado knows them. They don't. They know it when they see
it, but they don't know it to talk about, let alone to make one themselves. So there is a real separation between the makers of these representations, the film professionals who do it all the time for a living
and have done it for years and years, and the people who watch these
works for entertainment or possibly for information (or maybe they
just get the information along with the entertainment, not having
asked for it and perhaps not really wanting it). One group knows
things the other doesn't. And so less-informed viewers can be "fooled"
or "misled," moral problems of representation I discuss at length in
chapter 8.

We can find the extreme opposite of this widespread knowledge of
how to use a representation of social life in the world of mathematical model–making. Such a model creates an artificial world of carefully defined entities with a few simple properties, which can interact and influence one another only in a few equally carefully defined
ways governed by specific mathematical operations (see chapter 9 for
a lengthier explanation of math models). The advantage of such a
model is not that it is a realistic depiction of how social life really
works anywhere but that it makes clear what the world would be like
if it did operate according to that model. And this is something worth
knowing. One of the models described later tells you something that
would interest many people: what the repertoire of a symphony orchestra would consist of if the orchestra replaced old works with new
ones by following certain simple rules strictly (not that anyone does,
but that's not the point).

Anyway, briefly, and maybe a little inaccurately: anyone who
knows how to read, interpret, and understand a mathematical model

also knows how to make one. That is, construing these models, understanding them, requires a general acquaintance with the way mathematicians reason and a substantial understanding of the area of mathematical reasoning used in the particular case. To understand the analysis of symphonic repertoire made in the example I just gave, and to be able to be properly critical of it, you would need to know something, say, about difference equations; for the analysis of kinship systems made in another example given later, you would have to be familiar with Markov chains. Not many people know these things, and the ones who do usually (though not always) know them well enough to make models themselves. (And if you've put in the time and effort to learn all that, which few social scientists, and especially sociologists, have, you probably want to put those hard-won skills to work.) So, to oversimplify somewhat, the community of users of math models and the community of makers of math models are essentially coterminous and identical. It's just two different activities engaged in by the same people. Sometime they make models, sometimes they consume the models others have made.

Boyle, as quoted above by Shapin, is talking about something like the world of math models, though that's not exactly the kind of mathematics he had in mind. His complaints suggest some of the features it's useful to compare in discussing what we can call "interpretive communities," the groups that share enough knowledge (how much is a question, of course) to interpret the representations commonly made and used by their members.

Note, to begin with, the empirical generalization Boyle is working with, which goes something like this: the more complex and technical the expression of the results, the fewer people will be able to read and understand them. In itself that's no cause for complaint. Plenty of technical matters interest no one outside the relevant community of specialists, and there are many other things specialists think outsiders have no need to know about. But it is a common cause of complaint, because people who are not specialists do want to know enough so that they don't have to worry that someone is pulling a fast one on them (complaints about medical doctors often take this form). Here are some specific questions we can raise about this.

Whom do the makers want to reach? Put another way, whom is their world organized to reach, and what does that aim impose on them as a standard of intelligibility? People who make the kind of representation I make usually do it because some group of people somewhere wants something like that, and I make what I make (film, math model, whatever) in such a way as to be intelligible, pleasing, and useful to them. With whom, then, does their world's organization make them want to communicate routinely?

If you know the audience the makers want to reach, you can understand the features of any particular representation as the result of the makers' attempt to produce something that will reach those people in a form they will understand and approve. They will understand it because they have learned how to understand things like that, and they will approve it because it meets the standards they have acquired as part of that learning.

But Shapin's example of Boyle's practice shows that a maker might in fact have a choice of audiences to reach and that the choice of audience would imply a choice of representational style. So Boyle might reasonably have aimed for an audience of other learned scholars for whom the shorthand language of mathematical formulas and geometric representations of physical phenomena would have been no problem. But he wanted to reach beyond them, to a larger and more varied audience of educated gentlemen, who would understand the arguments he had to make *if* he made them in the plain language of ordinary, high-class, quasi-literary discourse that all gentlemen, more or less, knew.

So he had to use a less economical form of representation than he could have used had he confined himself to the technically experienced audience of his scientific peers. And that entailed using not just different words but a different style of proof. Mathematical proofs relied on the force of logic. What you showed to be true mathematically was true *of necessity*. If you accepted the premises and the reasoning was sound, the conclusion was inescapable. But what you showed in the world of empirical research was true in a different way. It was true because it was what people had observed to happen in the real world of real material stuff, and you knew it was true because it had been *observed* to be true. Not by you, because you, the reader, couldn't be there to observe everything scientists were reporting, but because it had been observed to be true by someone who could be believed. And what kind of person could be believed? Gentlemen, who were bound by a code of truth telling. You, as another gentleman reader, understood the system of social controls that required them to tell the truth and so could decide to accept their report as credible for yourself, because you understood the risks to his own honor such a person would run if he lied.

These gentlemen-philosopher-scientists, further, needed a way to judge credibility that could avoid disputes. Disputes arose when someone refused to believe a report made by someone else, But gentlemen, in that time and place, could not question one another's word without giving serious offense and possibly provoking, at worst, a duel. A duel? Over a scientific finding? Though the penalties for misstating what you have observed are very serious today—loss of grants, jobs, and your scientific reputation—they aren't life threatening. If I said I saw X and you said I couldn't have seen such a thing, that was equivalent, in Boyle's time, to the terrible insult of "giving the lie," accusing the other of being a liar. And that was a true offense in a culture of honor, one that had to be dealt with in the appropriate way, which, even at that late date, was a fight, potentially to the death.

Boyle and his colleagues were unhappy with mathematical reasoning, because it aimed not just at precision but at certainty, which led to "civic disasters," disputes that could not be resolved without, in a very gentlemanly way, insisting that since someone was right, someone else had necessarily said what wasn't true. These scientists didn't want to fight over disagreements. They wanted to have a civil conversation about their disparate findings. They depended, after all, on each other's testimony for evidence, since they could not see everything for themselves. So they had to accept other men's sincere reports as possibly as right as someone else's contradictory, but equally sincere, reports about what might be the same matter.

This led to ways of investigating and reporting that were properly circumspect: "The naturalistic and the normative were systematically bound together. Practitioners recognized others as honest and com-

petent, and they told each other how they ought to behave, only in respect of a shared view of the world which they investigated. Experimental culture shared norms insofar as its members shared a view of
reality. It was this ontology which was the ultimate sanction on members' conduct. If you are a genuine investigator of the natural world,
then *this* is how your reports ought to look and *this* is the epistemic
status you ought to claim for them" (Shapin 1994, 350). Only by viewing the world as various, and not necessarily homogenous in the way
mathematical treatment required, could you have the conversation
among mutually trusting equals that would allow empirical scientific
activity to go on. This leads Shapin to a speculation:

> *Every* practice, however committed to the production of precise and
> rigorous truth about the world, possesses institutionalized means of
> telling members when "reasonable agreement" or "adequate preci-
> sion" has been achieved, when "enough is enough," when to 'let it
> pass,' when to invoke idiopathic "error factors" and not to inquire too
> diligently into the sources of variation in testimony. The toleration of
> a degree of moral uncertainty is a condition for the collective pro-
> duction of *any future moral certainty.* This toleration allows truth-
> producing conversations to be continued tomorrow, by a community
> of practitioners able and willing to work with and to rely upon each
> other. (Shapin 1994, 353–54)

The generalization of this statement that we need for the investigation of reports on society is that any interpretive community—
defined as the network of people who make and use a particular form
of representation—shares some rules governing what its members
should believe and when and why they should believe it. How some
members of that community represent and communicate what they
know, and how other members interpret the communications they
get, will be governed by more or less agreed-on rules, and those rules
will embody understandings about the kinds of people who will be
involved in each of these activities.

We needn't think that the definitions of the kinds of people involved will always be based on a code of honor and mutual respect. It
way well be just the opposite: many makers of representations of

society don't think that users will know much or that they can be trusted with much. As a consequence, the representations they make use conventions that presuppose users who won't know much and thus include many aids—they are (as we say now) user-friendly.

So? The work of making representations is divided among makers and users. The work that makers do is there for users to use. What makers don't do, users must do. They may not all know enough to do what the makers want and require, they may know how to do it but not do it consciously, or they may do it differently. When they do it in their own way, they may well produce results different from what the makers had in mind. Different worlds of representation making divide the work quite differently. What seems inescapably the work of the makers in one world—labeling the rows and columns of the analytic table, for instance—becomes the ordinary work of users in the world of documentary photography. Every kind of representation offers the possibility, and probably the fact, of a different way of dividing up the work, with consequences for the look of what's made and for the fact of what's made of it.

5

Standardization and Innovation

Let's take stock. Representations are organizational products. The organizations and communities that make and use them divide the labor of selecting, translating, arranging, and interpretation between makers and users in a variety of ways. We can never take for granted how that's done, because the division of labor keeps changing. The makers choose what to include and how to arrange it. Do they do it "the way we've always done it," or do they try something new?

Most often, makers produce representations in a standard form that everyone understands and knows how to make and use. Occasionally, however, for whatever reason, someone begins to make representations of a particular kind differently, violating some of the existing agreements and provoking disagreements and conflicts. Such situations, bringing into question standards that have until then been taken for granted, provide the best possible data for sociological analysis of the day-to-day work of representing society. The polarity of standardization and innovation brings many features of the process into relief.

Conflicts occasioned by innovations in representation frequently take the form of arguments over what the best way to do it is. To do what? To make whatever kind of representation you and the other people who make and use them want. Representations can be and have been made and used in many different ways, and makers and users always have strong opinions about how do it. It's never easy or obvious which way would be best. What is the best way to write a scientific paper for publication in a sociology journal? What is the best way to use visual materials in a report? What is the best way to present social analysis in a documentary film? How do I write my novel, for which I have sociological ambitions? Makers and users of representations of society ask themselves and each other questions like that, and everyone involved has to answer them from time to time in order to get on with whatever they're doing. These fruitless questions have no guaranteed answers. They mainly irritate people, provoking endless discussion, dissension, and bad feelings.

A more interesting approach than arguing takes advantage of the ideas in the preceding chapters to propose a principle: *Every way of doing things is perfect.* Every answer to every question raised about how to make the film or write the ethnography or make the statistical table is the perfect answer.

There is a catch to this wonderful answer. That's not the full text of the principle. The full text goes like this: Every way of doing things is perfect—*for something.* That is, every way is the best way to accomplish something someone wants done, under some specific set of circumstances. So the problem changes from what is the best way to do X to what is X such that this particular form of representation best accomplishes it? That identifies the core of whatever argument there is: the question of what people are trying to accomplish by doing X the way they propose to do it. And the answer to that lies in the organization they are doing it in, which presents makers with the users who must be satisfied, and users with the makers who do that kind of work and might not want to satisfy those desires, and presents everyone involved with all the resources with which the work is to be done and distributed. Not just the money, though that's important, but also the skills and training and needs and desires each party brings to the situation.

The resulting situations take innumerable forms. But these conflicts and resolutions also share some common aspects.

Standardization

Every developed representational world works with forms that are, to some degree, standardized. The social science journal article, one of the most standardized representations of society that exists, exhibits the main features of the phenomenon. Increasingly over a period of perhaps one hundred years, these articles have followed a strict format: a statement of the problem and the theory out of which it develops; a description of what people have written about the question in the past, the "review of the literature" which so terrorizes graduate students; a statement of hypotheses to be tested; a description of the methods used to gather and analyze data; a discussion that accepts or rejects the hypotheses in the light of the evidence reported; and a conclusion repeating, in summary, all that. Articles typically report data (from a census, survey, or experiment) in tables presented in a standardized form. Everyone who uses this standardized form takes it as unproblematic, the epitome of the transparent scientific window through which makers of representations can communicate what they know. This supposes that readers actually read and evaluate the evidence presented in the tables. If everything works just this way, then the world approximates the one Boyle and his colleagues were looking for, in which they could present ideas and results to each other in an unproblematic way.

Do the articles, and the tables they depend on as evidence, work that way? McGill's study of students' reading habits (1990) led him to conclude not only that many readers just don't read the evidence-containing table but also that "when representations of information are standardized, readers can develop standardized ways of reading them, including standard short cuts as well."

Standardization affects how articles are read in several ways. It saves readers time by letting them go directly to what they think will be interesting, feeling sure that if they ignore the rest they won't miss anything they need. It lets them see whether the article is interesting for them at all. And it lets readers discriminate among articles according to their level of statistical knowledge and interest. So readers often skip tables, trusting that they say what the text says they do or that figuring out what they say would not be worth the time it would take.

McGill distinguished four kinds of journal readers, according to how they dealt with tables. Theory people ignored the tables, going right to the ideas. Nonnumerates didn't know how to read the tables, so they skipped them. Interest-driven statisticians went through tables carefully if they thought the topic interesting and often treated the tables as what was interesting, ignoring the text altogether. Statistical purists routinely criticized tables, which contained, for them, the meat. At one extreme, some read a statistical article by examining the tables and formulas carefully, working through them and thus reproducing the work the author did. At the other extreme, some readers only skimmed the evidence or pretty much ignored it altogether. Recall that some were sure that the tables said what the author said they did; if they didn't, the editors would not have published the article: QED.

What do serious users hope to get from a display of numbers in a table or graph? These displays, remember, let readers compare two numbers and see if one is bigger than the other. If so, we learn that something (often called an "independent variable") has a consequence worth thinking about; if it doesn't, we learn that it doesn't. We take either result to be relevant to the ideas whose truth we are considering, giving us proof for one of them or failing to do that.

Standardization lets readers develop standard ways of making that assessment and standard shortcuts when the standard way is too tedious. It lets readers who want to take the quick path do that, and readers who want to take the slow, careful path do that too, achieving both results by putting everything in standard language, standard and thus easily recognized symbols, and well-known standard formats that make it easy to identify the parts relevant for you. You can evaluate those parts according to your taste and know that the material you read or ignore contains just what you think it does, because that is where everyone routinely puts it. Which means that the finished product's features must be designed to satisfy well-defined kinds of users. Must? It's imperative *if* the product is to continue to have the support of the variety of people who now use it, each in their own way, and thus produce the base for the continued making of products like that.

Are there analogues to these differing ways of taking in knowledge about society in other areas of representational activity? What are the standard features of any kind of representation, and who knows them and how they work? What are the quick and slow paths for a movie, novel, or play?

The quick path for one of these fictional representations is just to read it or see it and experience it at the moment, with maybe a little postmortem with your friends afterward—"How did you like it?"—and then it's over. You've seen it, "gotten the point," and added it to the store of memories of similar materials you'll consult when you see and talk about the next movie or book, when you compare how the plot developed this time as opposed to other times. It's all casual, tied to occasions of sociable interaction with people who have similar interests, although that sociable interaction might include serious talk about serious matters—government intrigues and wrongdoing, the damaging activities of large corporations, the evils of drugs—that one of these works addresses. (Understand that all the "empirical" statements here are invented, guesses as to what might be so, things to check up on with real research. They illustrate the function of comparison, even of imaginary data, as a way of generating researchable problems.)

McGill's argument suggests, by analogy, that standardized formats let us extract ideas and emotions from these works with a minimum of trouble. The standardized elements make up the language of dramas and films and novels: characters, plots, metaphor, description, and so on. And, also, the truly primitive elements of production: for films, say, the point of view of the camera, the nature of the transitions from one point of the view to another ("cuts"), the way cutting between points of view can create a story—everything that a textbook on film technique describes. (David Mamet's discussion [Mamet 1991, 9–55] with film students gets right down to the specifics of how separate short shots create a film's narrative forward movement. I also learned a lot about these technical matters from Kawin 1992.) The standardized shortcuts provided by standardized film language tell us, for instance, who the good guys and bad guys are, a topic that invades even the most scientific forms of representation (as we'll see in chapter 8). They signal what kinds of people the characters are and what they are likely to do, and so give us both the pleasures of being proved right and the surprises of being proved wrong. Users easily internalize these standardized shortcuts, especially but not only in the case of popular forms like film, seldom consciously realizing that any language at all is being used, it all seems so "natural."

Other viewers, more careful and critical, know at every moment that everything in the work results from choices the makers of the work have made and might have made differently. These sophisticated users have all the analytic and linguistic apparatus they need to make critical distinctions and judgments, to decide that this work is well done and that one not. Film critics view a film over and over, just as a statistician might review tables and formulas carefully. As a result, they consciously experience a film as made up of sequences of shots, each with its own assortment of points of view, lighting, combinations of long and medium shots and closeups, etc. They talk about how a sequence of shots produces an emotional and cognitive result for the viewer. A sophisticated viewer might time the length of successive shots in the hunting scene in Jean Renoir's *The Rules of the Game* to see how quick cuts produce tension, while an ordinary movie viewer might register the length of the shots without thinking about it, feeling the tension without dwelling on what produced it. Alternatively, a long take without a cut similarly produces tension, as in the famous three-minute tracking shot that follows a car across the Mexican-U.S. border and ends in the car's explosion in Orson Welles's *Touch of Evil.*

The audience for documentary films presumably exhibits similar types, although it may be that fewer people who don't really care that much view them in that casual spirit. Documentary deals with material about which viewers more likely have serious opinions, and so they may be more critical, more suspicious, more on their guard, less willing to trust the filmmaker. Therefore, they may be more consciously analytic about what they are watching, about the persuasive devices being used, and about possible deceptions that might be going on.

Standardized representations are easy to make and use, but not everyone makes or uses them the same way. Some uses evade the control the makers try to exercise over how they are used. Some makers want to do things not accounted for easily in the standardized methods. Since standards are tied to doing some specific thing in the best possible way, whatever that something is, makers who want to do something different innovate, creating new possibilities and new standards.

Innovation

The makers and users for whom the standard ways have been good enough don't welcome innovations. The old ways are plenty good enough for them, and many of the representational worlds we're interested in here experience periodic, sometimes chronic, quarrels about how their characteristic products should be made.

Witness the example of John Tukey, a great innovator in statistics and statistical graphics. His *Exploratory Data Analysis* (1977) is a classic, a gold mine of possibilities that has, somehow, had relatively little impact on my own field of sociology. When I first discovered Tukey's work, I wondered why my colleagues who worked with numbers didn't use his discoveries and inventions.

In an early article, Tukey (1972) lays out five areas where innovation in graphical displays of numbers could and should occur. These include mixing text and numbers, which are usually kept rigorously apart; devising more efficient ways of displaying cyclical data; condensation in plotting, so that we can attend "to what is often most valuable for us to see"; convenient ways to lay out "additive fits to two-way tables"; and improved histograms (bar charts). He intended his inventions to make the important results of research more apparent and readily available to readers.

He says, about these innovations, "In one way or another, as one would expect of significant innovations for familiar problems, these five advances all have the flavor of heresy" (Tukey 1972, 294). In reference to the first, he says:

The most institutionalized of all has been the separation of "table" and "graph," involving as it has special technical skills and the division of labor. Any exhibit containing numbers had to be set in letterpress by a printer, who could not be expected to understand what was to be made clear and therefore has little choice but to make sure only that his table could yield its facts, if not its insights, to those skilled in the archeology of numbers. Anything graphic was to be drawn by a draftsman, who equally could not be expected to understand what was to be made clear and thus had little choice but to draw for the eyes of an unperceptive viewer whose thoughts were not to be stimulated.

As we move through an era of photographic and xerographic reproduction toward an era of computer-controlled composition, we have the opportunity of taking back into the analyst's hand and mind the control of what is to be shown and how the key points are to be emphasized. (1972, 294)

Tukey thus makes a nice organizational analysis, linking the inadequacies of contemporary practice in statistical graphics to the division of labor among statisticians, printers, and draftsmen. But *heresy* is the crucial word. I don't know how serious Tukey was, but he surely meant that changes like those he was proposing were not changes that others in the statistics and statistical graphics business would regard as simple improvements. No. At least some of those people would take his suggestions as inappropriate and probably better not even thought about. The proof of that, in some way, lies in a simple count of how many articles in the two major sociological journals over a period of years have used either of two simple devices he recommends (results in a minute), which seem to me (though I don't myself ordinarily work with numbers that need summarizing) worth incorporating into the daily practice of the sociological trade: the "stem-and-leaf display" and the "box-and-whisker" diagram.

The "stem-and-leaf display" arranges data in an array like the one Tukey gives of the height of 218 volcanoes:

to

8	0	98766562	0 | 9 = 900 feet
16	1	97719630	
39	2	69987766544422211009850	
57	3	876655412099551426	
79	4	99988443319294333361107	
102	5	97666666554422210097731	
(18)	6	898665441077761065	
98	7	98855431100652108073	
78	8	653322122937	
66	9	377655421000493	
51	10	0984433165212	
38	11	4963201631	
28	12	45421164	
20	13	47830	
15	14	00	
13	15	676	
10	16	52	
8	17	92	
6	18	5	
5	19	39730	19 | 3 = 19,300 feet

The heights are given in units of 100 feet; the numbers to the right of the vertical line are the heights of individual volcanoes in hundreds of feet; the numbers to its left of them are thousands of feet; and the number to the far left is the cumulative count of volcanoes that are at least that tall. So the third line tells us that all the volcanoes listed there are 2000 feet plus a number on the right side of the vertical line: the first is 2600 (2000 + 600) feet, the next two are 2900 feet, and so on. The number to the far left tells us that when you have counted all the volcanoes in this line and added those from the previous two lines, you have accumulated 39 volcanoes out of the total of 218. I've explained that in such painful detail to avoid the problem McGill alerted us to (of users' not reading the numbers).

You can see at a glance the general outline of the distribution in a graph—it's sort of a bell-shaped distribution centered in the lower altitudes—and simultaneously have all the individual numbers that make it up immediately available. The length of the line of type containing the list of the individual numbers in an altitude category is just another version of a bar in a bar graph; it's visually equivalent to the number of members of the category. Tukey describes this, nicely, as a "semi-graphic," which gives "the coarse information by position and [gives] the detailed information by the character or characters, the numerical text, that are positioned." (Tukey 1972, 295) He also demonstrates the use of a "slightly graphic list," a table with only a few numbers in it, so placed as to reproduce the essentials of a curve or chart.

Another Tukey innovation, the "box-and-whisker plot," provides a large amount of data about an array of numbers in a convenient, easily read, and easily compared form. It displays graphically (and the relevant numbers can be attached to it) many important facts about a numerical distribution—the median, the hinges (the points marking its approximate quartiles), the full range of the distribution—and makes it easy to identify the outlying cases for special attention. Most of the numbers are omitted in this example, but they could easily be added (from Tukey 1972):

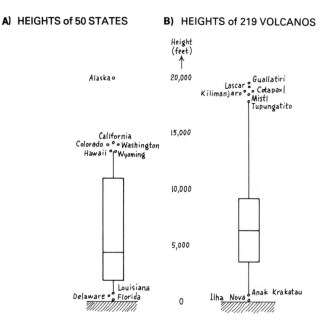

A) HEIGHTS of 50 STATES   **B) HEIGHTS of 219 VOLCANOS**

Those seem like good things to know about a distribution. And this way of communicating them solves the problem I will discuss in the next chapter, how much detail to include. We often want to know only a few things about a distribution: its range, dispersion, and central tendency. But we also want to know about the extreme cases. We typically display the former in a table and the latter in a scatter diagram. The box-and-whisker plot provides both economically. Additional numbers can be inserted or substituted: the mean for the median (or you can have both), the standard deviation, and so on.

The most obvious advantages of these plots are how much information you get at a glance, almost intuitively, and how easy it is then to compare distributions, just by looking at the pictures.

Do sociologists object to Tukey's inventions? No, they don't. They just ignore them. I undertook a small and (I'm sorry to say) very tedious piece of research, going through two major sociological journals, the *American Sociological Review* and the *American Journal of Sociology*, and seeing how many of the articles published in the year 2001 made use of the stem-and-leaf displays or box-and-whisker diagrams Tukey recommended. No reason to think 2001's output would differ much from adjacent years, so I let boredom convince me that one year was enough. None of the 77 articles published in the two journals uses any of those devices. (Sixty-eight of the 77 articles use numerical data for which Tukey's inventions might have been appropriate.) Critics could argue that the kinds of research problems presented in the articles weren't suited to those techniques. But many of the articles presented quantitative data in just the ways Tukey meant to avoid: pages of numbers that, instead of clarifying what had been found, obscured the results and provoked exactly the shortcut responses McGill's interviewees described. It's easier to take authors' claims at face value than to check them by tedious cell-by-cell comparisons; most readers of such articles probably do the former.

Would anyone — does anyone — find Tukey's simple statistical displays heretical? Was Tukey being a little paranoid? Do such sober objects provoke disproportionate responses? Latour says that though the methods section may not look it, it is the most polemic of all the sections of a scientific article, the one that fights with other authors and articles and fends off their attacks (1987, chap. 1, esp. 45–60). Methods, including methods for the display of data, carry a heavy moral charge. Using them correctly, according to the standards accepted by honorable practitioners in the field, signals the researcher's honesty and respect for those colleagues and their opinions (echoes of Shapin's discussion of Boyle and his colleagues). Not using them correctly signals arrogance, incompetence, dishonesty, or immorality.

Using standard methods of representation incorrectly or replacing them with alternative methods attacks how things have been done and therefore attacks the status system(s) of the world in which those kinds of reports circulate. Everett Hughes (n.d.) laid out the logic of such reasoning in a discussion of Action Catholique, a Canadian political movement of the 1940s. He began with two premises from William Graham Sumner—"status lies in the mores" and "all sects are at war with the mores"—and carried the syllogism to its logical conclusion: "Sects are at war with the society's status system." Sumner and Hughes were talking about religious groups and parties, but the syllogism applies to representational worlds too. When you attack standard methods, you attack the people who use those methods and the system that awards high prestige to people who use them.

So Tukey was on solid sociological ground when he called his innovations heresies. He says of his inventive variations on standard bar charts (histograms): "The idea that a histogram must have an area proportional to count seems to be deeply ingrained. Why? There seem to be a few clear answers. The argument is far from impregnable that (1) impact is proportional to area and that (2) impact ought to be proportional to count. We all know that one more case in the tails has far greater importance than one more in the middle" (1972, 312). He says a standard histogram often fails to show what most needs to be known: deviations from a pattern. So he first constructs a "rootogram," which plots each bar's height proportional to the square root of the count it expresses. More interesting yet, he then constructs a "hanging rootogram," in which the bars of the histogram are fitted, at the top, to a normal curve, so that their deviations from "normality" appear more clearly.

Neither innovation produces a bar whose area is proportional to the amount it represents; that's where it departs from standardized practice. It shows what it has to show differently, by the height of the bar above or below a line. But, the standard critical argument against innovations goes, people in general (especially laypeople) automatically see the area of the bar as what's crucial and so will inevitably misunderstand a bar with greater area as symbolizing more "real number" than a bar constructed in the standard way.

So, to push the interpretation maybe farther than is reasonable, conservatives, status quo defenders, speak to protect the ignorant and innocent, who will be misled by this breach of standardization. That's one element of the differential status the Sumner-Hughes theorem talks about: the division into "us" who know and "them" who don't, with "us" having the burden of protecting "them" against those who would take advantage of them. (This is a version of what's discussed in chapter 8 under the heading "Insidious.")

The other element has to do with the internal hierarchy of the statistical profession. If we've always done it this way and now you say we have to do it differently, what we do will no longer be considered as good, as important, as canonical as it used to be. Your way of representing data will, if it's accepted, usurp the place of honor held by our old way. And you will be more important and respected, and we will be correspondingly less so, in whatever the status system of the business is. To which a not uncommon response is "Oh, yeah?" Experts don't take being dethroned lightly.

The Classic Situation

Changes are proposed by people who don't like the forms of representation currently available. They want to do something else, or do what's to be done more easily, or do it better, and can't with the standard methods.

We can find this classic situation in every world of representation: a standard way, known by all or most people who use the form; people whose dissatisfaction with those standards, for whatever reason, leads to a disagreement about them; and some resolution of the disagreement in the form of, perhaps, a new standardization of representational forms and some new standardized habits of reading and viewing among users.

What makes people dissatisfied with the representations they currently have? Some complain that the way everyone has until now accepted no longer solves the problem our professional world (including its users) want solved. And we've found, or one of us has invented, a terrific new way that does what we all want, while avoiding some difficulties and problems the old way provokes that we had all learned to adjust to. Now we needn't adjust to them. Let's change.

Take the difficulty I referred to earlier of displaying more than a few dimensions of classification in a cross tabulation. Many sociologists have occasion to do that. The two-dimensional table is easy: the rows show the categories of one variable (age, for instance), the columns the categories of a second variable (let's say income).

	Income	
	Rich	Poor
Age		
old	old/rich	old/poor
young	young/rich	young/poor

Each cell contains one of the possible combinations of the categories of the two variables. When you add a third variable (gender, say), you have to repeat categories.

	Income			
	Rich		Poor	
Gender	Men	Women	Men	Women
Age				
old	old/rich men	old/rich/ women	old/poor/ men	old/poor/ women
young	young/rich/ men	young/rich/ women	young/poor/ men	young/poor/ women

Four or more variables use even more space, are harder to interpret (because the two numbers you want to keep in mind are farther apart), and more of the cells are likely to have no cases in them. What are some alternatives? The Boolean truth table recommended by Charles Ragin (1987, 2000) summarizes such data more compactly. (X means the feature in the heading is present, 0 that it is absent.)

Old (+60)	Rich ($100K)	Gender (Male)	# of cases
X	X	X	500
X	X	0	125
X	0	X	800
X	0	0	875
0	X	X	250
0	X	0	175
0	0	X	900
0	0	0	900

This shows all the possible combinations of characteristics and the number of people who exhibit that combination. So (in my invented data) there 500 old rich men (line 1), 125 old rich women (line 2), and so on, down to the 900 young poor men in the last line. This displays the data more economically and intelligibly than the eight cells of the conventional table, making comparing the numbers and interpreting what they mean much easier. This method has been adopted by some political scientists but is still not found very often in sociology (zero times in the year of articles I examined).

My brief scan of the major journals showed that sociologists don't use this device or any of the ones Tukey developed in his very large book. Why not? Here's a guess. It isn't the standard way. So some people don't know how to use these devices or are more at home doing something else they learned in graduate school and have done ever since. Furthermore, such people might say (and they might be right), users of such devices, people who read statistical charts and tables, might not know how to read them and could be confused or misled. And that would be too bad, because the statistical object's point is to give users correct, usable information, rather than confusing, misleading information. Standardized formats of the kind McGill describes provides correct, usable information for people who know standard ways of reading them. Changes interfere with that.

Susan Cotts Watkins (1985) presents an in-depth look at graphic devices proposed but never adopted in the study of population. (Chapter 10, below, goes into the question of different kinds of charts, numerical and nonnumerical, at length.) It's easy to see why they didn't: complicated and confusing, a welter of solid and broken lines, capital and small letters with prime signs attached, three-dimensional arrays—all excellent ways to present some special thing, but confusing to anyone unwilling to spend a lot of time deciphering them. Who will be prepared to make that extra investment of energy for information that they might not need or can get in a less adequate form but in a familiar and therefore less time- and energy-consuming way?

People also get dissatisfied with a standardized form of representation because it is actively misleading in some way it wasn't previously seen to be, as in the case of the so-called North-South map, which shows the world just as it is now shown in the Mercator projection, but upside down, as though we had turned the map on the wall top for bottom. Change the lettering and it's the same map. Its proponents argue that this rectifies a Eurocentric view in which (because we think "up" is more important than "down") the Northern Hemisphere (including Europe, Canada, the United States, and Japan) seems more important than South America, Africa, and Southeast Asia. Which, after all, is a political rather than a geographical judgment. (More sophisticated arguments are made against other versions of Eurocentrism displayed in maps.)

Participants in such worlds as drama, film, and fiction consider change inherently good. Artists generally don't want to do or be caught doing the same thing over and over. Change in the arts is the natural state of things. If each new piece innovated in form or method of display, no one would complain. The change would be done because the writer or filmmaker or producer wanted to express something that the old way couldn't accommodate, and that's enough reason. Of course, people in those worlds do complain when change occurs, and loudly, but their complaint is that the new goal is not worthwhile. The case of hypertext fiction, which requires writers and readers alike to learn new, nonlinear ways of dealing with narrative made possible by speedy personal computing, is a good example (see Becker 1995).

Tukey used the word *heresy* to refer to what seems like a minor variation in statistical charting. You hear a lot of language like that when makers of representations discuss how knowledge about society is represented. That, in turn, indicates how these representations are tightly attached to important interests and beliefs about the relative status of groups and about how participants in these relations should behave.

When the intelligent graduate students in my seminar discussed the collection of charts and tables I had gathered to provoke them (which I will describe at length in chapter 10), their moralistic language surprised me (even though I had already read Tukey and noted his anomalous mention of "heresy"). They complained—about a chart the authors of *Deep South* (Davis, Gardner, and Gardner 1941) had created to show how they arrived at and substantiated their analysis of clique structure and class in the white community of Natchez, Mississippi—that the authors had not labeled the chart clearly enough. No key in some easily accessible place gave the meaning of the chart's symbols. They complained indignantly that the authors "should have" done this, that they "owed it to us." When I pointed out that they had provided just that information to the side of the chart, the students relented a little, deciding that, OK, this "duty" had been fulfilled, after all, but still not as well as it might have been.

I thought I heard one student say that the author of another graphic had "failed us," by not labeling it sufficiently clearly. I had misheard him, but the mistake was instructive. What the student had said was that when he was in high school, a teacher had "failed us" (that is, the students) when "we" didn't label similar graphs clearly. The same student also thought the author whose work we were discussing had, in fact, failed us in the way I thought he meant, and the confusion perhaps gave a clue to the origin of some of this moralizing. It may be stretching things to say this, but I wonder whether learning about representations in the authoritative (and authoritarian) situation of the school, where an adult teacher punishes children for "doing it wrong," is part of what gives such rules their force.

I don't mean to treat the students' upset unseriously, but their concern was largely that because the tables and charts I gave them were not in a standard form, they had trouble reading them and thus might have trouble remembering and reproducing what they said for an examination. That meant that the authors hadn't taken the trouble they should have to make their handiwork clear. The students complained, in other words, about the division of labor: that they had to do too much work they should not have had to do, that it wasn't their responsibility to puzzle through a complex chart, it was the author's responsibility to make that puzzling unnecessary by making the chart in a standard way they could recognize and understand without undue thought.

They used the moral language of responsibility, assigning blame for what was, after all, a mutual failure: the joint failure of the two parties (authors and students) to communicate successfully about the subject matter at hand. The students wanted to say, "It's the authors' fault," while the authors might well have said, "Hey, we're trying to explain something complicated, there's no standard way to do it, do a little work, for chrissake." Since we are only analysts of this situation and not participants, we don't have to assign blame; we can just note that assigning blame is what's at issue.

The same problem arises in another, very different context, when readers complain that an author's prose is "hard to read." Many people in my generation complained that Talcott Parsons's theoretical works were inordinately hard to read (as they complain today about Pierre Bourdieu's). The word *inordinately*, with which I've summarized these complaints, is itself a moral judgment, meaning that I, the reader, should not have to work so hard to recover the meaning that might (or might not) be buried in these complications. The same complaints were made in the 1990s about "postmodern" prose, some of whose practitioners insisted, equally moralistically, that the difficulty is necessary and put there purposefully, because users should not be able to extract meaning too easily. And the sociology in many artistic representations of knowledge about society certainly requires users to work to extract it, as we've seen in the case of photography. Harvey Molotch (1994) raises the especially instructive question of opportunity costs: "If it takes seven hours to read an article by scholar X, we may never read three articles by other scholars (or learn something in a bar). It may be that X is wonderful, but is X three times as wonderful? Parsons was very smart, but was he ten times smarter than Mills? Or Goffman? Or Merton?" (Molotch 1994, 229). And if he isn't, am I within my rights not to read him? (And I'd add the further question of what court you would go to to recover your loss.)

The participants in the seminar gave an excellent example of this, putting themselves in the position of the students McGill had interviewed, a position they said, feelingly, they had often been in, confronted by a large number of articles to read to prepare for an exam or for a dreaded ritualistic review of the literature. You can do the job only by using the shortcuts McGill described, and you can use the standard shortcuts only if the article has used standard representational devices. If the author goes beyond that in difficulty, they'd like to be excused from having to know what he said. (Sometime in the 1960s a Harvard graduate student told me that to protect themselves from Parsons's frequent emendations of his theories, he and his peers had jointly agreed not to read anything he wrote after 1953, at least until they finished their dissertations. I wish I could vouch for the veracity of this story.)

My students' language also expresses the morality of efficiency. Readers commonly explain why something should be done in a particular way by saying that it makes things "easier," often using the telltale *just* as an intensifier. "It just makes it easier to read that way." The *just* says that it's so obvious as not to require justification; the *easier* invokes the logic of efficiency, according to which whatever makes a thing go faster and without effort is necessarily better. Users of representations often feel that their time is too valuable to waste learning new methods; they want to get right to the knowledge they can put to use. Experimental forms of literary and artistic social investigation— the works of people like David Antin (chapter 9) and Hans Haacke (chapter 4)—do demand, often successfully, that their users, perhaps more accustomed to paying that kind of price, make the extra effort.

The resolution of these conflicts probably takes certain generic forms. A new form can completely supplant the old. C. P. Snow told of such a change in his early novel about crystallography, *The Search* (Snow 1959), in which a highly mathematical form of representation completely supplanted an older form and left all the oldtimers who lacked the math needed for the new form out in the cold.

Another resolution—probably what has happened to mathematical modeling in sociology—is that the innovation becomes a specialty that has only a tangential relationship to the larger field. It replaces nothing; it adds a new something that some people use but most ignore. I think math models are more useful than a lot of people do, so a part of chapter 10 is devoted to them.

Some fields never do settle these questions. The arguments go on without end. Documentary film seems to be like that. What is allowable? How far must filmmakers go to avoid contaminating the reality they want to film? How does that compromise the result? (The relation between reality and representation gets an airing in chapter 7.)

Who's Involved?

We've been looking at intramural quarrels among makers of a particular kind of representation. Makers seldom, if ever, have complete control of their work situation or its results. Users also play a part, alluded to by makers who worry that "they" will be misled. But users are seldom so passive and stupid as that implies (as the studies of digital culture consumers reported in Karaganis, forthcoming, make clear). They actively participate in the process, choosing what to pay attention to and interpreting what they find, independent of the makers' intentions.

Users typically have a choice of "representational products." (I use that awkward expression to emphasize users' role as consumers in a marketplace of ideas.) They can go to this movie or that, read this book rather than that one, favor this genre over that one. In the sciences, they can believe and make use of material presented in this way rather than that. Users vote with their feet.

So the resolution of an argument among professionals—in those fields where the users get to vote that way—may not depend on "expert opinion" at all but rather be decided by the choice among alternatives made by end users, whom the professionals may think too ignorant to decide such matters as whether to use Tukey's graphic innovations. You could say that that's how the choice about statistical innovations has been made. Sociologists just don't use them and so far have no reason to explain to anyone why they don't. It's been said that this is how most "theoretical" disputes in sociology actually get settled: not by logic or evidence but by users' voting with their feet, getting interested in this idea rather than that one, even though they are only ordinary practitioners and not experts in theory.

Users also often use what's presented in ways the makers never intended and may be appalled by. I created my representation as the embodiment of an argument, carefully arranging problem, hypotheses, methods, results, and conclusions in a standardized way to provide a conclusion readable in a standardized fashion, and then find that readers are using the data in ways I never intended, as a file to ransack for evidence supporting conclusions I don't agree with, totally ignoring my careful construction. This happens all the time in the natural sciences but also, of course, in the arts, where each of the many layers of professional personnel involved, as well as the lay public, may make something different of the work (editors edit, directors stage, audiences make what they want of the result).

6

Summarizing Details

Every way of representing knowledge about society reduces the amount of data that users have to contend with. Latour (1987, 234–37) describes this as the process of producing nth+1 order descriptions, combinations of more detailed descriptions that take up more space, the combinations standing for the whole, as an equation stands for all the combinations of numbers that fit its requirements. Survey interviewers record very little of what they learn about interviewees, and their bosses soon mingle the little they recorded with the answers of other interviewees and summarize them as a cell in a table, the cell in turn condensed into a statistical summary like a mean or, combined with other cells, a correlation coefficient. And all of that is reduced finally to a conclusion said to be supported by all this evidence. Most of the evidence one might have used or thought interesting has been distilled away.

Not to make fun of the process. Data reduction isn't scientistic foolishness, it's a necessity, simultaneously theoretical and practical. Try this thought experiment. You don't summarize what you've found at your observational site. You bring it all back, the entire physical, biological, and social contents. What would that accomplish? It might be easier to get to the data you wanted to work on—no need to travel thousands of miles, or hundreds of years in your time machine. Get up in the morning, have some coffee, then go into the world you've stored nearby and watch it.

That doesn't accomplish anything useful if you want to tell someone else what you know about what you studied. You're Funes the

Memorius in Jorge Luis Borges's story (Borges 1964, 59–66), who remembered everything, forgot nothing, and could not separate what was important from what wasn't. Knowing everything means knowing nothing. Knowledge results from weeding out extraneous detail and exposing basic structures, the part we're interested in. Not everything is interesting or useful to us.

So we cut what we feel we can cut and combine the now-summarized pieces of information, which gives us more control of what we know. How do we make that reduction? How did Latour (1995), when he studied scientists working on a problem in soil science, leave behind the soil scientists and botanists, the Brazilian forest they were working in, with its trees, monkeys, heat, rain, soil, and plants—and produce an article in a scientific journal which settles a question of scientific and philosophical interest? The scientists solved their problem by turning the forest into a laboratory, getting rid of the confusing "other stuff" that hid the "essential story" they wanted to know. They numbered parts of the forest and thus turned it into a grid of meter-square plots, each of which could be represented by a small clod of earth . . . this and succeeding reductions finally ending in a chart in an article. Latour did the same, turning what he saw and heard into photographs and field notes, which he summarized as a story, which he then turned into some reflections on how one gets from the signified to the signifier, and wrote— a scientific article.

How do workers reduce what they observe in the various media and genres that report on society? How did Marcel Proust reduce the welter of details he knew about some parts of French society at the end of the nineteenth century to a story with a plot about some characters? How did playwright Caryl Churchill reduce the results of several weeks of interviewing and observation in post-Communist Romania to the three-act play *Mad Forest* (1996)? Are there principles? Are there describable techniques?

The Example of Maps

Reducing the detail of what we know and turning it into a formalized representation poses an insoluble problem. Bernard Beck has often remarked that sociology studies how people do what, in principle, cannot be done: they solve insoluble problems by relaxing some of the constraints laid on them. Cartographer John P. Snyder (1993) explains the unavoidable distortions of mapmaking:

> For about two thousand years, the challenge of trying to represent the round earth on a flat surface has posed mathematical, philosophical, and geographical problems that have attracted inventors of many types.
>
> . . . It was soon apparent that preparing a flat map of a surface curving in all directions led to distortion. That distortion may take many forms—shape, area, distance, direction, and interruptions or breaks between portions. In other words, a flat map cannot correctly represent the surface of a sphere.
>
> A globe also has drawbacks in spite of its basic freedom from distortion. A globe is bulky, of small scale, and awkward to measure; less than half its surface can normally be seen at one time. . . .
>
> The systematic representation of all or part of the surface of a round body, especially the earth, onto a flat or plane surface is called a *map projection*. Literally an infinite number of map projections are possible, and several hundred have been published. The designer of a map projection tries to minimize or eliminate some of the distortion, at the expense of more distortion of another type, preferably in a region of or off the map where distortion is less important. (Snyder 1993, 1)

It can't be done. You can't turn a sphere into a flat surface without distortion. The price of having a map at all is distortion the user learns to live with.

But a flat surface, because it's easily transported and can be superimposed on other flat documents (Latour 1987, 215–57), is what users want for scientific and practical purposes, especially for the creation of the cascades of increasingly abstract representations that give users control over what's depicted. Adam Gopnik (2000) described the map of New York City that bureaucrats use to make superimposable maps that let them see the relation of streets, water mains, electrical lines, and other features of the landscape, so that different city departments can coordinate their work. You can't do that with a globe, but you can with a flat computer representation.

Every way of making a flat projection is good for showing some things and not so good for showing others. If you're only interested in one particular area, you can make it the center of a map which maximizes a desired kind of accuracy there and ignore the distortion in places less important to you (though they might be important to someone else). "Mercator's chief purpose in developing the [1569] projection was navigational. All lines of constant bearing (loxodromes or rhumb lines) are shown straight. The projection thus became valuable to sailors, who could follow a single compass setting (adjusted for magnetic declination, or the variation of true from magnetic north) based on the bearing or azimuth of the straight line connecting the point of departure and destination on the map" (Snyder 1993, 46).

According to Mercator himself:

In this mapping of the world we have had three ends in view: first, so to spread out the surface of the globe into a plane that the places shall everywhere be properly located, not only with respect to their true direction and distance, one from another, but also in accordance with their due longitude and latitude; and further, that the shape of the lands, as they appear on the globe shall be preserved as far as possible.

Mercator further explains how his projection will do what sailors need and want done, and why the resulting distortions won't interfere with navigation on the high seas, whatever else they mess up. Similarly, some map users are mainly interested in very small local areas. Stereographic projections distort larger surrounding areas, but the small one of interest to specialized users is just fine. (Snyder 1993, 20)

As cartography developed into a separate professional specialty, its products acquired many new uses (e.g., for the administration of political entities) and mapmakers increasingly used complex mathematical methods. Which led to the invention of projections whose greatest virtue was that they were difficult to do and so would please a professional audience appreciative of the technical obstacles that had been overcome. "More complicated projection developments were in some cases carried out for the reason often given for climbing mountains: because the challenge was there. Beyond the achievement of placing a world map in a triangle, for example, there is little to recommend such a projection. The inventors of many of these mathematical novelties generally did not promote their work beyond modest scientific publication" (Snyder 1993, 155).

Summarizing

Any representation of social reality, then, has to make a little out of a lot. How do you take a great deal of material on something and turn it into less material, so that it can be comfortably and practically taken in by its intended reader or viewer?

Students of society hail new technological developments because they let us make our representations "more complete." Now (I write this in early 2006, but who knows what will be possible when you read it?) we can record all the voices in a room, without distortion, on our tape. We can videotape our surroundings for four hours without having to stop to put a new tape in the camera. We can put every word of the extant literature of ancient Greece and Rome on one CD-ROM. Awesome!

What good is that ability? It doesn't solve a problem. It makes the problem worse. Carry the premise to an extreme. Imagine that we can, finally, reproduce, in all its complexity, at full scale, every single aspect of a social situation. Now we have it all.

Ariane Lodkochnikov, the heroine of Eric Kraft's comic novel *What a Piece of Work I Am* (1994), embodies the problem. She has turned her life into a work of art that consists of . . . her life. She lives on the stage of a theater. People buy tickets and come to watch her live, watch her entertain guests, eat, read, watch television, sleep. She has been there for years and has devoted fans who come regularly to catch up with what's going on.

But what she has created is no longer a representation of anything. It's the thing itself. If we make—if we could make—an exact duplicate of what we want to understand, a duplicate from which none of the original has been subtracted, then what we have is, after all, the thing itself. And we are no further along the road to understanding this thing than we were before we made the replica. Which emphasizes that the point of making the representation was to get rid of a lot of that reality so that we could see clearly and focus on just those things we want to know about, without being distracted by what we don't care about. (That's why, remember, newspaper editors tell photographers to "get rid of all that clutter" in a photograph, perhaps by intentionally blurring everything that isn't the "main subject." See the discussions in Hagaman 1993, 1996.)

But summarizing always threatens to lose something we really wanted. Summarize too much, and you no longer have enough. Enough for what? That depends on what a representation maker wants to accomplish. What's too much for me isn't enough for you. Not just because we have different tastes but because the enterprises we're engaged in need a different kind of information. "How much is enough?" always has to be understood in the context of a particular group that wants the representation for a specific, situationally based purpose.

The problem of summarizing just the right amount crops up in many places. Two prominent ones, very different, are summary statistics and ethnographic accounts.

Statistical methods aim to reduce the bulk of the data we have to deal with, to turn an array of measurements into a chart, or into an average or some other measure of central tendency (median, mode). But not to reduce it too much. An average, after all, doesn't tell you a lot about the collection of numbers it summarizes, other than that it represents in some ways and for some purposes (but not all the important ones) what the collection is like. People who use numbers also often want to know something else: how much variety does the collection contain—or, put another way, how different are its members? One answer is to tell you the extreme values your collection of cases contains, perhaps the largest and the smallest, the range of the distribution. Still another answer tells you how closely clustered the members are around the average, summarized in a number called the standard deviation.

When we want to describe how closely connected two or more

things are—height and weight, or income and years of education—
we use measures that produce a number that can be compared to
other similar measures, so that we can say these two variables are
more or less closely associated in this population than they are in
some other one. Statisticians have invented many such measures of
association, which differ in what they emphasize or give weight to. No
two of them give exactly the same measure of how and how often the
two variables go together, even though they summarize the same data.

All of these measures lose information. Once you have reduced a
collection of measurements to an average, you cannot manipulate it
to recover the full array of individual measurements that produced it.
They're gone (unless you saved them somewhere else).

Each way of summarizing loses different information. Correla-
tional methods turn cases into scores on individual items and then
calculate the relationship between items. The unity of the individual
cases, the variety of ways those two items connected with each other
in particular cases and with the rest of their context, disappears.
Other methods preserve the connections in the individual case.

When we decide to collect certain kinds of information and present it in a certain way, we simultaneously decide not to collect or display some other kinds of information. For every way of summarizing
data we can ask: What is usually left out? And can we retrieve some of
what was lost and put it back in? Social scientists have very conventionalized notions of what's to be included in a social science description and what can be safely let go of. Think of all the information participant observers collect, when they are in the field, that they never
use. Their field notes never contain everything that went on in their
presence.

When I taught field work, I made students crazy in the first weeks
of the class by insisting that they write "more." A student who spent
four hours in an auto repair shop would give me one page of notes, and
I'd say it wasn't enough. It took weeks for them to see that I really
meant they should write down "everything," at least try to do it, and
many more weeks for them to see that they couldn't do that and that
what I wanted them to do was think through what they really wanted
to know and write down as much as they could about that. And that

only delayed the hard question, which was, what did they want to know? Because the trick in observing is to get curious about things you hadn't noticed before.

Still, there were limits even to my pedagogically inspired curiosity, and I seldom demanded that they make a complete inventory of smells in the place where they did their research, even though you don't have to be Georg Simmel to recognize the possibility of a sociology of smells—where they come from, how people interpret them, how social life is organized to notice or ignore them, legal and informal ways of capitalizing on desirable ones and getting rid of bad ones, and all the other things any inventive person can think of in a few minutes.

Try another experiment. Tell a social scientist that he or she will be told only a small number of facts about some people whose behavior is to be explained (a condition not very different from the actual constraints that typical survey interviewing imposes on what can be discovered, but what I'm talking about isn't confined to that method). What will they pick, no matter what their theoretical or methodological persuasion? Age, sex, race, income, education, ethnicity—the usual causes (or "independent variables"). A social scientist would blush not to know these things, and yet there are plenty of other things that have an arguable claim to inclusion. How about height-weight ratio? Or hair color? Or "general attractiveness," however measured? Or aggressiveness/timidity? Or general physical handiness as opposed to awkwardness? Not to mention the variables that are specific to an occupation or a neighborhood or a region of the country. If I'm studying musicians who play for weddings, bar mitzvahs, and other social events, or in neighborhood bars and restaurants, the variable of how many songs they know and can play without needing written music would surely be more important than any of the standard list (Becker and Faulkner 2006a, 2006b).

How much to summarize and how much to report in full erupted as a question in ethnographic work in the 1980s, over somewhat similar issues (examined in Clifford 1988). Anthropologists, following the lead of Margaret Mead, Bronislaw Malinowski, and A. R. Radcliffe-Brown, had in the 1920s developed and standardized, at least somewhat, a way of doing and reporting anthropological fieldwork, which Clifford characterizes this way: (1) a professional fieldworker with special skills (2) "used" rather than "commanded" the native language, (3) relied more on visual observation than on talk, (4) used scientific abstractions and methods based on them, (5) focused on particular institutions (e.g., Mead on childhood), and reported their results in "the ethnographic present." This, among other things, allowed people to write long books based on relatively short stays in the field. It was, Clifford says, "an efficient ethnography based on scientific participant observation." This combination based the authority of the fieldworker on a "peculiar amalgam of intense personal experience and scientific analysis." Participant observation consisted of "a continuous tacking between the "inside" and the "outside" of events: on the one hand grasping the sense of specific occurrences and gestures empathetically, on the other stepping back to situate these meanings in wider contexts" (Clifford 1988, 32, 34).

How could these fieldworkers make a coherent summary combining what they had learned from their own observations and what they had added as interpretations of the materials they had gathered? For these were not the same thing. Experience let fieldworkers claim, as the ultimate authority for what they reported, "I was there." Experience made workers sensitive to cues and meanings that might be difficult to specify but were nevertheless real. Such materials, however, did not arise in dialogue and thus were subjective rather than intersubjective—and so were arguable.

Anthropologists realized that fieldworkers came home with something more than their raw experience. They brought back notebooks, writing that carved certain things out of the flux of experience, named and described them, and so turned them into objects of ethnographic work. Events became field notes. In the typical case, such textualizations, combined and summarized, produced the "culture" the work reported on, or some portion of it.

All this writing inevitably reduced the field experience, leaving out details the fieldworker thought dispensable (though others might not agree) or just hadn't thought to include (as no one thinks to include odors in their field reports). Most important, it typically left out the talk with indigenous people from which anthropologists distilled the generalized descriptions of "the culture" that the standard anthropological research report consisted of. Anthropologists summarized what they had learned from observation and interview in statements like this: "the Nuer think X" or "the Samoans do Y."

Some anthropologists became uneasy with these summaries, and that raised, as an important question, how to incorporate the voices of others than the anthropologist into the anthropological report. A polyphonic style of reporting would reveal and recognize the cooperative character of ethnographic work and let the multiple voices of the people who had cooperated on that work be heard. As early as the 1940s, Clyde Kluckhohn (1945) worried about how life history materials, long personal stories told by someone to an anthropologist, should be reported. His wonderfully utopian conclusion, which somehow seemed less impossible to do then than it does now, was to publish them in three versions: a transcription of the anthropologist's notes just as they were written or recorded on audiotape, though there are questions about the accuracy of that too (Blauner 1987); an edited version that removed the "irrelevancies" of ordinary talk (which conversation analysts might think essential); and a reduced version in a less conversational style for lay readers. To suggest such an array of productions is to see how impractical it would be to actually do.

In any event, summarizing anthropological findings and understandings is very complicated, especially raising the question of how much of what actually happened is to be incorporated into the report. Clifford describes several experimental forms of reporting, whose authors don't intend them solely for consumption by anthropologists but rather want them to be read by nonprofessionals, especially perhaps by the people whose own testimony makes up part of the work. This might lead, Clifford says, to publications that will look old-fashioned, in the sense that they contain compendia of uninterpreted indigenous materials, of little use to nonindigenes but of great interest to the indigenes who furnished them.

And so far I have only talked about which people to include. What about the situations in which the behavior we're interested in occurs?

Trying to describe situations leads to the problem of representing what some social scientists like to call "lived experience."

Some representations of society aim to give users a sense of what the lives and experiences of the people and organizations described are like. (Some other forms, of course, promise no such thing, searching instead for uniformities of behavior that lead to lawlike statements of invariant relationships.) These representations want to go beyond reporting on regularities and patterns of behavior, statements of social rules and norms, and other such collective phenomena. They want the reader or viewer to experience, to feel personally, what it would be like to be in those situations themselves as participants.

Representations of "lived experience"—this elusive stuff of feeling and sensation—may be based on very close observation, on detailed interviews, or on access to such privileged documents as letters and diaries. In the extreme case, the representation may be based, implicitly or explicitly, on the experience of the reporters themselves, who may belong to the same social category (they are black or gay or musicians or whatever the relevant social category is) as the people they have studied and thus have shared this experiences, accidentally or coincidentally, or because they have deliberately exposed themselves to those experiences in doing their research, as Mitchell Duneier (Duneier 2000) shared the sixteen-hour days of the street vendors he studied and many anthropologists have proudly shared the meager diets and housing of "their people." Researchers and artists who do this know, in a way others don't, just how cold you get sitting on a New York street all night long in November or what it feels like to be hit by a cop who calls you a demeaning name referring to your race or sexual orientation. Some social scientists and artists who claim to portray the experience of others have had this kind of firsthand experience of what they portray, but not many.

Suppose you do have that kind of intimate knowledge of what it is like to walk, as they say, in someone else's shoes. How do you convey the fullness of that experience to others who haven't had it themselves? What good is it to know all that if most of it gets lost in the translation?

Different representational formats vary in how much of the full experience of the lives they describe gets through. Some give very little and have no intention of providing more than that: a street map, for instance, from which you will never know such simple things as how steep the climb up a particular San Francisco street is, let alone what kinds of buildings it contains, what kinds of people live in them, what's it like at night or in the rain, what the trees smell like. (Mr. Bixby's explanation to his apprentice steamboat pilot Mark Twain of what a Mississippi river boat pilot had to know about that river contained much more information of the kind picked up by going up and down it than any printed chart of the river could hold.)

A street map is the extreme of abstraction: just the bare facts relevant to geographical orientation, everything else gone. Statistical tables and charts are like that too: a limited number of things described in a limited vocabulary. I don't criticize these abstractions. They pay off in their ability to describe a large number of things in a systematic and comparable way. At the cost, of course, of losing detail. A well-known tradeoff.

Historical, biographical, and ethnographic prose tries to get us close to the experience itself. Authors in these styles usually have some of this more detailed, experiential knowledge, often think it is the essence of what's worth knowing, and want to share it with their readers. They want us to know the details of people's daily lives, what they wore, how cold and hungry they were, the details of their sexual activity, and, above all, what they thought and felt while they were experiencing all that. How to convey that knowledge? Not just the facts of the story but the inner world of the players, and especially the world of emotion.

A lot of historical and anthropological prose tries to convey such subtle aspects of human social experience. The lists of kinship terms, descriptions of technology, and lists of magical spells and religious beliefs in anthropological monographs alternate with lengthy, sometimes poetic, usually consciously literary attempts at prose that will produce a sympathetic emotional response in readers. Similarly with historical and biographical accounts, which layer "facts" between slabs of authorial interpretation based on and attested to by material from letters, diaries, observation, and interviews.

Authors like these, dissatisfied with ordinary scholarly prose, use all the literary artifices they know about and have the nerve to try to draw readers into a world distant in time or space or culture. They invent the inner thoughts of the people they write about. They write fiction, as in Carter Wilson's "anthropological novel" *Crazy February* ([1965] 1974). They experiment with multiple voices, represented by multiple type faces, like Richard and Sally Price's account of the lives of the multiethnic peoples of Surinam (Price 1990; Price and Price 1995).

If you want readers to experience what the people studied actually experienced, these attempts all have an irremediable defect. In the end, they give users no more than what they can learn reading in an armchair at home. They don't experience what the people the book tells them about lived through. The reader can't see what they saw, only imagine it on the basis of a verbal description.

That leads to using photographs and film to supplement or replace the writing. These have many advantages and create many problems this book can't avoid for long. The main thing about photographs, for now, is they let you see what things look like; they give you a lot of visual detail that resembles what you would see if you were there to see for yourself. They don't really do that, of course, since the photographer and author selected what you see so as to make the points they, as the representation's maker, wanted you to get. Purists complain about that screen between the user and the lived experience. Still, in such definitive ethnographic works as *Balinese Character* (Bateson and Mead 1942), you learn and have available for study a lot that prose would not give you, or would not give you so economically. The book, consisting of one hundred pages of photographs, five to eight or more on a page, with a facing page of anthropological interpretation, shows the attentive user, to take one small example, details of posture and touching between adult and child that might affect the development of personality (as Bateson and Mead thought and meant to convey). The photographs often show successive stages in the development of some event, large or small—a dance, a trance, a child's tantrum—all shown in great detail but with great economy. It's hard to imagine the prose you would need to convey what one of these pages of photographs tells you.

The same advantages and problems exist for motion pictures. Films add to the visual detail of the still photograph the continuity of continuous action and thus the possibility of both a straightforward ongoing narrative and the fragmentation of that straight narrative through the use of flash-forwards and flashbacks. But none of these media really go very far in delivering "lived experience." Even the most avant-garde scholarly presentation ends up summarizing that experience out of existence. Which is not to say that it can't be done. Artists, who don't subject themselves to the constraints of scholarly standardization, have some important things to show us.

We all "live experience" in situations. Situations are physical. We all know that the physicality is important for our understanding of what goes on in them, but social science representations almost never give users a way to experience it. Makers of representations, even those deeply concerned to present us with "lived experience," don't usually propose that we experience its physical reality.

But we could give our users that experience, at least in principle. Not in the conventional formats we usually consider (and often consider as paradigmatic in this book), such as film or the theater, let alone ethnographic prose. Movies have made sound more "realistic," but attempts to add something so elementary as smell to film presentations have been no more than commercial gimmicks: scratch-and-sniff cards, to be scratched at appropriate moments, or odors sent through the theater's ventilating system just don't get it. And the same difficulties would arise in theatrical performances.

Site-specific theater, however, goes a way toward meeting this challenge, including many of the physical details other modes of representation leave out. What is site-specific theater? Theatrical performances in places that are not conventional theaters, often rooms or places that seem to be the rooms or places in which the events we watch have actually occurred (or which, on occasion, *are* those very rooms). Antenna Theater of Sausalito, California, has long specialized in such performances. (I don't know of other companies that produce similar events, but there probably are some; Antenna is the one whose work I have followed for years.) *High School* took place in Tamilpais High School in Mill Valley, California (and has since been done in other communities and schools, with the collaboration of local students and faculty). Audience members put on a Walkman and, one at a time, followed taped directions that led them through classrooms, gym, locker rooms, assembly hall, and bathrooms as they listened to an audio collage of interviews with students from that school and the sounds of everyday school activities. The rooms smelled the way high schools smell, and why wouldn't they? It *was* a high school. The walls echoed with talk, just as in a real high school. And why wouldn't they, since it was a real high school? Boys even got the thrill of going into the girls' bathroom. You finally arrived at the outdoor assembly area for your graduation and received a diploma from a silent actor standing just where the principal would stand if the occasion were real. The Antenna Web site describes many of its productions, including the ones I discuss here (www.antenna-theater.org/productionheadings.htm).

Antenna productions don't use speaking actors, and sometimes they employ no actors at all, relying on interviews and recorded ambient sound to fill the tapes. If you have ever taken the National Park Service tour of Alcatraz, the former federal prison in San Francisco Bay, you heard an Antenna tape of prisoners and guards talking about the spaces you were walking through and have a sense of what their productions feel like.

On Sight (In Sausalito), an outdoor Antenna production, told the history of that waterfront town in the bohemian 1960s, describing colorful characters who had lived there—Jean Varda, the artist, and Sterling Hayden, the actor, among others—in the words of people who knew them, while the audience tramped around the outskirts of the houseboats and old shipways where those people had lived and done the things that were being recounted.

These productions provide exactly the physical experiences the typical representational genre slights because no one can think of a practical way to get them to an audience. Antenna's way may not be practical for a lot of purposes, but it is perfect to give ninety or so people a night such an experience.

Audience members often "experience" directly what is being talked about. In *Artery*, a mystery, viewers walked through a simple set, consisting of seventeen rooms, as they listened to dialogue and followed taped instructions. At one point the voice called your attention to a cutout wooden figure pointing a wooden gun at you across a tiny room, then to a cutout wooden gun hanging on the wall beside you, and told you that the other guy was going to shoot you. Then the voice said, "Take the gun. Take it! Now! Shoot him! Before he shoots you!" Which I did, and so did other viewers I surveyed later. In another room, the taped voice instructed you to "steal" a (dime-store) necklace from a jewel case on a shelf, which I did, and later to "deposit" it in a safe (by means of which it was returned to the place I had stolen it from). These sound like childish maneuvers, but I, and others I talked to, had the odd feeling that we had actually committed "crimes."

In *Etiquette of the Underclass*, you lay down on what might be an operating table and were pushed through a door into a dark space, hearing doctors in an emergency room talk about your death from injuries sustained in an automobile accident, and then you were pushed into a lighted space, thus being "born" into poverty, into the underclass. You spent time in a jail cell and in a hospital clinic and eventually died violently. The Alcatraz tour provides the emotionally heavy experience, which not everyone volunteers for, of being locked in a solitary-confinement cell for a short period. The door shuts, and you stand in complete darkness and silence for a minute or so, realizing what it might have been like to spend days or weeks there. The physical sensation is very immediate and worth much more than a thousand words of description.

Some academics have experimented in this style, trying to add something that conventional social science forms leave out. Victor and Edith Turner (1982) describe a number of these performances, including the time they and other members of the University of Virginia Anthropology Department—students, faculty, and staff—performed a middle-class American wedding (the Turners played the mother and father of the bride). Dwight Conquergood (Conquergood 1992; Siegel 1990) studied the performative aspects of society and embodied the knowledge he gained in performances of rituals he had studied (such as the swearing of the Latin King oath by members of that Chicago gang).

I don't insist that we aspire to this level of realism in telling users about society. But not to do that is a choice. We could do it if we thought it was important enough, and being aware of this possibility makes us realize that every choice of what to include or leave out is, in fact, a choice, not a necessity forced on us by theoretical or practical impossibilities. (I'll take a longer look at the possibilities of dramatic representations in chapter 12.)

7

Reality Aesthetics
Why Do We Believe It?

I twice cotaught a course with Dwight Conquergood at Northwestern University called "Performing Social Science." We wanted to explore the possibilities of communicating social science ideas via public performance (other than the routinized performances of a scholarly "talk"). Twenty of our students came from Dwight's department, Performance Studies, and its neighboring department Theater, and half from social science, mostly sociology. Neither Dwight nor I had much idea about how to perform social science, and we counted on the students' inventiveness to give us something to work with. We gave them a simple assignment: perform something that might, under a very loose interpretation of the term, be called "social science."

The students' inventiveness exceeded our hopes. I had the feeling that they had all done the only thing they could think of—but no two did anything similar. One performance raised the problem of this chapter in an acute and interesting way.

The class had argued at length about the importance of the truth of the material you presented in your performance. Did it matter if it was something that had really happened? What if you tarted up the details to make it more "dramatic"? Or presented a result that had been disproved? Not surprisingly, the social science students insisted that the material performed had to be true; if it wasn't, how could you call it social *science*? And the students from theater and performance thought the truth of the material didn't matter if people responded to the piece as an aesthetic work. The arguments were heated. A traitor to my own people, I said that the truth might not matter.

For many of the students' performances, this question didn't arise. One student simply read from an article in the *American Sociological Review* reporting correlations between expenditure on education, race, and income in some school system. He did something simple but effective: he read the article "with feeling." When the text said that there was "fully a twelve per cent difference" between educational expenditures on blacks and whites, he said: "There is *fully!* a *twelve percent!* difference," his voice rising in high-pitched outrage as he indicted the variables "correlated with" (for which the author had clearly meant us to understand "were to blame for") the discriminatory results. The emotional reading exposed the ideological subtext of the sober scholarly report. Most interestingly, while the student's recitation sounded a little silly, it didn't sound "wrong." He hadn't misplaced the emotion, nor did he misrepresent what the author intended; he had just brought it to the surface and made it evident. No one questioned the truth of the findings or of his assertion that an article in the journal had actually contained the words he spoke.

But some performances did raise the question of truth. Tom, an ingenious and mischievous theater major, came into the room and passed out 3×5 cards to everyone. Each card had a woman's name written on it. He told everyone to look at their card and then to ask him whatever they liked. "Who is Mary Jones?" "She was my first-grade teacher." "Who is Betsy Smith?" "She's the first girl I ever kissed." "Who's Sarah Garfield?" "She's my aunt. She's married to my mother's brother." And, after a beat, and in the same conversational tone, "She and my father have been having an affair for the last five years." Someone immediately asked, "Is that true?" Tom considered this judiciously, then said, "I don't think I'll answer that question," and grinned. The room exploded. And, oddly enough, the theater and performance students insisted, much more than the social scientists, that the truth, goddamnit, did matter. They insisted that he tell them, and he wouldn't. These were the same people who, two days earlier, had said the truth didn't matter.

I pointed out the inconsistency and insisted that these defenders of "it doesn't matter whether it's true" had just proved to us that it does matter, even for an aesthetic work, and that we'd better devote ourselves to understanding how it matters and how to communicate the truth of what we performed.

Users care about the truth of what they're told, even when the message comes in an artistic genre, and certainly when it's science, and makers incorporate reasons for users to accept what they present as true in their work. But all these terms are ambiguous.

Truth: Questions and Answers

Is it true? The question, so filled with philosophical traps, becomes more tractable if we put it more simply as a problem of questions and answers. I'll use the example of documentary photography to keep the discussion down to earth, and I'll begin with these premises:

1. Every photograph can be interpreted as the answer to one or more questions.
2. We care whether the answer the photograph gives to our questions is true.
3. Every question we ask of a photograph can be put, and therefore answered, in more than one way.
4. Different questions are not the right or wrong way to ask (or answer); they are just different.

Saying that we can interpret photographs as answers to questions doesn't mean that we always do, only that we often do, in principle we always can, and that is a useful way to think about photographs. We can ask simple descriptive questions: What does Yosemite look like? What does the Republican candidate for president look like? How did our family and friends look in 1957? Or historical and cultural questions: How did people make photographs in 1905? How do the Yoruba make them? What did the battlefield at Gettysburg look like? Sometimes we ask scientific questions: Is this lung tuberculous? What happens when I bombard an atomic nucleus this way? Or psychological ones: What is the true character of the Republican candidate for president? Sometimes we ask for an abstraction: Tell me the essence of virginal innocence, or Mexican peasant life, or the urban experience.

Different people can ask different questions of the same photograph, not always the question the photographer had in mind. Some questions interest many people, who ask it in the same way. News photographs answer common questions about current events. Scientific photographs answer questions arising from the common concerns of a narrower professional community. Its members ask the same questions and find the same answers in photographs offered as evidence.

Other questions interest a very small circle, because they ask about personal relations and personally experienced events of no concern to most people. A photograph of me in front of the Eiffel Tower interests only me and mine. But pictures that once had only personal interest can, years later, answer questions interesting to a larger audience: childhood snapshots of people who later become famous or photographs of places in which events of general interest later took place.

We care that photographs that tell us about society give credible answers to our questions. Different people ask different questions of the same photograph. (Chapter 11 shows how this can be done from the perspectives of documentary photography, photojournalism, and visual sociology.) So there is no general answer to "Is it true?" We can say only that its answer to a particular question is more or less believable.

When we interpret a photograph as saying something about some social phenomenon, we suggest an answer to a question that might have a different answer. That raises the problem of truth. Because questions about society involve interests and emotions, people can disagree about the answers, often suggesting that they're not credible because the photographs are biased, misleading, subjective, or an unfair sampling.

Many problems arise over this ambiguity: A series of photographs suggests X is true; we don't deny it but think Y is true too. Do the photographs suggest that X *and only* X is true, or allow for the possibility that, while X is true, Y is true too? Specifically: many people think Robert Frank's book *The Americans* (1969; a sequence of eighty-four photographs made all over the United States in the 1950s) tells us that American life is bleak, nasty, uncultured, and materialistic—and that that's all it is. Without becoming an apologist for "the American Way of Life," it is possible to cite images by other photographers giving a different view. Does Frank's book suggest that this is *all* there is to American life? The book's length, long enough to allow for the inclusion of a greater variety of imagery, prompts that interpretation. If it does suggest that this is *all* there is, you could say the statement is wrong, because other kinds of evidence exist. (Photoessays can be seen as a kind of *specified generalization*. See my discussion of John Berger and Jean Mohr's *A Seventh Man* [1975/1982] in Becker 2002.)

Skepticism and the "Plenty Good Enough" Criterion

Suppose we do believe some of what we are told. Some skeptics won't accept that and will call attention to the shakiness of all knowledge about society, reminding us that all statements purporting to communicate such knowledge rests on a basis of "facts" that have been selected and interpreted in ways so hopelessly biasing the results that you just can't believe anything. If so, there's nothing to talk about and we can call the rest of this off.

People who talk that way don't really mean that they don't believe any representation of social reality. Do they believe, for instance, in the telephone directory, which presents itself as a more or less accurate listing of who is at the other end when you call a number? Skeptics might point to the inevitable errors committed by the clerical workers who type in the original information, or to the errors that arise because of changes that occur between the time of information gathering and printing, and between that time and the time you consult the list, or to the refusal of some people to be listed or to be listed under their real name. But those skeptics probably, like the rest of us, use that list and its numbers, for lack of anything better. The data aren't accurate, but they are "plenty good enough" for the purpose we will put them to, which is to call someone.

The same thing is probably true of a map of city streets, which purports to tell you how to get from here to there by using surface streets with names and numbers. With all its inaccuracies and omissions, it's good enough for most people's purposes. When a cabdriver turns on the overhead light and looks in a street guide for an address, the address is probably there and the way to get to it is probably more or less clear. If I want to drive from Seattle to San Francisco, and then to a particular address in San Francisco, a few state maps and a city map will show me the way. The maps will not show where the hills are in the city (though they will indicate the height of various mountains and mountain passes the highway goes through), but they will get me where I'm going. "Plenty good enough," knowledge good enough for what I want to do with it.

What about the U.S. Census? This is more complicated, because many people use the census for many purposes, and while it's good enough for some people and some purposes, it's not good enough for others. It wasn't good enough for several purposes when the 1960 enumeration seriously undercounted young black men by as much as 20 percent. That miscount wasn't good enough for the constitutionally required apportionment of seats in the House of Representatives and of electoral votes. It wasn't good enough for the calculation of crime rates, because undercounting the denominator of a fraction like the crime rate inflates the rate over its true value. If you don't count all the people in a particular population category, such as "young, black, and male," but you count all the criminals who fall in that category, the resulting ratio will be larger than it would be if you had an accurate count of the denominator. This undercount had political consequences, as well as mucking up social science thinking and research with faulty data.

Such flawed findings might once have been good enough, at least for people who were in a position to make that judgment in an effective way. But now new people began making their own assessments, and it wasn't good enough for them. Accepting a number that affects congressional representation because it's "plenty good enough" has a political component.

Which is not to say that science is "all politics" or that all epistemological questions can be settled by political means. It does mean that when you look at even so scientific an operation as the census, some of what's done has no "scientific" warrant but rests on an agreement among interested parties to treat something as good enough for some purpose, flaws and all. Users accept the resulting description not because it has an incontrovertible epistemological basis but because it's better than nothing for something they want to do.

So we all believe some of these representations all, or most, of the time, and some of us believe some of what we are told some of the time. No one disbelieves all of it all the time. Even with all these troubles, users treat representations as "essentially correct," which is the way physicians talk about laboratory findings that, they know perfectly well, have many errors built into them but are "plenty good enough" for what they will use them for.

But user communities ask different questions and use the answers for different purposes, and what's good enough for one won't be good enough for another. My map doesn't have to be accurate to the nearest foot, because I'm just using it to get to my friend's house. If I were using it to settle a property dispute, I'd need a different kind of geographic knowledge expressed in a different way. The two uses and the two question-answer pairs aren't competing with one another to see which is most accurate or "best"; they are different animals in a different environment.

As an epistemological judgment, "plenty good enough" has no philosophical justification. It's a social agreement based on another kind of justification. That doesn't make all knowledge totally relative, though. Once users enter into that agreement, they can and do arrive at reliable conclusions by following the agreed-on rules of evidence.

The Social Agreement to Believe

What justification does "social agreement," as a way of creating social knowledge that is "plenty good enough," have? For one thing, everyone accepts these agreements, and much work in the particular field has been based on them with no apparent ill effects. Latour's (1987, 21–77) parable of the doubter who questions a scientific result explains this mechanism. The doubter arrives in the scientist's laboratory demanding evidence for what everyone else in the lab accepts, refusing to "believe" in what is well attested to in the literature and by the use of accepted tools and techniques—and his questions become so ludicrous that no one takes him seriously and he finally slinks ignominiously out. Which leads to Latour's rule of method: believe in scientific results just as much as the scientists do, but no more than they do.

That's not an epistemological judgment either, it's the practical judgment that if you start doubting what everyone else believes, it's likely that you'll be eliminated from the dialogue altogether as a nut. But you can doubt what others will accept as possibly dubious.

Further, the social agreement allows scientific work (or any kind of collective activity) to proceed, which is no small thing. Thomas Kuhn (1970, chap. 3) made the point in connection with episodes of scientific progress: the only way any science ever gets done in is that workers in a field agree to concentrate on one or a few related problems, which they all approach the same way. The premises of the approach may be false, but work can proceed when everyone agrees and can't when everyone is working on different, idiosyncratically defined problems. Agreement on a paradigm lets researchers do collectively whatever they're going to do.

More generally, we could say that people who make and use a particular kind of representation (a film or table or novel or mathematical model) have come to some agreement as to what will be "plenty good enough" for their purposes. Plenty good enough for the purposes of the makers, whoever they are and whatever their interests are, and plenty good enough for the users, whoever they are and whatever their interests are. Not perfect, not as good as everyone would like, but good enough, given the circumstances, to rely on for guidance.

Participants in a representational world agree on an object that everyone involved knows how to make, read, use, interpret, discount. It's what John Hersey, as we will see in the next chapter, claims about journalism, when he says that of course journalists leave relevant facts out of their stories but since everyone knows they do that, no one minds. Readers just discount for that source of error as they read.

Where such an agreement exists, we believe the statements made by an object that bears the marks of living up to it. If it shows, in its presentation, that it was made the way users and makers have agreed on as the way to make things like that, then the results will be plenty good enough for the agreed-on purposes. If it's a documentary film, there's no fiction in it. If it's a statistical table, it follows agreed-on procedures guaranteeing a user that appropriate safeguards have been taken and potentially misleading practices have been avoided (e.g., the area of the bars in a histogram are proportional to the numbers the bars represent). If it's a "realistic" novel, it doesn't include factual stuff that, if you look into it, isn't factual.

Is my characterization of representational activity itself true? Do representational worlds work that way? All the time? Some of the time? Now and then? The answer isn't "all the time," because every trade that produces reports about society is usually rocking with some kind of conflict over exactly what I've described, a few paragraphs ago, as matters of peaceful agreement and harmonious consensus.

Criteria of Believability

Whether to believe what you're told and why are matters of agreement. Fair enough. But what criteria of believability, specifically, do people accept and use in everyday life?

We frequently compare what we are told with our own experience of life. We all have plenty of that and are usually unwilling to believe anything we're told that runs counter to it, at least until we are given pretty good reasons to change our mind. If what we are told resembles our own experience, we accept it. People who have experienced recreational drug intoxication typically dismiss the exotic fairytales people with no firsthand experience believe. Their own experience tells them that smoking marijuana has not made them crazy.

We evaluate what we are told in the light of other knowledge we have of a more academic or secondhand sort. If we have read a lot about Russia and what we read here is congruent with that, then OK, we'll believe this too.

We imagine the method the maker probably used to get what we're being told and then criticize that method. We don't believe what someone with no firsthand knowledge of an event or activity says about it.

Since makers don't always give this information, users reconstruct it, if necessary, from fragments. A friend complained to me about David Remnick's descriptions of Russian politics and, by extension, about the *New Yorker* school of reportage, which he described thus: "They just go in with a tape recorder and write down everything they're told, which is aimed at an American audience, and then string it together." I disagreed, feeling sure that, for instance, Remnick spoke Russian fluently, though I couldn't say why I thought that, and that it counted toward the believability of what he wrote that he seemed knowledgeable about Russian literature and history.

We also reconstruct the methods that make a report believable from our understanding of what someone would have to do to get "good stuff." We are suspicious of people who have visited some place for a few days, don't speak the language, and have an explanation for everything. The proverbial *Life* photographer, parachuted into wherever-it-is for a few days and then airlifted out, is not a believable documenter, for some of us, of that place's way of life.

We judge believability from the consistency of what we see and hear. Anna Deveare Smith described riot situations in Brooklyn and Los Angeles on the basis of long interviews with participants, which she reenacted for an audience (Smith 1992, 1993). We put together a picture of the chaotic event from the fragments she gives us, the little bits of testimony offered by many different participants. Gradually, we acquire enough knowledge to crosscheck, however crudely, remembering that if *this* one said that it happened this way, then there's a conflict with what *that* one said and we'd better be wary. (The playwright Caryl Churchill, as we'll see in chapter 12, uses a similar method to create a theatrical report on a major political event from interview fragments.)

Passing Tests

In all these procedures, users compare the representation to something else they already believe and sees how it stacks up: is it congruent with what I already know and believe? The representation has to prove itself in competition with what's already on the accepted list. That's a version of a process that Latour speaks of as undergoing "trials of strength" (1987, 53–56, 74–79, 87–94). In this way: if the representation suggests a conclusion or fact that isn't congruent with what I know or believe, it has to pass a lot of tests and find allies in other reports and sources before I will believe it.

Many representations do convince us to accept facts we didn't accept before. So this feat can be accomplished, just as, despite the obstacles to acceptance that Latour describes, new scientific facts do get accepted. But a maker doesn't achieve that just by announcing the new idea or fact or interpretation. Skeptical users insist on tests.

Makers can construct representations to produce the effect of obstacles overcome and tests passed. The standard journal article does this by providing all the facts conventionally required in a standardized format, allowing skeptics to convince themselves that all the potential sources of error have been avoided and all the potential sources of information investigated. The idea that investigators should guard against "threats to the validity of their hypotheses," formulated and propagated by Donald Campbell and his colleagues (Campbell and Stanley 1963; Cook and Campbell 1979), is a systematic way of listing what has to be dealt with.

You can also produce the effect of obstacles overcome and convincing proof produced by using data so widely accepted that the possibility they could be false doesn't arise. Hans Haacke's "Guggenheim Project," mentioned earlier, rests on easily verified facts about the trustees of New York's Guggenheim Museum, including their names and addresses, their family connections (they are mostly all Guggenheims, whatever their names), and the other organizations on whose boards they sit (large multinational mining corporations). Finally, we learn that Chile's soon-to-be-dead (assassinated or by his own hand) president Salvador Allende had made the mistake of confiscating properties belonging to one of these companies.

There's nothing to argue about factually. Any user can easily check everything stated in these panels in any well-furnished library or by using Google. But the user needn't check them, because it's obvious that, were the facts not as Haacke states them, someone would have said so. People who found Haacke's work distasteful (there were plenty) would have been glad to dispute any disputable facts. The reliance on what is publicly available disarms mistrust and suspicion. You can criticize the reasoning, but that's all. Here Haacke uses the

ploy discussed earlier, leaving all the reasoning and conclusion drawing to users, who do the rhetorical work, convincing themselves that
the conclusion is justified.

Natural scientists get very upset when they are told that they just
"believe" things rather than having "discovered the truth." They think
this means that their proofs have no real epistemological justification,
that anyone can in principle believe anything they want to, and that
such a stance, opening the door to rampant mysticism, is the death of
real science.

George Polya, a mathematician, argued that compelling proof, the
kind scientists like to think is provided when Nature speaks (Latour
1987, 94–100), is available only in the fields of logic and mathematics,
which make no reference to the empirical world and whose truth
rests on demonstrative logic; what is true is so by definition and by
logical deduction from those definitions (Polya 1954, 140–41). Everywhere else in the empirical sciences, and not just the weak social sciences but the strong natural sciences as well, we can only estimate
degrees of credibility or believability, and those only roughly.

Polya illustrates how scientific conclusions are contingent on evidence with a small detective story. A yacht explodes. We discover that
the owner's son-in-law, with whom he does not get along, bought
some dynamite a week earlier, and so we think it likely that he "did it."
But then we discover that the son-in-law used all the purchased dynamite to blast out a tree stump in his backyard. That makes it less
likely that he did it. And so on: each new bit of evidence changes our
assessment of his guilt.

Empirical science, Polya says, works like that. No matter how well
proved a statement may seem, new facts can always cause us to reconsider our belief. Latour calls well-established conclusions "black
boxes," like the ones in computer science, whose workings we no
longer inquire into but just accept their outputs (derived from our in-
puts in ways we don't inspect and may not understand at all) as reliable bases for further work (Latour 1987, 2, 131).

Instead of definitive knowledge, empirical science gives us degrees
of credibility and procedures for agreeing on them. Polya provides a
collection of diagrams (1954, 3–37) showing how different empirical

results produce different degrees of credibility. When you inspect them, you see that they codify the practices of your own reasoning. Scientists needn't get upset about this, because the analysis of degrees of credibility shows that scientists can use these procedures just as they use the criterion of truth. Nothing changes in the day-to-day world of scientific work if you do that; in fact, that is how scientists work, talking about "truth" in order to deal with the rest of the world and convince nonscientists that science is, after all, worth supporting.

So when we discuss alternative formats for the presentation of social science ideas, conclusions, and research findings, we should look for the procedures people use that lead them to find different kinds of reports more or less credible.

Aesthetics

It's not clear what "aesthetic" means when we consider representations as objects conveying information and ideas about society. From a purely "artistic" point of view, it might refer to what are usually spoken of as the formal aspects of the object: the harmony or balance displayed by the relations between its parts. We often just use vague words like *beautiful*, by which we mean things like gorgeous sunsets or natural landscapes that appeal to us in so obvious a way as not to require explanation; it's enough to point and say "Wow!" to register our response. Others will know what we mean. That kind of judgment would never pass muster among serious students of aesthetics, who require a more philosophically defensible justification of our responses and criteria of judgment (Becker 1982, 131–64).

Let's consider the criteria makers and users apply to representations of social reality that could in some way be taken as "aesthetic."

Even the most relentlessly realistic representation, we've seen, results from the selection and reduction of material to be represented, the translation of the raw material of experience into the language of the maker's medium, and the subsequent arrangement of the translated items. Are there better and worse ways to perform these operations? Is there craft involved, and if there is, is it being done as well as it could and should be? That's the kind of thing people discuss as the aesthetic issues of representing society. Let's consider some common criteria of aesthetic worth.

Craft standards influence judgments, perhaps more among makers than among users, and certainly more than anyone would like to admit. Does the author write properly elegant prose? Critics disapproved of Theodore Dreiser's novels of urban America for his failure to meet that standard. Are the photographs in focus and printed appropriately? Photo critics of the 1950s complained that the images in Robert Frank's *The Americans* ([1959] 1969) didn't exhibit a full tonal range, from a pure black to a pure white with as many shades of gray as could be managed in between—an aesthetic criterion that Ansel Adams, the photographer of Yosemite, had successfully installed in the world of high art photography. Did the journal article fail to cite "relevant literature"? Many studies fail to be published in the best journals only to reach their users via book form, which doesn't require meeting that particularly restrictive set of craft standards (I speak from experience). You can find similar examples in every artistic and scholarly form.

This problem arises in an illuminating way in the difficulties of making films in a *vérité* style. *Vérité* requires the filmmaker to avoid pushing the people being filmed around too much and instead to let them do whatever they would do in the kind of situation being filmed if the filmmakers weren't there and to shoot what happens as best you can given those constraints. But the resulting footage is often badly lit, out of focus, and in other ways not up to "professional standards."

Editors, the people who have to make cinematic sense of documentary films, complain that the results of *vérité* shooting do not give them the material they need to create the sense of continuity, or continuous intelligible flow of the action, that marks a properly edited film. Because the filmmakers used just one camera or because they did not anticipate what might be needed, the editor may have no material for a "cutaway," in which you break up a continuous shot of someone talking, for instance, so that you can use just a few parts of it, by going to a shot of something else that covers the discontinuity the jump from one part to another might create. Or the editor may not have an available "establishing" shot, which prevents viewer confusion by showing them where the action is taking place. Charlotte Zwerin, who edited *Salesman*, a classic documentary about a Bible salesman made by David and Al Maysles, explains to an interviewer:

> As I began editing I found I needed certain establishing shots, and Al went back and got them for me. I think these shots included things like the exterior of the motel in Boston, and some stuff around the Florida motel.
>
> [I'm interested in the question of continuity in editing vérité style films. Did you find this much of a problem in *Salesman*?]
>
> Sure, it was murderous. Al goes into a place and has so many things to think about—lighting, reasonable camera angles, how to shift position without falling all over everybody—that, consequently, he can't really consider how it's all going to edit smoothly. . . .
>
> [Can you give me an example of a sequence that was hard to edit?]
>
> One of the funniest but also most difficult scenes, was when Charlie and the Rabbit go in to sell a Bible to this old Irish lady and her daughter in Boston. The two women were marvelous characters and very amusing, but the sequence drove me mad for a couple of months because Charlie and the Rabbit kept shifting around from the piano, to the coffee table, to the door; they went all over the place and Al didn't do a thing about it. He obviously couldn't tell them to sit or stay rooted to one spot, but every time Al cut away it looked as if Charlie and the Rabbit had gone to another house. The lighting of the room was also maddening and didn't help the cutting. The salesmen were in one end of the room which was black, and were wearing dark clothes, while the two women were sitting on the couch wearing very light clothes in a very light situation. There was no room to get back and get an establishing shot, and after looking at the rushes I was left with the feeling that the two groups weren't even in the same room. (Zwerin 1971, 90)

Because *vérité* produces these results, the very "imperfections" become guarantees of the "authenticity" of the film and convince viewers to take the film as "true," even when the blurs and shakes did not actually result from the conditions of shooting. Gillo Pontecorvo's 1966 *Battle of Algiers* was entirely a movie fiction, artfully rehearsed "events" with paid actors and extras, but it mimicked the imperfections of documentary footage so perfectly that audiences had a hard time accepting that they were not seeing newsreel footage of real incidents from the uprising that led the French to leave Algeria.

Criticism based on craft standards permeates the making of almost all representations of society. Most representations are made by people who belong to some craft community. That community maintains standards of acceptable craft, and its members criticize products that do not meet them. Makers of representations accept those standards and apply them to their own products, knowing that their craft peers will criticize any failure to meet them. And they will share that judgment. They try to live up to those standards, even at the expense of some other value they want to maximize, like "documentary truth." Users who want truths about society, not just an entertaining movie, worry that filmmakers may sacrifice truth, however defined, to craft standards.

How do these considerations affect the work's truth value? Does making a scene dramatically effective simultaneously make it impossible to have it tell some kind of truth?

When we consider representations that, at least in part, describe social life and social events—in the realm of "art," that includes photographs, films, novels, and plays—we find ourselves dealing with a criterion different from the perfection of formal relations mentioned earlier. In these cases, we're interested in the relation of what the work depicts to the "real world," in the truth or accuracy of what the work tells us about social reality. We take the work seriously, in part, because it claims to tell us something we didn't know before about some aspect of society.

Dickens's prose is magnificent, his plots complicated and engrossing, his characters memorable. But an important part of the effect of his later novels rests on our belief that they tell us the truth, however caricatured, about the social and economic institutions of Victorian England. Imagine, as an experiment, that historians, working with masses of court records, discover that lawsuits did not drag on for years, like *Jarndyce v. Jarndyce* in *Bleak House,* until the lawyers had gobbled up all the money involved in fees. We would feel differently about the novel, regard it as a fantasy rather than a realistic account of events that might well have happened, and probably judge it a smaller achievement. We could not take what we read there as fact of some kind on which to base a response to social conditions, we could not answer questions about Victorian institutions credibly, and we would not find the plot and characters so affecting. It would be a different book, even though the words were all the same.

Dickens apparently feared that some, refusing to believe that British courts could behave so badly, might think he had invented his story. Proud of the accuracy of his reporting (he had, after all, been a journalist), he defended himself, in a preface to *Bleak House*, against such a charge and insisted on the story's substantial truth, which he evidently thought necessary to the book's aesthetic success:

> Everything set forth in these pages concerning the Court of Chancery is substantially true, and within the truth. The case of Gridley is in no essential altered from one of actual occurrence, made public by a dis-interested person who was professionally acquainted with the whole of the monstrous wrong from beginning to end. At the present mo-ment (August, 1853) there is a suit before the court which was com-menced nearly twenty years ago, in which from thirty to forty counsel have been known to appear at one time, in which costs have been incurred to the amount of seventy thousand pounds, which is A FRIENDLY SUIT, and which is (I am assured) no nearer to its termi-nation now than when it was begun. There is another well-known suit in Chancery, not yet decided, which was commenced before the close of the last century and in which more than double the amount of sev-enty thousand pounds has been swallowed up in costs. If I wanted other authorities for Jarndyce and Jarndyce, I could rain them on these pages, to the shame of a parsimonious public.

Adam Hochschild deals with Joseph Conrad's *Heart of Darkness*, a classic exploration of the relations between Europeans and "others," that is, the indigenous people of countries that once were European colonies. In the story Mr. Kurtz, an agent of a European trading outfit, has gone wild and established a personal fiefdom along the course of the Congo River in what was then the Belgian Congo, eventually became Zaire, and is, as I write this, the Democratic Republic of the Congo. Hochschild recalls a particularly gruesome image in the novel:

> Something we especially remember is the scene of Marlow [the nar-
> rator] on the steamboat looking through his binoculars at what he
> thinks are ornamental knobs on top of the fence posts near Kurtz's
> house and finding that each is "black, dried, sunken, with closed eye-
> lids—a head that seemed to sleep at the top of that pole, and with
> the shrunken dry lips showing a narrow line of white teeth." Even
> many people who haven't read the novel remember the severed heads,
> because Francis Ford Coppola included a few when he transferred
> "Heart of Darkness" to the screen in "Apocalypse Now." (Hochschild
> 1997, 40–41)

This bothers Hochschild because the book is now routinely read as being about almost anything but the reality of Africa, a reality Conrad had firsthand knowledge of, as Hochschild painstakingly documents.

Writers and academics have looked at the novel in terms of Freud and Jung and Nietzsche, of Victorian innocence and original sin, of patriarchy and Gnosticism, of postmodernism and post-colonialism and post-structuralism. But, as hundreds of monographs and Ph.D. theses pour out, with titles like "The Eye and the Gaze in 'Heart of Darkness': A Symptomological Reading," it is easy to forget that the novel was closely based on a real place and time. It is also easy to over-look, as almost all Conrad's many biographers have done, certain real people: several likely models for the novel's central figure, who is one of the twentieth century's most notorious literary villains—Mr. Kurtz. . . .

When scholars talk about the more bloodthirsty aspects of Kurtz, they often assume that Conrad made these up, or borrowed them from indigenous practices in the region. . . . Norman Sherry writes, "As for the shrunken heads on poles around Kurtz's house, these might be a macabre transference by Conrad of the fate of Hodister [a Belgian active in the ivory trade at that time, who was massacred by rival traders who beheaded him] and his men."

We know from other witnesses that the local warlords along the river at this time did indeed display the severed heads of their victims. But did Conrad have to make a "macabre transference" to imagine

Kurtz doing the same? Sherry and others have chosen to ignore several other prototypes who share a feature of Kurtz that the critics prefer to think of as phantasmagoric: they were white men who collected African heads. (1997, 40–41)

Hochschild does not accept this as just the way academics go on about anything. He sees it as having a submerged political motivation:

> Europeans and Americans have long been reluctant to regard the conquest of Africa as having been on the same genocidal scale as the deeds of Hitler and Stalin. For this reason, we find it more comfortable to think of Kurtz's head-collecting as a "macabre transference" and to locate the sources of this murderousness in Conrad's imagination. We have eagerly pulled "Heart of Darkness" loose from its historical moorings and turned it into a universal parable. The most macabre transference of all is our insistence on moving the novel out of Africa. [He cites film versions set in Spain and Vietnam.] Would we not think it strangely evasive if a director filmed Solzhenitsyn's "One Day in the Life of Ivan Denosovich" but didn't set it in the Soviet Union, or filmed Elie Wiesel's "Night" but didn't set it in Auschwitz? (1997, 46)

What's at stake here? Hochschild wants to see the book as descriptive, telling the truth about a particularly cruel practice the central European character engages in. He produces evidence to substantiate his claim and explains why others have ignored this crucial aspect of the book. He's taken something usually thought of as an aesthetically motivated invention and turned it into the simple factual report of something the author saw. And though he doesn't say this, you could take that as an element in the aesthetic experience of a reader who knows it—it shocks you by telling you that this is a way our kind of people really did behave when they had the chance and no one whose opinion they cared about was watching.

Hochschild's complaint suggests a general point. Many more works of art than we ordinarily so understand can be taken to be, and their makers very likely meant them to be, literal descriptions of some social fact, a verifiable description of a particular social organization at a particular time and place.

We can go further. The presumed truth of an artistic representation of a social fact is an essential element in our appreciation of the work as art. That is, art and truth do not work at cross-purposes, so that you can have one or the other but not both. In a lot of works, you can only have both, or neither: no art without truth. The truth of the work's assertions about social reality contribute to its aesthetic effect. That's why the class got so angry at Tom. If the story about his aunt and father was true, it moved and upset us. If not, it was just a silly joke. No truth, no art.

8

The Morality of Representation

Representing society raises moral questions for participants, for makers and users. These come in several varieties: misrepresentation as a moral wrong; the way common techniques shape our moral judgments; the related questions of assigning praise and blame for the results of action and of casting participants in social action as heroes and villains.

"Misrepresentation"

Sociologists in my tradition routinely seek understanding of social organizations by looking for trouble, for situations in which people complain that things aren't as they should be. You can easily discover the rules and understandings governing social relations when you hear people complain about their violation. Fields of representational activity undergo periodic violent, heavily moralistic debates over the making and use of their characteristic products. The cries of "It's not fair" and "He cheated" would sound like the games of five-year-olds were the stakes not so much higher and the matters dealt with so much more serious. The problem of *misrepresentation* invites us to begin our analysis by looking for these conflicts.

Anthropology students at the University of Papua New Guinea complained, in the *Nova* program "Papua New Guinea: Anthropology on Trial" (*Nova* 1983), that Margaret Mead's *Growing Up in New Guinea* was "unfair" because it repeated the derogatory stories her informants had told about the students' ancestors, for whom the informants' people had a traditional contempt. The students didn't complain that Mead had reported what had been said inaccurately; they agreed that those people had said such things. Nor did they complain that Mead had presented the stories as fact; she hadn't. No, they complained because their own ancestors, whom Mead had not studied, used to say equally terrible things about those other people, and Mead had not given them equal time.

These complaints exemplify the class of complaints that arise from self-interest: "You made me [or mine] look bad!" The first assistant physician of the mental hospital Erving Goffman studied and wrote about in *Asylums* complained (in the footnote Goffman donated to him) that for every "bad thing" the book described he could have produced a balancing "good thing": for the victimizations of patients Goffman reported, he might have told about the newly painted cafeteria (Goffman 1961, 234). Similarly, the citizens and politicians of Kansas City, Missouri, complained that the 1960 U.S. Census underreported the city's population by a few thousand, thus keeping it from sharing in the benefits state law gave to cities over half a million (a law that had been designed to help St. Louis out of financial trouble some years earlier). Almost everyone whose organization Frederick Wiseman has filmed complains that they didn't realize they were going to end up looking like that.

The practice of more or less fictionalizing reportage, as practiced by Norman Mailer, Truman Capote, and Tom Wolfe, among others, provoked a more general complaint. The well-known journalist John Hersey (1980) pointed out that these writers not only made things up but insisted on the right to make them up in the name of a higher truth. He argued that an author can invent details and incidents in writing labeled as fiction, which carries on its license the legend "THIS WAS MADE UP!" but not in journalism. There "the writer must not invent. The legend on the license must read: NONE OF THIS WAS MADE UP. The ethics of journalism, if we can allow such a boon, must be based on the simple truth that every journalist knows the difference between the distortion that comes from subtracting observed data and the distortion that comes from adding invented data."

Hersey adds, interestingly, that distortion by omission is acceptable, because "the reader assumes the subtraction [of observed data] as a given of journalism and instinctively hunts for the bias; the moment the reader suspects additions, the earth begins to skid underfoot, for the idea that there is no way of knowing what is real and what is not real is terrifying. Even more terrifying is the notion that lies are truths" (Hersey 1980). But many critics have complained that print and broadcast journalism (e.g., Molotch and Lester 1974; Tuchman 1978; Gitlin 1980) leave out exactly those things people need to be able to assess issues properly. And it's easy to imagine that many readers would "instinctively hunt out" additions in just the way Hersey goes after subtractions, if they knew that they should; many of Wolfe's readers, as well as newspaper readers and television viewers, probably did just that.

Hersey, whether or not we accept his judgments, identifies the sociological core of conflicts over representations of social reality. No report in any medium or genre, following no-matter-how-strict rules, will solve all problems, answer all questions, or avoid all potential troubles. As we've seen, people who create reports of any kind come to agree on what is "plenty good enough," what procedures should be followed to achieve that good-enough condition, and that any report made by following those procedures is authoritative enough for ordinary purposes. That protects professional interests and lets the work of the people who use those procedures proceed, guaranteeing the results as acceptable, believable, and ready to bear the weight that routine use for other people's purposes puts on them. The agreed-on standards define what is expected, so that users can discount for the shortcomings of representations made according to them and at least know what they are dealing with. Hersey's analysis accepts this state of affairs as normal, standard, and proper. It is what I had in mind earlier when I said that every way of making a representation is "perfect," good enough that users will accept the result as the best they can get under the circumstances and learn how to work with its limitations. Critics claim that misrepresentation has occurred when someone doesn't follow the standard procedures and misleads users into thinking a contract is in force when it is actually not being honored.

Quarrels among documentary film makers often revolve around

methods whose difference from a previous standard seem to create the possibility of confusion about what the film alleges to be true. Michelle Citron provoked a storm of criticism by including "fictional" passages in *Daughter Rite* (Citron 1979), an otherwise "factual" film. Some more conservative filmmakers complained that viewers would be misled, "tricked" into thinking that what they were seeing had actually happened when it hadn't. Citron, not unreasonably, argued that her film displayed a more generic "truth."

Users and critics also claim "misrepresentation" when the routine use of acceptable standard procedures harms their interests by leaving something out that, were it included, would change not only the interpretations of fact but, more importantly, the moral judgments people make on the basis of the representation. That often happens when some historical shift makes new voices audible. The people Mead studied did not read anthropological monographs and so could not criticize them. But their descendants, studying at the University of Papua New Guinea, can and do.

In either case, the problem of misrepresentation is a problem of social organization, a problem that manifests itself when a bargain once good enough for everyone is redefined as inadequate. Many "moral" problems that crosscut genres and media can be similarly analyzed as organizational products, including the ethics of representation and the problem of the authority of a representation.

"Insidious": The Moral Community of Makers and Users

Frederick Wiseman's film *Titicutt Follies* (1967) describes, in an uninflected, nonjudgmental way, the day-to-day life of the Bridgewater (Massachusetts) Hospital for the Criminally Insane. No description will do justice to this complex work, but here's a short version. Mostly in very long takes without a cut, it portrays scenes in the life of the institution which, you come to believe, recur repeatedly for staff and inmates: meetings in which staff discuss patients and decide on their treatment; hospital personnel force-feeding recalcitrant patients via an intranasal tube; a patient shouting gibberish for minutes on end without stopping; a holiday show featuring members of the staff and inmates; Vladimir, a patient, explaining to an apparently unreachable staff why he should be let out. It's easy to see how such a place would drive a person crazy, but it's also easy for most people to see that a lot of the people in there were probably already very crazy when they arrived. The film leads almost anyone, however, to conclude that the institution is a terrible place that ought to be closed and that the staff are cruel and unfeeling. Unlike most documentaries of its era, *Titicutt Follies* has no titles or voiceover commentary telling viewers what to think. Nevertheless, just as in Haacke's "Guggenheim" piece, the selection and editing of the film leads any reasonable viewer to conclude that this hospital is a terrible place.

A student in the "Telling" seminar objected that Wiseman's film, which I had presented to the students as a wonderful piece of documentary work, was "insidious," meaning (she said, when I asked her to explain what she meant) that it used all sorts of film devices ("tricks") to get viewers to believe that what they saw was "true": the lighting, the harsh, unceasing noise, the men's frequent nakedness (not commented on by anyone in the film), the very long takes, which led viewers to think that this material was not simply a collage of cleverly edited short moments that might hide a larger and different reality. She wasn't clear about why that was "insidious," but I thought then and still think that it was a wonderful word.

Why? "Insidious" implies that an effect was achieved by means that you, the viewer, weren't fully aware of and therefore can't be critical about. When a voiceover in a film tells us something, we know a voice is speaking to us in intelligible sentences, and many, if not most, of us have learned that, most of the time, we should suspect authoritative voices. But we may not understand in the same way that when a camera points up at someone to film them from below, they will look bigger and more awe-inspiring or scary and, conversely, that someone filmed from above, by a camera pointing down at them, will look smaller, less authoritative, and more childlike. When we know what's being done we're on our guard, we look for reasons not to accept the idea urged on us, we recognize the tricks and are wary. When we don't know what's being done, when it's insidious, we aren't on our guard, don't take proper intellectual precautions, and are likely to be "fooled" or "lulled" into accepting a statement or idea we wouldn't accept if we had had all our antennae up to detect trickery.

People vary in what tricks will fool them. These insidious forces may be less likely to affect professionals than amateurs or the general public. We can guess, not unreasonably, that people who make films for a living know what's up and take care not to be fooled. Some presentational tricks are so well known that they aren't "tricky," which may be what Hersey had in mind in distinguishing the common journalistic practice of not putting everything in a story, which he thought was OK because "everyone" knows newspapers do that, from inventing dialogue that never took place, which ordinary readers might not be accustomed to watch out for.

The distinction is important. Inaccuracy or corner cutting or other "illegitimate" practices presumably do not fool users who know that makers routinely use such practices. These alert users discount for the distortions introduced by such expectable routine activity and are skeptical about conclusions based on material produced in ways that contain these routine "errors" or "distortions." But people who don't know about routine distortions or omissions may accept conclusions and ideas they would never accept if they only knew the routine tricks that were leading them that way.

If these naive users knew how the trick was done, they would know that these "invalid" methods do not produce "real evidence" that would withstand crucial tests. And then they would know that the conclusion was "no good," having been "justified improperly." I put all those words in quotation marks to indicate that the informed readers I invented in the last paragraph might take this view, not that I accept all those criteria and all that reasoning myself.

Which suggests a generalization. For every means of telling about society, there will be some group for whom that way is justified by a moral pact between makers and users, which specifies permissible ways of persuading users that what's alleged is valid and therefore can be publicly acknowledged as acceptable, and which identifies sneaky and unacceptable ways. People who use sneaky means will be seen by parties to this pact as cheating, violating the moral agreement that makers and users have entered into. Users who are parties to this moral pact will be knowledgeable, within the limits set by the agreement, and so will not be easily fooled; they will expect makers to abide by the agreement and avoid means of persuasion not already agreed to. ("Insidious" implies what might not be true, that users would object, if they knew, to being persuaded by means they're hardly or not at all aware of.)

We needn't imagine that this pact has been agreed to in some self-conscious, document-signing way, or even the way agreements are invoked when you buy computer software (by opening the envelope containing the disk, you accept all the terms of some contract). We can just suppose that people agree to accept it the way so much is agreed to and accepted in ordinary social activity, by continuing to participate in the activity, even as one becomes aware of all these tacit understandings. (Keep in mind the standard ethnomethodological warning: participants often honor agreements after the fact by figuring out, on every occasion, what they might or must have had in mind when they said they agreed to whatever it is.)

Other users, not parties to such a pact, may not know what to look out for and could therefore be easily fooled by the unscrupulous. But we might say of users like this that they have no business using stuff they don't know enough about, that it's not the maker's fault if they insist on fooling with what they don't understand and can't properly evaluate.

We can say all that—if we insist on taking sides in such a potential dispute, which we needn't. I'd rather avoid taking sides on such issues and instead just observe who disagrees with whom about what—treat it as a sociological phenomenon to study rather than as a court case for us to decide.

For every form of telling about society, we should look for (as a possibility, not an inevitability) a moral community of makers and users, whose members know and accept some standard methods of communicating ideas and conclusions about society and of persuading others of the validity of what's communicated, even though those methods are riddled with faults and flaws. Users know all about what makers do. No "insidious" persuasion is going on. Makers are not doing secret things to fool users; there are no secrets. (The highly professionalized and esoteric world of mathematical models, discussed in chapter 9, is like that. The only people who consume these models regularly are people who themselves could make them, and maybe do.)

We can ask all the standard sociological questions about these representational communities. How do they recruit members and socialize them into the way they do business? Which participants know all about the persuasive means makers use? Where did they learn that? Which users know less and are more likely to be taken in by insidious means? What selection process divided users into knowledgeable and not so knowledgeable? Did those who don't know have a chance to learn but not take it (as I can imagine many people reading this book might decline a free ten-week class in mathematical modeling)?

In many of these worlds a small group of makers produces representations viewed by a large group of not-very-knowledgeable users. Most people who see movies in theaters or on the small screen wouldn't know how to make one. Not knowing how to make a film, of course, is not the same as not knowing how to watch films critically. On the other hand, the statistical tables and charts presented in newspapers and popular magazines may well fool people not trained to spot trickery. They may know that statistics lie but not know what kinds of lies are told and how to detect them, something only experts know. (Which produces books like *Damned Lies and Statistics* [Best 2001], which aim to set them straight.)

Are all the less knowledgeable participants in these worlds being duped? Many people might not care much that "insidious" means of communication had fooled them. Suppose you told viewers that the makers of *Titicutt Follies* had manipulated their emotions and conclusions by the cutting and pacing of shots, so that they had come to believe what might or might not be true. Many of them might say (might not, of course) that they didn't care, that they believed the evidence of their senses, what they had seen and heard, independent of such influences; that no such influences could change their judgment of the doctor's failure to take Vladimir's logic as seriously as we end up taking it; that no instruction on the artful use of montage, camera angle, lighting, or sound recording could change their conclusion that the treatment people receive in hospitals like this one eventually kills them; that an awareness of sequencing and editorial decisions can't take away from the inhumanity of the lockup procedures and the way the guards tease inmates they saw in the film.

So "insidious" implies what might not be true: that users would object, if they knew, to being persuaded by means they're not aware of. That points to another level of moral agreement involved in maker-user relations. I'm going to speculate about possibilities here, not report research results.

Some users might well be mainly interested in the "big" conclusions of the work, for which there is plenty of what seems to be straightforward evidence, for which the insidious means are only "incidental," as the mood-establishing background music of a documentary film might be. These users could say that all that incidental stuff just helps them grasp the message; they aren't fooled by it, they welcome it as a reader might welcome an easily read typeface. Readers might welcome a graphic device they're minimally aware of which emphasizes some element of a table more than it "deserves" (by using a device that professional statisticians think is misleading) because it helps them see what's important to them. Critics might say that that just shows how fooled they really are.

Who gets to decide that someone else doesn't know enough to make judgments on serious questions for themselves? We routinely assume that is true of children below a certain age, probably without thinking much about why we're entitled to assume it. Can we similarly assume that we know better than adults, who know less than we do about the matter at hand?

Questions about who can and should protect less knowledgeable users leads us to consider varieties of social organization surrounding the making and using of representations and the learning of the morality that surrounds these activities. One way to learn what that variety is would be to ask about different methods and organizations of socialization into the making and use of representations.

We learn about some representations as part of growing up: how to watch movies or read books, for instance. Others require specialized training: learning to read a complex statistical table or a technical map. Many representations come in a variety of forms, some readable by any ordinarily well-socialized member of a society, others only by experts and the specially trained. The difficulty is not an intrinsic property of any representation, it depends on what people have been trained to do. If everyone in a community learns, as a matter of course, to read complex weather charts (as might happen in a seafaring community or at an airbase), that's ordinary socialization, although in other places only the highly trained know how to do the same thing. This varies historically too. What was esoteric in another generation is grade school stuff now. Conversely, fewer people now have skills — how to make a dress from a pattern you buy at the store — that were once more common.

Hersey argued that we needn't worry about users' being fooled by the journalistic practice of not telling you everything you need to know, because readers know how to protect themselves against that form of trickery. They will, he thought, do the work of protecting themselves, reading carefully, thinking about possible other materials the journalist might be leaving out, assessing what those materials might contain, and deciding how what might be in those materials could alter their judgment on the issue being discussed.

That's a heavy responsibility for an ordinary reader, and it returns us to the question of the division of labor. Do people actually do that work? Average newspaper or magazine readers probably aren't that careful or skeptical about what they read (something for a researcher to nail down). They might be more like the students McGill interviewed, who didn't think they had to read the tables in scientific articles because the editors have already ensured that the tables say what the text says they say and support the author's argument.

Praise and Blame: Who and What Are Good and Bad

Social science and historical analysts almost always, explicitly or more or less covertly, make strong moral judgments about the subjects they write about. Historians don't just argue about whether the Civil War was inevitable; they want to establish, say, that it wasn't inevitable and so the people responsible for it happening are guilty of causing it. Had they behaved differently, it never would have happened, and all those lives would have been saved. Or they want to establish that the war was inevitable, given the configuration of forces and events at the time, and so those same people are not guilty.

In the late twentieth century, sociologists and anthropologists, and others as well, argued about whether poor black people in the United States—who no one denied were not as well off as other people, in many different ways—contributed in some way to their own troubles (just as people argued about whether European Jews had done something that made them complicit in their own deaths in the Nazi camps). Scholars and others were arguing about "the culture of poverty" or, in another form, "black culture": Do poor (or black, or poor and black) people more or less willingly participate in a system of understandings and practices that makes their victimization by a system of exploitation, repression, and oppression inevitable? Or could they, by somehow not participating, improve their situation?

Even though social scientists may seem to argue about specific factual findings and specific technical problems, you can almost always find behind the arguments a desire to show that something is just the way it should be or not at all the way it should be, although the "should" is generally left unargued and unsupported. When the student in our Performing Social Science class read the article on race and educational expenditure "with feeling," he made that animus evident.

The Rhetorical Value of Being Neutral

Most ways of telling what we know about society try to appear neutral and avoid looking like they're just raving and ranting in a way that would convince only the already convinced. They present facts and let users arrive at conclusions.

Some makers keep their moral beliefs to themselves. They run the tables, present the materials germane to a problem they have made a serious moral judgment about—racial discrimination, for instance—and then let readers come to their own conclusion: a standard scientific stance often recommended by authorities (e.g., Ogburn 1947).

Makers who do this count on all or most of their users sharing their moral position. Most U.S. social scientists (sociologists, certainly—maybe this is less true in other fields) are more or less political liberals as Americans use that expression, more or less left as the rest of the world understands these things. They can, as a result (or so they think), take certain premises for granted. If I demonstrate an income disparity between blacks and whites, I don't have to say it is a bad thing. Almost everyone who reads what I write will agree it's bad. The moral conclusion follows automatically from the statistical result (which, nevertheless, does not logically lead there).

Such disguised judgments appear in other ways of telling about society. It's not only social scientists who assume an ostensibly neutral stance. Haacke's "Guggenheim Project" and many of his other works use the same strategy, presenting more or less well known facts, arranged to lead users to a moral conclusion he expects them to work out for themselves. Wiseman's films have a surface air of simply presenting what you could see if you'd been where he's been.

In twenty-first-century Western societies (and many other places as well), being scientific means being neutral. When you pursue almost any public goal, the strongest ally you can enroll in your campaign is science, precisely because everyone thinks it is neutral and therefore not influenced by what we would like to be true, but only by the results of impartial, objective research. Opponents who disagree with your religious beliefs and question your moral imperatives have a tough time arguing with science, which, everyone thinks, just tells it like it is. Which is to some large extent true, despite all the critiques and social constructionist arguments. I accept most such arguments, but I still trust a neutral scientific study more than an argument based on religious revelation or deduction from a moral imperative that I don't accept (or even from one I do accept).

By presenting my findings and analyses neutrally and objectively, then, I can communicate my moral judgments effectively. As long as users share my moral premises, simple logic will bring them to my moral conclusions.

You get a great rhetorical advantage from this roundabout way of doing things: you can present your moral judgments as the findings of disinterested science. But the moral judgments, hidden though they may be, can cause analytic trouble. It's a problem of language. Scientists try to use neutral terms that collect things that resemble each other enough that you can find verifiable generalizations about the conditions that lead to them. They want their language to be precise and don't try to make it include a moral judgment. Medical scientists don't usually treat germs and viruses as requiring moral condemnation. They want to know how those organisms work, and what their reproductive cycle depends on, in order to interfere with it effectively. Of course, they think the germs and viruses are "bad" for us and need to killed off and gotten rid of. But they don't spend time condemning them and calling them bad names.

Why not? Because everyone agrees that tuberculosis and syphilis and measles are bad. The diseases and the germs that cause them have no defenders. (Although George Bernard Shaw made a pretty good case for them in his 1932 play *Too True to Be Good*, in which a germ is an important and sympathetic character.) As a result, scientists can describe them in technical language and no one will accuse them of moral irresponsibility. But if they discuss the causes of lung cancer and whether the manufacturers of cigarettes are responsible for cancers that develop as the result of a life of smoking tobacco, neutral language has a moral consequence. (And recall the discussions of "good" cholesterol and "bad" cholesterol.)

The language that makers use to write about social life is always engaged in a game of expressing moral judgments, trying to avoid them, or making them in a disguised way. There are serious reasons to avoid name-calling in social analysis, which I'll treat in chapter 13, in the discussion of Erving Goffman's carefully neutral analytic terminology. Some representations come very close to a nonjudgmental, quite neutral recitation of plain uninterpreted fact. James Agee did it in *Let Us Now Praise Famous Men* ([1941] 1988), and novelist Georges Perec made experiments in this vein that I'll discuss in chapter 15.

Causes and Blame

Social scientists routinely look for the causes of the phenomena they study; it's the most common way of describing what we do. Moral judgments frequently take the form of assigning blame. Social scientists routinely assign blame by announcing what caused something to happen. If we know what causes something, we know what has to be changed in order to change some social consequence we disapprove of. If we don't like the situation of black people in the United States and want to change it, and if we know what causes that situation, then we know what to change in order to get the result we want. If we can identify X as the cause, we know we should do something about X so that it no longer produces the result we don't want. When you explain what caused something bad, you blame that cause for the untoward result you've analyzed.

That's a misleading, and in the end mischievous, way of thinking. The justification for that harsh statement comes from an alternative way of thinking about how social phenomena happen. (For longer discussions of this complicated question, see Ragin 1987, 2000, and Becker 1998, especially 63–66 and 183–94.) Looking for causes misleads because it supposes an additive model of how things happen. It's mischievous because it leads analysts to assign blame in an incomplete and morally questionable way.

Suppose that the deplorable situation of black people in the United States is caused by a number of things: flat-out racial prejudice, institutional racism, industry's leaving the cities where black people live, the prevalence of the crack habit and trade in the neighborhoods many blacks live in, and so on. We could reasonably and correctly add many other things to the list, but the completeness of the list doesn't affect the point I want to make.

In conventional causal analysis, each cause influences the thing we are interested in. In conventional analytic language, the causal (independent) variables affect the effect (dependent) variables to some measurable degree. So racial prejudice adds (I'll invent the numbers) 10 percent to the bad situation, industrial flight from inner city neighborhoods adds 30 percent, and so on, until all the variance in the situation we want to explain is accounted for by a combination of these variables. Any of the independent variables could do the whole job of producing the unwanted result by itself, if it were strong enough, but none of them ever are. And any combination of them would do the trick if they were collectively strong enough. The causal variables are substitutable. To say it another way: you can add the causes' influence up, and any result that brings the total to the right number will produce the effect.

The alternative, a multiplicative analysis, looks for the "conjuncture" of variables that produces the result. What combination of variables has to be present for the effect we're interested in to happen? This approach says that each of those things is important. If any of them are missing, the effect won't happen, or won't happen in the way we want to explain, though something else unpleasant might occur. That's why it's called multiplicative. Remember grade school arithmetic. If you multiply some number, any number no matter how big it is, by 0, the result will be zero. Analogously, if any of the conditions necessary to the final result is missing, you won't get the final result. With respect to the situation of blacks in U.S. cities, Mario Small's 2004 study of a community in the Boston area makes this clear.

Good Guys and Bad Guys

The problem arises in nonscience forms of telling about society as well. Storytellers almost always, implicitly or explicitly, take sides. Stories have heroes and villains, and the storyteller usually lets us know who is who, either by explicit labeling or by providing easily read clues. In stories for grownups, we expect some subtlety. The villain doesn't always wear a black hat and have a long, droopy mustache, but by the end of the story we know who to cheer for.

Most people who do sociological research, or even just read sociology for pleasure or profit (that is, for some pragmatic purpose), think of it as one of the "social sciences," and the word *science* is often, though not always, taken quite seriously. As the previous chapter suggested, users imagine that what they read is not merely the expression of someone's opinion, consisting of and shaped by wishful thinking and pious hopes, but that it is in some way dependent on what is "actually happening" somewhere in the "real world." They prefer to think that what the report they are reading tells them rests on materials systematically gathered and analyzed, the "results" justified by something beyond the writer's genius or intuition.

Users want to know all this because what they "really" want to know is who's to blame for this mess, who can be held to account for these injustices, whose fault it is. They want to sort the actors in a social situation—the participants in an organization, the opponents in a political dispute, the parties to a quarrel—into Good Guys and Bad Guys, those doing the right thing and those acting badly. This rests on a simplified notion of cause: bad results are caused by bad people acting badly.

But you can't get from the results of a scientific study to moral judgments like that in any direct way. You can sometimes show that *these* actions have *these* consequences (it's not easy, but suppose you can). But you can't derive the judgment that some people are good and have behaved well and others are bad and have behaved badly directly from the results of empirical investigation. You can decide, on the basis of a philosophical argument, that certain kinds of acts or consequences are bad and then show "scientifically" or empirically that those people have done those acts and that their acts have had those consequences.

Many people find this troubling. They want to strengthen their moral position by demonstrating that what they disapprove of is bad *scientifically*. My own experience as one of the participants in the development of the "labeling theory" of deviance (Becker 1973) gives an example. Labeling theory analyzed "deviance" as the result of complicated, many-stage interactions involving accusers, accused, and a variety of official and unofficial organizations. Such an approach generally cast doubt on conventional assignments of praise and blame, on the allocation of actors to the Good Guys or the Bad Guys, by showing that the process of accusation and proof of guilt was a social process, not a scientific procedure. Critics, appalled by such relativism, often asked something like this: "Well, what about murder? Isn't that *really* deviant?" They implied that while many acts might exhibit the definitional variation that was the key insight of the approach, some acts are so heinous that no reasonable person would ever define them in a way that excused the person or persons or organization that had committed them. It never helped, when this accusation was made, to point out that whether something was murder, as opposed to justified homicide or self-defense or acting on behalf of your country or supporting law and order, was exactly a definitional matter. This criticism, by the way, was made from both the left and the right, the right upholding "traditional values" and presenting such crimes as murder and incest as the killer counter-examples, while the left offered up crimes like "imperialism" and "colonialism" to accomplish the same end. (See Becker 1973, 173–212.)

What was at stake was this: most people interested in problems of society want to say something more than identifying what they don't like as deviant according to community standards as applied in that community. They want to say that those community standards of badness were not just the community's standards but were standards science had shown, *scientifically,* to be bad. Critics didn't want the word *deviant* to have a simple technical definition as "something some participants in a situation call bad"; they wanted it to mean "bad, and science has proved it's bad."

"What about murder?" challenged me to deny what was obvious to any reasonable well-socialized member of our society: that something we all know is bad, like murder or incest, really is bad. When I said that I agreed with them and did think that murder is bad and was willing to say so, they were not happy; my agreement that it was bad didn't satisfy them. So I asked: Why isn't it enough to say that murder is bad and evil? What do we gain if say it's "deviant" too? What is gained is obvious: the authority of science. Because a judgment of "evil" can be justified only by theological argument and a judgment of "bad" by ethical argument. And even those who are firm in their own belief know that they cannot convince nonbelievers with arguments like that. They want an argument that works with nonbelievers too. That argument is science, which any well-socialized member of contemporary society presumably believes in.

Maybe that example is enough to show that users of social science reports want a way to distinguish good and bad, good and evil, good guys and bad guys. And the people who make social science reports are, for the most part, not only willing but eager to supply that distinction. It doesn't take an acting student, reading a scientific report with great emotion, to show that either right on the surface of a social science research report, or barely beneath it, the makers are assigning moral praise and blame, even when they profess "objectivity" and "scientific neutrality." Historians do this openly and as a matter of course; critics may blame them for not doing it. They assign blame, as I suggested, for wars. If Lincoln had done this or that, maybe the Southerners would not have been so angered as to want to secede. They assess the moral character of historical actors. If Thomas Jefferson was really the father of his slave Sally Hemings's children, and given the undisputed fact of his slaveholding, does he deserve the respect we accord him as a founder of the nation?

Many social scientists will not recognize themselves or their work in the preceding paragraphs. William Fielding Ogburn, who brought statistics to American sociology and sociology to the American government, thought that, since sociology was a science, sociologists should be neutral in a way that permeated their writing. He wanted objective and nonemotive prose that replaced evocative words with precise words with clear meanings (Ogburn 1947).

Most social scientists routinely follow Ogburn's advice, whether they know it or not. What they write still contains villains or heroes, usually disguised as the attribution of causality to variables. Take an excellent example of the genre, one in which the labeling of virtue and vice is not hidden. Stanley Lieberson wrote *A Piece of the Pie* (1980) to answer this question: How come American blacks have not achieved the kind of individual and communal social mobility other ethnic groups managed? Why could the Jews and the Italians and the Irish and the Poles do it and the blacks couldn't? Is it because of discrimination, or does this failure reflect inherent differences in ability? Whose fault is the lack of black mobility and social success? Blacks', for not being good enough? Or whites', for not letting blacks have a fair chance? This factual question, to be sure, can be answered factually, with enough careful defining of terms and critical inspection of all the available sources of information. But it's simultaneously a moral question because, given the way Americans think about blame, if it's discrimination it's the white folks' fault; if it's not discrimination, if it's something about black folks, if it's "their fault," well, too bad, maybe we can do something about it, but it's not our fault.

Not to keep anyone who hasn't read Lieberson's excellent book in suspense, the answer, arrived at after inventive and exhaustive analysis of a mass of imaginatively discovered data, is that the culprit responsible for the low mobility scores of blacks is indeed discrimination, no doubt about it. Though Lieberson's prose is as scientifically chaste as Ogburn could have wished, the moral animus of his argument is perfectly clear. The chaste prose, by the way, has an important rhetorical consequence: it helps convince readers who might not have fully made up their minds on these questions that the author who produced these results has no ax to grind. If the data had shown that it wasn't discrimination, he would have told them that just as forthrightly, so they better believe this; there's nothing left to support any other conclusion.

Christopher Jencks routinely writes this way, taking seriously propositions that outrage most routinely liberal American academics and subjecting them to a rigorous examination. His prose is so antiseptic and his analysis so evenhanded that when he concludes, after a careful and systematic assessment of the available evidence, that Arthur Jensen's notions about the low intelligence scores of black Americans are hogwash (Jencks 1980), you believe him in a way you would not, quite, if he had begun with some conventional pieties about how reprehensible Jensen and his ideas are.

Most social science reports bury their judgments deeper than that. Perhaps it's better to say that they routinize them, so that the moral judgment is present simply in the choice of a problem. Why study the distribution of people of different races in the ranks of a large organization, if you don't think that there is some injustice going on? But once you've chosen the problem, no more moral talk, or not much. Your readers will supply it automatically.

Most users of scientific representations are content to let the moral go unsaid. Users of works in artistic genres seem more often to require that moral condemnation be expressed explicitly. I'll discuss the interesting case of Wallace Shawn's play *Aunt Dan and Lemon*, which provokingly refuses to make such judgments, in chapter 12.

Part II : Examples

9

Parables, Ideal Types, and Mathematical Models
Useful Analyses We Don't Believe

We ordinarily want reports about society to be factually correct, to tell us something true we didn't know before. In artistic forms as well as scientific ones, the truth of a representation is generally quite important to users. But there are three important exceptions to that generalization, three kinds of analyses of society we don't expect or want to be true. We know that someone just made them up, that they have no basis in carefully gathered evidence. We don't worry about that because we don't think anything will be added to their value if they do have a counterpart in the "real world." And unlike our performance class confronted with Tom's story about his aunt and his father, we don't care if anyone says "That's not true." Their effect on and for users doesn't depend on truth.

Parables—stories we think describe a sort of Platonic ideal that lies underneath what we can see (I'm extending the dictionary definition, which is "story that illustrates a moral attitude or a religious principle")—serve purposes truth can't get to, at least not easily. Similarly, the *ideal type*, the theoretical tool refined and used so expertly by Max Weber, does not describe anything we will find in the social world around us or available to us through historical study. *Mathematical models* create a mathematized ideal type, even more abstracted from reality than Weberian models. No one expects to find, anywhere in the real world, anything like the social organizations whose workings these mathematical inventions describe.

Users understand that the utility of these three "unrealistic" representations lies elsewhere than in their fidelity to a real-world original. Instead, they make clear the inner workings of a form of collective action obscured by the historically contingent details of particular real-world settings, although they may be quite detailed themselves. The analyst makes these idealized descriptions by removing details that needn't have the form they take in some historical case and, in so doing, reveals the idealized ("perfect") organizational mechanisms an empirical example hides. Representations like these show you how things would work if that were the way they worked, if the forces in play, unencumbered by irrelevant and extraneous detail, could reveal their essential nature. Being unrealistic doesn't deprive these representations of value or usefulness. On the contrary, social scientists and others all use important tools of this kind.

David Antin's Parables

You can't easily describe David Antin with a single occupational title. Charles O. Hartman, whose chapter on Antin's work (Hartman 1991) I've relied on extensively, lists some reasonable possibilities for a quick description: "a linguist, an art critic, an engineer, a poet, a technical translator, a curator, a teacher," also mentioning that Antin "draws from an exhilarating range of the linguistic, scientific, sociological, and aesthetic thought available to a cultured contemporary mind" (77). I'm very imperialistic, always wanting to call smart people who do interesting work "sociologists," so (agreeing with Hartman's inclusion of sociology in the list) I will treat Antin as someone who does and reports his own social science research. Since he called one of his works "the sociology of art" (Antin 1976, 157–208), he might be willing to accept this dubious honor.

Antin's work takes the form of improvised "talk pieces," which he delivers, more or less impromptu, before a live audience, and then records, transcribes, and publishes in an unusual format, economically described by Hartman like this:

1. no capitalization;
2. no punctuation (except for quotation marks);
3. unjustified left and right margins;
4. pauses made visible as gaps about seven ems wide;
5. line breaks arbitrary;
6. (added in *tuning* [Antin 1984]) something like paragraph breaks;

a part-line is dropped straight down or (if the previous partial line is too long) three-quarters of a line of white space is added. (Hartman 1991, 86)

He has talked about a great variety of topics, including (these are his titles) "the invention of fact," "tuning," "gambling," "real estate," "the fringe," "what it means to be avant-garde," and "the price."

"the currency of the country" (Antin 1984, 5–47), a not very realistic story, produces, in Antin's hands, an insightful and useful analysis of social, political, and economic organization. He begins by describing some experiences at his own university, where he had trouble understanding other faculty members' talk about the first, second, and third worlds, and wonders why he has been asked to participate in a meeting about technology and the arts in the third world (does anyone in the third world really care, or care even a little bit, about technology and the arts?). He moves on to a conversation with a friend in which he's surprised to learn how much a steelworker makes, considers how much the price of a cup of coffee has gone up, and begins to speculate about how commodities (coffee, for instance) and services (a taxi ride) have a sort of standard price you get used to and how surprised you are when the price changes dramatically, when coffee starts costing $2.50 a cup instead of 50 cents. He realizes that his vague notions of how much a "worker" makes and how much a cup of coffee costs and how much a house costs connect with one another, in a vague and unverbalized general scheme of value, all of whose parts are linked and described in amounts of money. Then he tells a story.

In the story, a friend gets a fellowship to an unnamed (and, as the story develops, unlikely to exist) European country. In its monetary system, based on powers of 2 (rather than being decimal, like most Western currencies), the smallest coin, no longer in circulation, is called the *unum*. He names all the other coins (his knowledge of linguistics helps him construct a plausible set of terms) from the *diplum* (worth two *unums*) to the *bregma,* worth 1,280 *unums*. For various reasons, many of the coins are no longer in use, and the people use only *sards* (8 unums), *nerors* (32), *slekts* (64), *arkts* (128), and *bregmas.*

In this little country, nestled in a valley between two polluting industrial countries, the air is so unbreathable that purified air must be delivered to houses and other buildings, public and private, as well as to public transportation vehicles. Citizens have to buy it for their homes and other uses, the way people in the United States buy water for private use. Though it costs only one slekt for a *droz* (three liter-minutes) of pure air, the slekts add up, so that people pay a large part of their income to make their houses livable. People with ordinary incomes can afford to keep only one room full of breathable air. Antin then calculates how many bregmas it would take to ventilate a house, or perhaps only a portion of a house, and tells us how much of the salary of, say, a senior city planner would necessarily go to ventilation. He tells us how people seek work that lets them spend their workday breathing air the employer pays for, which means they can turn off the ventilation at home, and how they put their children in day care for the same reason.

The relationship between salaries and the price of air needed to ventilate houses and apartments forces people to find ways to economize by sharing living quarters: "it really worked out that three or four people living in a room was the most economical way of paying this rather outrageous price for air while still providing a reasonable physical space for the occupants but it did cut down on privacy and you can imagine what effect it had on the social life" (Antin 1984, 30).

And on everything else. Phone calls made from a (ventilated) booth cost one *slekt*, what the amount of air you consume in three minutes in the booth would cost you at home. The price of television (ostensibly one slekt for three minutes) is related to how much air several people watching the same set in the same room would breathe. But that is so expensive that broadcasters, who would otherwise not be able to attract the audience their advertisers seek, subsidize and distribute a special "hexagonal" slekt, called a *vizuslekt*, which you can put into the slot through which you pay for the TV (making it possible for several people to be in the room and watch, thus increasing audience size) but cannot spend on anything else.

Because privacy is so expensive—two people who want to be alone have to provide themselves with a special air supply—young people who want to make love must take special measures. They can buy a tank of air and take it to the country (where they have to be quick about it, because the tanks are expensive) or take advantage of the stratified system of clean air on public buses, by riding in closed (therefore private) compartments with a special air supply—this, however, costs much more than riding in the open part of the bus, where the air is much worse, with the general public.

Antin shows how these financial facts of life permeate the language; he invents a vaguely Central European language in order to illustrate these points. It takes his friend some time to understand what people are saying in ordinary conversation, because he doesn't at first understand the metaphorical content of the money terms in common expressions, doesn't see what they have to do with anything else. Someone who wants to describe something as completely worthless might say, "na vodjie tviijnii na vizuslektduvar" (it's not even worth a hexagonal slekt), which gets its force from the hexagonal *slekt*'s being worthless for anything but television. Similarly, young people who go to the country to make love are called "people who bring air to the mountains," and everybody snickers when that is said, because they know what is meant, though it takes Antin's friend awhile to decipher it.

In the currency of this country, a full night in a private compartment on a bus would cost a couple 8 bregmas. But even a city planner makes only 950 bregmas a month, while a workman might earn only 400 or 500 bregmas and a student might only have an allowance of 100 or 200 bregmas. So a couple's spending two nights a week together (72 bregmas) might use up as much as 75 percent of a student's allowance or 15–20 percent of a workman's income.

Popular expressions embody these financial realities. If you want to describe a man as "fabulously wealthy," you would say he is *tij vlazcescu mberie bregmadziu na dumobru ezadjie* ("a man rich enough to make love in his own house," rich enough, that is, to fill at least two rooms with breathable air, one for him and his partner, the other for everyone else). No wonder, then, that this society has the verb *medra-bregmadzian*, whose metaphorical meaning refers to something like "rolling in sensuality" but whose literal meaning, according to Antin, is "spending the whole night screwing" (1984, 35). Antin provides a thorough linguistic analysis of this word's morphology (built on the root *bregma*, the monetary unit) which means an impossibly large amount of money (*bregmas*).

> [*medrabregmadzian*]
> is a compound verb built on the infinitive *bregmadzian*
> that is transparently composed of the verbalizing infinitive
> ending plus the stem *bregma*   while *medra* is an adverbial
> prefix   itself composed of two parts   *med-a*   meaning
> more than   and the infix *r*   an intensifier expressing
> the notion of surpassing all possibility   so that *medra* meant
> "impossibly many" or "much"   or simply "too much"
> because to make
> love in a closed compartment for a whole night

was clearly overdoing it.

So in this society, as revealed by the evidence of common idioms, the meanings of money include (envelop, absorb) all kinds of other meanings that relate air, privacy, sex, and many other things.

The story, not to keep you in suspense, ends tragically. The American student meets a young woman of the country who calls herself a sculptor but isn't what we would think of as one (she doesn't produce physical objects made of durable materials). She calls herself that because sculptors, who do physically hard work, get government-subsidized air, and she wishes to express solidarity with the laboring classes. But she is actually quite thin and looks like a brainworker rather than someone who does physical work. Brainworkers and physical workers are enemies, and the first night that the young woman invites the American, shyly, to "ride the bus" with her, their bus is stopped by members of the brainworker party for the purpose of political indoctrination of the captive riders. The police come to break it up and, in the ensuing scuffle, mistake her for a brainworker, and she is killed (or so we end up thinking, though it isn't that clear).

The American goes home and is, of course, interrogated by the CIA. When he tells them this story, they are disgusted. They don't believe that the country's political conflict is as he describes it and tell him he has wasted the money spent on his fellowship.

You might at first think this story is true. I did. Some of the stories Antin tells in his "talk pieces," so called because they are oral improvisations, are true or sound as if they could be true. ("the price" recounts the breakup of his mother's liaison, in an old people's home, with a fellow resident, who eventually leaves when the new management refuses to let him continue to spend the night with his sweetheart in her room; as he tells Antin, that residence was nicer than the place he has moved to, but in this new place "the price is right.") The extensive detail Antin provides about the geography of the country with its associated air pollution and the elaborate linguistic analyses of common sayings in his fabricated Eastern European language eventually convince you that the story is not "true" but rather a parable, according to the dictionary "a simple story illustrating a moral or religious [or, in this case, sociological] lesson."

Not being true doesn't make much difference—it didn't to me, and I don't think it would to you—to the value of the story's social analysis. The story lays out the intricate connections between common belief, language, class structure, environmental conditions, personal relations, and many other theoretically important things in a clear and convincing way. True or not, the connections are such that you can see how they would, or might, be true in almost any setting. Not in the particular details presented in this case, but in ways that knowing this story would help you to discover. Or, if not true, they are laid out with such a reasonable logic that you would want to use them as guidelines for your own research on similar topics.

Antin does not make much of the connections as theory, though they have considerable theoretical interest. The user has to extract the theory from the story and from Antin's wise-guy, mock-innocent remarks. Antin leaves a lot of work for users to do. He gives you categories, concepts, varieties of possible social facts—all the parts from which you might construct similar social arrangements. While the stories aren't true, we don't care, because they teach us something about society we can apply elsewhere, in our own attempts to understand what is going on. They tell us how things would be if they were something like the way they are in his invented country, with its poor air-starved citizens.

Ideal Types

Social scientists know ideal types in the version proposed by Max Weber (1949, 89–95) who gave, as an example, the economist's idea of a market and its associated exchange economy:

> This conceptual pattern brings together certain relationships and events of historical life into a complex, which is conceived as an internally consistent system. Substantively, this construct in itself is like a utopia which has been arrived at by the analytical accentuation of certain elements of reality. Its relationship to the empirical data consists solely in the fact that where market-conditioned relationships of the type referred to by the abstract construct are discovered or suspected to exist in reality to some extent, we can make the characteristic features of this relationship pragmatically clear and understandable by reference to an ideal-type. This procedure can be indispensable for heuristic as well as expository purposes. The ideal typical concept will help to develop our skill in imputation in research: it is no "hypothesis" but it offers guidance to the construction of hypotheses. It is not a description of reality but it aims to give unambiguous means of expression to such a description. . . . It is a utopia. Historical research faces the task of determining in each individual case, the extent to which this ideal-construct approximates to or diverges from reality.

You make an ideal type by abstraction from the mess of reality, as Weber suggests with the idea of "handicraft": "One can work the 'idea' of 'handicraft' into a utopia [by 'utopia' he means an idealized version] by arranging certain traits, actually found in an unclear, confused state in the industrial enterprises of the most diverse epochs and countries, into a consistent ideal construct by an accentuation of their essential tendencies. . . . One can further delineate a society in which all branches of economic and even intellectual activity are governed by maxims which appear to be applications of the same principle which characterizes the ideal-typical 'handicraft' system."

Weber used this procedure often. He described several kinds of authority—charismatic, traditional, legal-rational—in ideal-typical terms. In his studies of world religions he did not expect, and we don't expect when we do our own research in other areas of social life, to find any pure cases of these kinds of leadership. The types tell us how things would be if people really did follow a leader because they thought he had special gifts, or because that was the way they had always done things, or because this person was the one the rules said they should follow. But no society or organization exists, and we shouldn't expect to find any, in which people act purely on one or another such basis. Weber pictured bureaucracy as it would be if an organization actually had all the characteristics he attributed to the pure type: administrative activities governed by rules, the work done by full-time professionals organized in a hierarchy whose careers consisted of doing such work, workers who did not own the means of administration, with an income from a salary rather than profits or fees, and so on. But he didn't expect to find any organization in the real world with all those features (Gerth and Mills 1946, 96–104).

Researchers use ideal types as a way of getting to what is crucial in the case they are studying, stripping away the historically contingent and accidental, everything that isn't necessary to the idea whose essence they want to expose. This gives them, as a result, concepts and working ideas that are logically consistent and coherent yet have enough relation to what's observable to be useful in dealing with empirical materials. Maybe the city government I'm studying doesn't have all the characteristics of an ideal bureaucracy, but I can identify enough of them to give me clues about where to look next, what kinds of investigations might lead to further discoveries, and so on: a kind of thought experiment, in which you ask yourself what would happen if certain tendencies specified in the ideal type operated unchecked. That lets you see traces of those possibilities in what actually does happen when those tendencies operate only partially, because something else in the organization checked their full-blown expression.

The ideal type is never "true"; truth isn't a relevant question to bring up about one. If they do what we want them to do, they show us interconnections between elements, let us see how things influence each other in the pure case, so that we can detect their operation in the less pure conditions of the real world. Weber said: "There is only one criterion, namely, that of success in revealing concrete cultural phenomena in their interdependence, their causal conditions and their significance." It's like Antin's story, in which what might have happened, could have happened if that had been the way those things happened, can lead you to an understanding of what did happen in some situation you are trying to understand. It's not true, but it's "useful," a very different criterion. A useful type alerts us to things present in the real cases we study, as Weber's typology of authority helped him detect different ways of organizing collective action in religious groups.

To say that an ideal type portrays how things would be if that were the way they are means that the maker of such a representation specifies a set of conditions and a process from which you can figure out what will happen next. In the purest case of an ideal type—a mathematical model—you would call these a beginning state and transition rules and identify what happens next as the succeeding states of a system.

Mathematical Models

Antin's stories exemplify the interconnections of elements in a society. Weber created ideal types of organizations in words. They both make social reality less realistic and more understandable.

The purest version of these idealizing operations is the mathematical model, which gives numerical or abstract mathematical values to the elements it contains. Models specify a population of elements, the kinds of states each element can be in, the operations one can do on such elements. Members of a subclass of models important for sociology list the initial distribution of elements among possible states and delineate transition rules that say how elements can change between successive states of the entire system and what the resulting distribution of the elements among states will be. Even less detailed than an ideal type, they produce correspondingly clearer results.

John G. Kemeny, J. Laurie Snell, and Gerald L. Thompson outline a simple and productive model: "In some primitive societies there are rigid rules as to when marriages are permissible. These rules are designed to prevent very close relatives from marrying" (1974, 451). The rules specify who belongs to a marriage type (think of it as a clan), which members of which marriage types are permitted to marry, what type the children of such a union belong to, and so on: "These rules can be given precise mathematical formulation in terms of permutation matrices" (451).

They define a permutation matrix (think of it as a table, with rows and columns) as "a square matrix [like a table] having exactly one 1 in each row and each column, and having zeroes in all other entries" (1974, 453). If you label the rows and columns with the names of the clans into which such a society is divided, then the 1s and 0s represent marriages that are allowed or forbidden. The mathematics of such matrices tell you how to perform addition, multiplication, and other arithmetic operations on them, and the results of these operations tell you the makeup of the next generation.

Of course, not many societies have such rigid and complex marriage rules, and those that do obey them only "more or less," so the utility of such a scheme for studying a real society is limited. But as a model it has a lot of utility, because it tells you what sorts of systems are possible and gives you a way of identifying how and when rules are violated and many other things of interest to students of kinship.

Harrison White studied the complex kinship systems of Australian indigenous peoples, as well as the system of a group that lived along the Indochinese border with Burma, to demonstrate the possibilities of modeling (White 1963, especially 94–105; his discussion overlaps with that of Kemeny, Snell, and Thompson). He concludes that "unambiguous prescriptive marriage [of the kind outlined by the kind of rules mentioned above] is a limiting case, an ideal type. One should ask not whether a tribe has a prescriptive as opposed to a preferential marriage system, but rather to what extent the tribe conforms to one or some mixture of ideal types of prescribed marriage systems, either as an isolated unit or as part of an interacting network of tribes. There remains the difficult task of developing a more general framework of analysis within which one can meaningfully and with precision define the extent of conformity. . . . I have succeeded only in deriving the ideal types" (148–49).

A mathematical model, for instance, might be constructed which would make this kind of analysis of symphonic repertoires; this is my own invented example of William McPhee's analysis of the general class of social phenomena he identifies as the "survival of items in culture" (1963, 26–73):

> Let's collect what all the symphony orchestras in the United States play in a given year, and let's classify those works, say, by nationality of the composer (it needn't be that, it could be year of composition or birthdate of the composer or length of the work or even the key). We discover that x per cent of the works were written by German composers and y per cent by French composers, etc. (There will be ambiguities and troublesome cases, composers with dual nationalities, for instance, as there would be for any criterion, and these will have to be solved by somewhat arbitrary definitions, which will not, perhaps surprisingly, affect the usefulness of the model.)
>
> Suppose further that the repertoire, still defined as what all the orchestras play in a year, changes by two per cent annually. Every year two per cent of the works played the year before are dropped and two per cent are added. Suppose further that the added works differ in ethnic composition in some specified way from the present composition of the repertoire. While the current repertoire has 30 per cent works by German composers and ten per cent by French composers, the works added this year are 25 per cent by German composers and 15 per cent by French composers. And suppose still further that, the repertoire changing every year, the new proportion persists for ten years. What will the ethnic provenance of the repertoire then be?
>
> If that seems like a frivolous example, consider that the problem so stated is formally identical to the problem of how long it would take to achieve a certain percentage of women of the rank of colonel in the U.S. Air Force, given that the present proportion of women is x per cent and the rate of replacement is z per cent a year. Whatever we have found out about the way proportions of composers of different nationalities change from year to year will, in general, be true of any situation in which a fixed number of elements of several different kinds are replaced at known rates at regular intervals.

Just as with Weber's ideal types of authority, it's irrelevant to complain that that isn't the process by which the symphonic repertoire changes. That isn't what the analysis tells us. It just tells us what would be true *if* that were the way it changed.

And we would want to know that for much the same reasons we

want to know about the ideal types of authority or the ideal form of a kinship system of a certain kind: as a way of understanding the dynamics of how something might be working, even though it doesn't work just the way the model specifies. So it might be helpful to know how an organization would look if it actually were a bureaucracy of the kind Weber described, perhaps in order to say that, for instance, whatever else the Chicago city government is, it isn't that kind of bureaucracy.

Because mathematical ideal types are instances of mathematical forms that are already known and about which many theorems have been proved and for the manipulation of which many operations have been created—Markov chains or difference equations or directed graphs, for instance—anything that has been proved about those entities automatically applies to any particular use of that entity for purposes of social analysis. If I display the workings of a hypothetical kinship system as a Markov process ("a random process whose future probabilities are determined by its most recent values" [Weisstein n.d.]), once I make the appropriate connections—identify the varieties of clan membership, for example, and specify the rules governing interclan marriage and the rate at which they occur—everything that is known about Markov chains (which is a lot) is logically (therefore automatically) true of the system I've described. If I describe the connections between people in an organization as a network, everything that has been proved about directed graphs becomes available to me as a result about the organization I've studied, without my doing any further empirical work. The logic of the math guarantees the accuracy of those results. Not empirically, of course. To repeat, it doesn't matter that there is no such kinship system anywhere or that some specific real-world kinship system I'm describing doesn't really work like that. The model establishes what would happen if it happened that way. And that is a useful thing to know.

Thomas Schelling (1978) used this property to explain still another gift of mathematical thinking to social scientists. Many things that interest us are true by definition. They are what mathematicians call "identities," the terms on one side of the equation adding up to the same amount as the term on the other side. Schelling gives some simple examples: the number of sales in a market *must* equal the number of purchases: you can't sell something unless someone buys it, or buy something unless someone sells it. That's obvious, but many examples are much less so. I'll quote one at length:

> We are often interested in the ratio of two populations in several locations. An example is a dozen dormitories and a college population three-quarters male. Lots of combinations are possible, all subject to one numerical constraint. There is, for example, a unique ratio that can be common to all the dormitories: 3 to 1. There is a unique way to divide the men and the women so that all women live in dormitories that are half men: six may be half and half, the other six all men. If two dormitories are women only, the ratios in the other ten must average 9 to 1. Exactly two houses can be half and half if two houses are all women. And so forth. The principle holds true for freshmen, black students, married students or any other group. If black students are one-twelfth of the college they can be all in one dormitory, 50-50 in two dormitories, or 1 to 3 in four dorms. There is no way to get whites living, on the average, with more than one black student out of twelve.
>
> On a smaller scale, the indivisibility of people becomes important. Distributed among four-person rooms nobody can be less than 25 per cent of his local population. If blacks are a twelfth of the total, only three-elevenths of the whites can have any black roommates at all. If every black prefers one black roommate, and if whites feel the same, the only acceptable ratio will be two and two, with ten-twelfths of the rooms in the college being white only. The same applies to hospital wards, military squads, and, in the extreme case, pairs of police in two-man squad cars where all integrated cars are 50-50 and nobody in an integrated car is with anybody his own color. (Schelling 1978, 58–59)

There is nothing to argue about in these conclusions; you don't need to gather data, they follow from simple arithmetic. But that doesn't make them obvious: "It is astonishing how many hours of committee meetings have been spent on proposals to mix men and women in dormitories, or blacks and whites, or freshmen and sophomores, in ways that violated the simple arithmetic principle that no matter how you distribute them, the numbers in all the dormitories have to add up to the numbers that there are" (Schelling 1978, 59).

It's Not True and So What?

Oddly enough (it seems odd until you start thinking about it in a properly abstract way), Antin's story and similar analyses stated as parables have much in common with mathematical models, just as those are like Weberian ideal types.

How so? Antin's story is a fiction. The country he describes doesn't exist. The story he tells never happened. But neither does the bureaucracy Weber's type describes exist, and no collection of symphony orchestras planning their programs follows so precise a strategy from year to year as my imagined mathematical model described. The model and the type are just as fictional as the story. All three resemble each other, too, in being analytic, in dissecting real situations to find their important components and then constructing a model of how those components influence and depend on one another.

But stories, types, and models also differ substantially, and the differences are instructive. Mathematical models state the relationships they analyze in terms simultaneously precise and abstract (the two needn't go together). They work metaphorically, likening the concrete social phenomena they model to an abstract mathematical object (just as people calculate distances by likening their sightings of places and stars to the abstract geometrical shape of a triangle) and reasoning from the properties of the abstract object to the properties of the specific topic they're looking into. So Kemeny, Snell, and Thompson describe the marriage rules of a society as the working out, modeled as permutation matrices, of seven axioms embodying the workings of a kinship system that assigns group membership to children and prescribes some marriages between groups and forbids others. Their analysis shows, interestingly, that the number of possible systems is, if people actually act the way the system says, very limited.

The relations analyzed in such a model are necessarily "true." If the specifications of the system are met, the results follow automatically, just as the sum of the squares of the two sides of a right triangle necessarily equals the square of the hypotenuse. That's the simple, inevitable logic of geometry. But the model makes no claim that anything in the world is like that; it just says that if anything were like that, this is what would be happening.

Since hardly any human activity resembles any of these mathematical objects very much, the purveyors of models have a hard sell. Because, though we don't require them to be true, we do often require them to be "similar to" actual social phenomena we are interested in. And while we can show how an abstract object could be constructed, the more mathematically precise, clean, and elegant it is, the less it tells us about the thing we want it to model. But that is partly a matter of our ingenuity in finding similarities. I don't give up hope about this, partly because of the successes of the other two varieties of "unrealistic" representations.

Ideal types, less subject to this criticism, look a lot like the real thing. If you walk into a government office, it will surely have files, as Weber said they would. They may be on a computer's hard drive, but they are files that serve the functions Weber assigned to them. And the office personnel can usually describe an employment system that has many of the features Weber assigned to the careers and job contingencies of bureaucratic employment systems.

The relations between the elements of an ideal type aren't true of necessity, but they have a kind of connection in human logic. We can see and understand how those attributes would go together that way, how having files would give a certain predictability to action. Still, these relations are not true of logical necessity, and they do claim to be about something in the actual social world, though perhaps not exactly like those things. Not like any real bureaucracy, but like the things we think of as bureaucracies. So it might turn out that the model doesn't work for the class of things it claims to work for. In assessing such a model, we can go to our own experience of situations and organizations "like that" and see if what's proposed makes sense or not.

Antin's story is quite specific, even though he invented all of it. He wants to show us how we recognize how much things are worth, monetarily, and how that folk recognition is built into language. He wants us to understand how an environmental situation could ramify into every aspect of life: how bad air quality could lead to a loss of privacy, which in turn could lead to people's using public facilities to make love; and how a system of allocating air according to how hard one worked, surely a just and reasonable system, could lead to sculptors' being "workers" while painters and writers weren't, and how that could lead, in turn, to political conflict of a kind that could kill a friend. The details of Antin's story are compelling, even as we recognize their fictional character. The linguistic objects he analyzes for us, complete with all the paraphernalia of a technical linguistic analysis, sound good enough to be true, even though to see how that would be you have to inspect a language you do know for similarities.

Antin's story does not have to be like a real anything, as Weber's type does, and the regularities he calls attention to are not stated in an abstract form; rather they are put as the specifics of a specific environmental and political situation and language. We don't have to think anything is like that. But we probably do.

Each of these not-true but nevertheless worthwhile analyses satisfies some set of users. Mathematical models are made for and used by the relatively small number of sociologists and anthropologists who have the technical knowledge and interest that might let them make such models themselves, although they also find a receptive audience among playful dabblers like me. Ideal types have become a standard piece of sociological apparatus, used by many researchers in sociology and beyond its borders, though I think relatively few people invent new ones for their own purposes, as Weber did for his. Parables have yet to gain many sociological adherents. I don't think I'm the only one, though we're probably a small number—maybe only those who have had the chance to see Antin perform one of his "talk pieces." I think it's a form of reasoning whose use social scientists might consider, one that would let them do some kinds of thinking they might find useful. And one that reminds us that truth is a big thing, but not the only thing.

10

Charts
Thinking with Drawings

Data Pictures

Eugene S. Ferguson, a historian of technology, emphasized the visual component in thinking in an eye-opening article called "The Mind's Eye: Nonverbal Thought in Technology" (Ferguson 1977), which showed how technologists and scientists used pictures and diagrams, rather than words and numbers, to convey ideas and possibilities. Inventors and engineers thought through how a machine worked in pictures and presented their results to each other as pictures. An exploded view of a machine could show skilled readers everything they needed to understand the relations of the parts, how the machine's elements meshed to produce its desired result, and how to make one yourself.

Much of the creative thought of the designers of our technological worlds is nonverbal, not easily reducible to words; its language is an object or a picture or a visual image in the mind. It is out of this kind of thinking that the clock, printing press and snowmobile have arisen. Technologists, converting their nonverbal knowledge into objects directly (as when an artisan fashioned an American ax) or into drawings that have enabled others to build what was in their minds, have chosen the shape and many of the qualities of our man-made surroundings. This intellectual component of technology, which is nonliterary and nonscientific, has been generally unnoticed because its origins lie in art and not in science.

As the scientific component of knowledge in technology has increased markedly in the 19th and 20th centuries, the tendency has been to lose sight of the crucial part played by nonverbal knowledge in making the "big" decisions of form, arrangement, and texture that determine the parameters within which a system will operate. (Ferguson 1977, 835)

Sociologists don't work with machines, so nothing in what they study is as easily charted as the meshing of gears or the turning of an axle. They have mostly used pictures to portray large conceptual entities, what Michael Lynch called, unkindly but accurately, "pictures of nothing": "the sketches, diagrams, and tabular arrays presented in theoretical arguments" (Lynch 1991). He illustrates with a "schematic rendering" constructed by Ralph Turner to describe Harold Garfinkel's implicit model of accounting, in which phrases like "Capacity for language use" and "Deliberative capacities" are connected (usually by double-headed arrows) to other phrases like "Capacity for indexicality" and "Stocks of knowledge." Some of the arrow paths are labeled with phrases like "contextual interpretation of gestures activates." Lynch describes this and other theory pictures as "orderly assemblages of nominal factors linked by causal or quasi-causal vectors" (1991, 3).

Such pictures of geometrical shapes containing words connected by double-headed arrows indicating causality running in both directions are common in sociological writing. The words in the shapes almost always express abstract concepts: "society," "culture," and "personality," for instance. These pictures produce what Lynch calls an "impression of rationality" and a "rhetorical mathematics," which is a fancy way to say they are about nothing at all. He contrasts pictures like these with pictures that have a clearer relation to some kind of shared reality.

I mention Lynch's analysis to distinguish those empty "theory pictures" from another kind of picture with a clearer relationship to an empirical reality the investigator studied, whose purpose is to do the important work, discussed earlier, of summarizing details. Drowning in details doesn't lead to sociological findings. Undigested detail that doesn't lead anywhere bores readers. Ignoring the detail of daily life leads to abstract conceptions whose relation to the social reality they propose to explain convinces nobody. We need methods for presenting as much data as users can handle in a way that makes handling it easy and intelligible, like those the technologists Ferguson described did. To make the workings of the sociological machines we study as immediately graspable as a technologist's drawing of a motor—that's something sociologists could try for.

This chapter has a modest aim: to show readers some possibilities that might be useful. These modest possibilities don't require arcane skills. They do ask users to do a little more work, but they pay off in increased knowledge and understanding.

Some classic works in sociology have used drawings and charts imaginatively to present complex materials whose presentation in prose would have taken many more words and been much harder to follow. These "data pictures" (in contrast to Lynch's "theory pictures") don't give up their meaning at a single glance, the way John Tukey suggested a good statistical graphic might. Although major points are established at a glance, the pictures require more work before they give up their full meaning,

This raises again a generic problem of representation: many users don't want to do that extra work. Finding a balance between innovation and standardization is a problem associated with pictures of the kind I find helpful. If we use a standard format to display our data, we lose a lot of specific information that might help explain the knowledge standard forms don't provide a place for. And users who know the format well may not actually inspect the evidence we do give them, like the students McGill interviewed who never looked at the tables in the articles they read.

But if we invent a new format every time we have something to say, we risk alienating users, who won't take the trouble to work out the connections. They don't want to discover for themselves the relationships buried in the lists of names and company positions in Haacke's "Guggenheim Project." A sociologist complained to me about Haacke's piece: "It doesn't have any conclusions! If the man has something to say, let him say it and not waste my time!" Even though the work involved is minimal, many think it is like trying to decipher Talcott Parsons's prose and won't do it. They do the cost accounting Harvey Molotch suggested, don't believe it will pay off, and resent the "extra" effort the work asks them to make.

In other words, if the picture is made to do just this one job, it will be unfamiliar, and users may balk at the extra work required to understand it. But if it is a standard format, it will not, almost by definition, have room for the idiosyncratic details of the particular case. It's not that every case is completely unique—as sociologists we certainly believe there are regularities in there somewhere—but that each case's features are expressed, you could say, in a local language. Translating from local idiosyncrasy to standard language loses nuance and maybe real meat as well.

I'll look at some classic data pictures to see what their creators did and with what results, focusing on materials that demonstrate facts and processes associated with hierarchical social arrangements. I have a prejudice: pictures like these are a resource waiting to be used, and, more in this chapter than anywhere else in the book, I'm in a proselytizing mood.

Class, Caste, and Networks

The sociological classic *Deep South* (Davis, Gardner, and Gardner 1941) reports on social inequality, both within and between racial groups, in the small town of Natchez, Mississippi, in the early 1930s. Allison and Elizabeth Davis, who were black, and Burleigh and Mary Gardner, who were white, lived there for two years, participating fully in the social life of their classes and castes and studying the class/caste system, in its social and economic aspects, thoroughly. It's a remarkable study and has become "interesting" again as experts in network analysis discovered it as an early ancestor of their concerns (Freeman 2003).

Some of the interesting diagrams and charts deal with the class system of the white caste as it manifests itself in family and social life (59–207). This study, and other studies associated with the anthropologist W. Lloyd Warner, have been criticized for not paying sufficient attention to ownership of the means of production and to the economic inequalities that support the entire social system. That criticism doesn't apply to *Deep South*, part 2 of which (259–538) examines with painstaking care the economic base of that society, the system of cotton production, and its economic and political consequences.

The book takes, as its subject, class in the specialized sense the authors give to the term: "As here used, a 'social class' is to be thought of as the largest group of people whose members have intimate access to one another. A class is composed of families and social cliques. The interrelationships between these families and cliques, in such informal activities as visiting, dances, receptions, teas, and larger informal affairs, constitute the structure of a social class. A person is a member of that social class with which most of his participations, of this intimate kind, occur" (Davis, Gardner, and Gardner 1941, 59).

The authors explain how they learned about the social classes:

> The researchers, both white and Negro, were initiated into the intricacies of class behavior at the same time that they were being taught how to act toward persons of the opposite caste. Whether it was a matter of accepting an invitation to a party, deciding to visit a family, or planning to attend a church, the participant-observers, who had been "adopted" by people of relatively high social status within their respective castes, were advised upon the important matter of "who" and "where." Certain people were to be approached, not as equals, but as subordinates. There were places where one "could not afford to be seen" having a "good time," or even worshipping, without loss of status unless it was for purposes of research. (1941, 59)

They explain how they heard people describe each other in stereotyped terms—"'leading families,' 'fine old families,' 'the four hundred,' 'the society crowd,' 'plain people,' 'nice, respectable people,' 'good people, but nobody,' 'po' whites,' 'red necks,' etc." (60)—whose systematic character they analyzed as a hierarchy of three social classes, each divided into an "upper" and a "lower" segment. "Not only do the whites frequently refer to these subdivisions within their own caste group, but they do so in such a manner as to indicate that they think in terms of a social hierarchy with some people at the 'top,' some at the 'bottom'; with some people 'equal' to themselves, and others 'above' or 'below' them. There are recurrent expressions such as 'He isn't our social equal,' 'She isn't our kind,' 'They are just nobody,' 'Those folks are the way-high-ups,' 'They're nothing but white trash!' . . . People tend to act in conformity with these conceptions of their 'place' and the social position of others in the society"(60–61). The book contains twenty-six charts of different kinds presenting conclusions and evidence about this system of unequal social participation. I'll comment on a few and then recommend that you read the book and work through the full variety presented there.

The authors immediately note that while everyone in the local society more or less recognizes these social divisions, the class system and the segments people recognize depend on their own position in it. They present their analysis of this difference in class perspectives in a figure titled "The social perspectives of the social classes" (see fig. 9; Davis, Gardner, and Gardner 1941, 65).

Quick inspection produces an immediate conclusion: each group has a somewhat different view of the system, though their various views do not conflict with one another. Lengthier inspection confirms two further, more interesting conclusions:

> While members of all class groups recognize classes above and below them, or both, the greater the social distance from the other classes the less clearly are fine distinctions made. (71)

And:

> Although an individual recognizes most clearly the existence of groups immediately above and below his own, he is usually not aware of the social distance actually maintained between his own and these adjacent groups. Thus, in all cases except that of the upper-lower class the individual sees only a minimum of social distance between his class and the adjacent classes. This is illustrated by the dotted lines. . . .
>
> In general, too, individuals visualize class groups above them less clearly than those below them; they tend to minimize the social differentiations between themselves and those above. (71–72)

The figure conveys all this and more as you inspect it carefully; it's an economical way to present complex conclusions, with their

UPPER-UPPER CLASS

"Old aristocracy"	UU
- - - - - - - - - - - - -	
"Aristocracy," but not "old"	LU
"Nice, respectable people"	UM
- - - - - - - - - - - -	
"Good people, but 'nobody' "	LM
	UL
"Po' whites"	LL

LOWER-UPPER CLASS

"Old aristocracy"	
- - - - - - - - - - - - -	
"Aristocracy," but not "old"	
- - - - - - - - - - - - -	
"Nice, respectable people"	
"Good people, but 'nobody' "	
"Po' whites"	

UPPER-MIDDLE CLASS

"Society" { "Old families"	UU
"Society" but not "old families"	LU
- - - - - - - - - - - - -	
"People who should be upper class"	UM
- - - - - - - - - - - - -	
"People who don't have much money"	LM
	UL
"No 'count lot"	LL

LOWER-MIDDLE CLASS

"Old aristocracy" (older) │ "Broken-down aristocracy" (younger)	
- - - - - - - - - - - - -	
"People who think they are somebody"	
- - - - - - - - - - - - -	
"We poor folk"	
- - - - - - - - - - - - -	
"People poorer than us"	
- - - - - - - - - - - - -	
"No 'count lot"	

UPPER-LOWER CLASS

	UU
	LU
"Society" or the "folks with money"	UM
"People who are up because they have a little money"	LM
"Poor but honest folk"	UL
- - - - - - - - - - - - -	
"Shiftless people"	LL

LOWER-LOWER CLASS

"Society" or the "folks with money"	
- - - - - - - - - - - - -	
"Way-high-ups," but not "Society"	
"Snobs trying to push up"	
- - - - - - - - - - - - -	
"People just as good as anybody"	

10.1 Allison Davis, Burleigh B. Gardner, and Mary R. Gardner, *Deep South* (1941), p. 65: The Social Perspectives of the Social Classes.

supporting detail. But you have to inspect it carefully. The authors leave plenty of work for users who want to verify things and work out implications for themselves.

A series of diagrams lays out the analysis of "social cliques in white society" (137–70). Preliminary diagrams (figures 3 and 4, 148 and 149, the latter reproduced here as figure 10.2) show social events on the horizontal axis and women's names on the vertical; an X indicates a woman's participation in the event. With a little work, you can see who participated with whom and how often. Miss Thelma Johnson and Mrs. Sophie Harris attended all nine events, Miss Kathleen Mills attended all but three, and the other three ladies fewer still, from which we can see that Johnson and Harris made up the core of the group. The authors do more work and give users figure 5 (p. 150, reproduced here as figure 10.3), which uses material from the preceding figures to show degrees of membership in each clique and when and in what ways the two groups overlapped. It suggests distinctions among core, primary, and secondary members of the clique, and users can see for themselves the detail of participation that these ideas summarize.

The authors use another kind of chart to show "social cliques in colored society" (208–27). Their figure 12 (p. 212, reproduced here as figure 10.4) shows the "social stratification of colored cliques" and is explained like this (I hope it isn't necessary to explain that criticism of Davis, Gardner, and Gardner's use of the term *colored* would be anachronistic, since that was the respectful way to talk in the 1930s and early 1940s):

NAMES OF PARTICIPANTS OF GROUP II	CODE NUMBERS AND DATES OF SOCIAL EVENTS REPORTED IN *Old City Herald*								
	(1) 6/27	(2) 3/2	(3) 4/12	(4) 9/26	(5) 2/25	(6) 5/19	(7) 3/15	(8) 9/16	(9) 4/8
1a. Miss Thelma Johnson......	X	X	X	X	X	X	X	X	X
2a. Mrs. Sophia Harris.........	X	X	X	X	X	X	X	X	X
3a. Mrs. Kathleen Mills........	X	X	X	X	X	X	....	....	....
4a. Mrs. Ruth Turner.........	X	X	X	....	....	X	X	....	....
5a. Mrs. Alice Jones...........	X	X	....	....	....	X	....	....	....
6a. Mrs. Julia Smith...........	....	X	X	....	....	....	....	....	....

10.2 Davis, Gardner, and Gardner, *Deep South* (1941), p. 149: Frequency of Interparticipation of a Group of Women in Old City, 1936—Group II.

Type of Membership	Members	1	2	3	4	5	6	7	8	9	10	11	12	13	14
Clique I:															
Core.......	1	C	C	C	C	C	C	–	C	C					
	2	C	C	C	–	C	C	C	C	–					
	3	–	C	C	C	C	C	C	C	C					
	4	C	–	C	C	C	C	C	–						
Primary...	5		P	P	P	–	P	–	–						
	6		P	–	P	P	–	P	–						
	7				P	P	P	P	–						
Secondary .	8					–	S	–	S	S					
Clique II:															
Secondary .	9					S	–	S	S	S					
	10						S	S	S	–	–	S			
Primary...	11							–	P	P	P	–	P		
	12							–	P	P	P	–	P	P	P
Core......	13							C	C	C	C	–	C	C	C
	14						C	C	–	C	–	C	C	C	C
	15								C	C	–	C	C	C	C
Secondary .	16									S	S	S	–	S	
	17											S	–	S	
	18											S	–	S	

10.3 Davis, Gardner, and Gardner, *Deep South* (1941), p. 150: Types of Members of, and Relationships between, Two Overlapping Cliques.

[The ordering] of a few of the most active cliques . . . has been shown. The second stage, of relating this system of ordinated cliques to the larger system of social classes, has been suggested by indicating class lines. Social space is pictured as having only two dimensions: (1) height, which represents the range of social status; and (2) width, which represents age range. A third dimension, depth, is not represented, for the relative size of classes, as well as status and age, is not considered. . . .

The fact that most of the cliques are represented by narrow, short ellipses, or by circles, signifies two general characteristics of cliques, viz., that both the age range and the status range of these informal groups are narrow. (Davis, Gardner, and Gardner 1941, 211–12)

Both kinds of diagrams furnish the raw material for still further analyses of such interesting questions as social mobility. How does clique membership facilitate moving up in the class system (137–207)? A reader who wants to benefit from them has to study them closely, following the lines and markings to see what kind of social

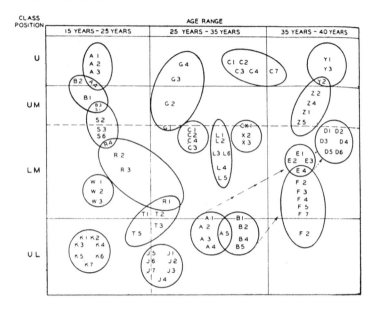

10.4 Davis, Gardner, and Gardner, *Deep South* (1941), p. 212: Social Stratification of a Group of Colored Cliques.

participation they refer to and evaluating ideas about social class and its manifestations in social life in the light of this evidence.

The students in the Telling About Society seminar complained that these charts, and the ones still to come in this chapter, were "hard to read." They meant what was true, that they had to learn some unfamiliar visual language (unfamiliar to all readers, since it had been invented for this specific study) and interpretive skills, though nothing very elaborate, and pursue the meanings of the new terms and their visual counterparts through a maze of little pictures. They didn't see why they "had to do that" and considered such demands a violation of their implicit contract with makers of representations (illustrating again the moral tone of criticisms of this kind). I invoked another kind of morality and said that that was ridiculous, all you had to do was pay attention. As we talked, it became clear that that was the problem. These books asked them to do work they thought the author should do, work they didn't expect to have to do when they read social science. Like the students McGill interviewed, they wanted the answer without having to do any more work than necessary—"unnecessary" meaning that, if the conclusion has been guaranteed by some external process, such as a journal refereeing system, there's no reason to go through all that work again just to find out the material was OK all along.

Class, Ethnicity, and Occupation

Everett C. Hughes's pioneering study of the industrialization process, *French Canada in Transition*, has several excellent graphic representations of social phenomena. Diagram VII, "Ethnic Composition of Interest Groups" (Hughes 1943, 134), is very Tukey-like. It gives the proportions of French and English in five different interest groups in the small Quebec city "Cantonville" that he studied, in the form of a simple two-part bar chart (reproduced here as figure 10.5).

In the context of the book's analysis of the ethnic division of labor in Canada, in Quebec, and in the town itself, this chart delivers its information efficiently: the "most powerful economic force of the community" is almost entirely English, and the other, less powerful business associations are predominantly French. This reinforces the book's

	English	French
Canadian Manufacturers' Association.		
Chamber of commerce.	17	64
Retail merchants' association.		
Proprietors' league.		
National Catholic labor unions		

The chart does not compare the size of membership of one organization with another, but only the English with the French membership within each organization. The proprietors' league and the labor unions both have some hundreds of members. We are reasonably sure that there are no English members whatsoever in the retail merchants' association and the labor unions. Perhaps as many as four or five people of the old nonindustrial English families belong to the proprietors' league. The French members of the Canadian Manufacturers' Association include the managers of the smaller industries and a few leading men of commercial interests who had a hand in bringing industry to the town.

10.5 Everett C. Hughes, *French Canada in Transition* (1943), p. 134: Ethnic Composition of Interest Groups.

analysis of the dominance of the English in economic affairs. The bars in the graph are unconventionally laid on their sides but otherwise don't pose a problem for users in a hurry.

Not so with diagram X (Hughes 1943, 164, reproduced here as figure 10.6), "Kin and Other Connections between a Group of Leading Men," which provides evidence for some reflections on the role of kinship in the organization of social and business affairs in the French community.

After distinguishing three other groups of well-to-do French ("two old families," a group of six "families of business and professional men, who . . . lead a 'quiet life,'" and "the sporty clique of recognized good social standing"), he focuses on

> the *arrivistes,* [who] present a maze of kinship and intermarriage, reaching down into the lower ranks and out into the surrounding rural counties. . . .
>
> This one web of kinship, intermarriage, partnership, and close friendships includes four of the seven lawyers, two physicians, several of the prominent businessmen, as well as some of lesser importance. The whole is tied with several bonds to the curé of the leading parish. Six of the men now hold public office, and others have done so; all are Conservative in politics, although they vary from extremely nationalistic to moderate and compromising in their attitude toward the English. While several of the men belong to the golf club and have important diplomatic relations with English people concerning matters of industry, business, and politics, no family of the group has any social contacts with English families. (Hughes 1943, 163)

Hughes points out the most crucial results for his exploration of ethnic mixing during the industrialization of Quebec but doesn't comment further, leaving exploration of the diagram to the reader. What could an industrious reader make of it?

Most simply, we can note that many arrows link members of this small group of men, showing them as a tight group with multiple social ties, from which we can deduce the obligations and responsibilities such connections produce. Or we could do a more detailed reading, noting each connection and assessing its potential for collective activity among this small ethnic elite. For instance:

DIAGRAM X

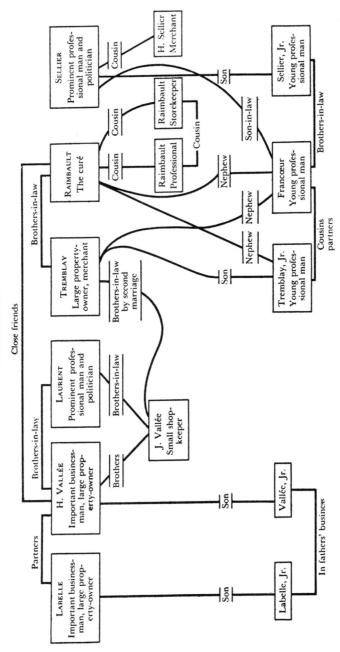

10.6 Hughes, *French Canada in Transition* (1943), p. 164: Kin and Other Connections between a Group of Leading Men.

Labelle and H. Vallée are in an important business together, and both employ their sons in the business. H. Vallée and Raimbault, the curate, are brothers-in-law, and H. Vallée is also the brother of J. Vallée, which makes both of them brothers-in-law of Laurent, a professional man and politician. J. Vallée married twice and so is also the brother-in-law of Tremblay, the merchant and property owner. Tremblay, by virtue of this marriage, is also the brother-in-law of Raimbault, the curate. Raimbault is cousin to two other Raimbaults, who are also cousins to one another, and the uncle of Tremblay's son, who is cousin to Francœur, with whom he is a partner in some business. Francœur, in turn, is brother-in-law to Sellier Jr., son of Sellier, another prominent professional and politician. This takes a lot longer to say in words, clearly, and doesn't give as clear and understandable a picture of the interconnections as all those lines of partnership and kinship snaking around the page. You don't need much imagination to guess that reciprocal communication and loyalties would be very influential for these men's economic, social, and political activities.

You can see how the English would have no chance to mix in this world, since they are unlikely to have any kin connections and the other relations that accompany them, and how the French would not have the time for interethnic mixing with the English and would be held back from it by familial/ethnic loyalty, if they had any opportunity to mix at all. We can also see how this web of connections would greatly enhance the possibilities of collective action within an ethnic group while diminishing chances for such action across ethnic lines (and we should recognize too that the web could just as well create possibilities of conflict that would hinder such action).

When the seminar students complained about these diagrams, they made a special point of something that seems to me a virtue — that they are tailored to the particular use they're put to. Each diagram takes its form from the specific job its book calls on it to do. If Hughes wants to demonstrate the close links within a group of people, his diagram solves that problem neatly and efficiently. But it might not work as well for some other group among whom the ties were differently distributed or were of a different kind, even though it might have in its favor that some people would already have learned how to read it.

Picturing Social Processes

William Foote Whyte's classic study of a poor Italian neighborhood in Boston in the 1930s, *Street Corner Society* ([1943] 1981), rests on four years of participant observation during which he lived in the neighborhood and took an active part in neighborhood activities. Summarizing all that data was a monumental job, and Whyte doesn't say a lot about how he did his analysis, though he gives a detailed account of how he carried on the fieldwork. He counted interactions between people, as recorded in his enormously detailed notes, and he also recorded interactions between people in their institutional capacities, as politicians or racketeers or members and officers of local clubs. He summarized some of these topics in diagrams that condense the information into a quickly readable form. You can read important results directly from the pictures (with a little explanatory help from the author).

The diagrams are especially helpful in Whyte's discussions of process, events that took place in steps. A simple instance is the discussion of the social distance between the college boys—more ambitious, socially mobile, less tied to the neighborhood—and the corner boys—more traditional, not going to college, mostly without jobs, more loyal to one another. Whyte says that in his experience the members of the two groups never interacted except through intermediaries whose own status was somewhat ambiguous (Whyte himself being the clearest example of someone in that position, available to both groups but not really a member of either). Then he shows you an instance of what his notes contain that supports this statement. After laying out three social levels in the neighborhood—college boys, corner boys, and intermediaries who could participate with either group—he verbally maps a street-corner conversation that shows how the three interacted:

> One evening in the fall of 1937 I was standing on Norton Street talking with Chick Morelli, Phil Principio [college boys], Fred Mackey and Lou Danaro [intermediaries], when Frank Bonelli and Nutsy [corner boys] came along and took up a position next to us. I was standing between the two groups. I talked with Chick, Phil, Fred, and

Lou, and I turned to talk with Frank and Nutsy. There was no general conversation. Then Lou and Fred stepped forward and turned so that they were facing the others and standing directly in front of me. At this point the course of the conversation changed, so that, for example, Nutsy said something to Fred, and Fred continued the conversation with Chick and Phil; Chick said something to Lou, and Lou continued the conversation with Frank and Nutsy. At no time did Chick or Phil communicate directly with Frank or Nutsy. After a short time, Lou issued a general invitation to sit in his car. Chick, Phil, and Fred accepted. Nutsy walked over to the car and talked with Lou for a while through the window. Then he returned to Frank and me, and we walked away. (Whyte 1943, 94–95)

He charted it as an interaction in three steps, a concise summary of what the text described (95, reproduced here as figure 10.7). We see everything simultaneously and can compare the three stages of the little event easily. But we can make sense of it only if we have first read the verbal description. We have to know what they were doing in order to *see* what they were doing. The symbols have a meaning special to this study.

That is less true of two other diagrams, "Making and Fixing a Pinch" and "Obtaining the Park Fence" (250–51, reproduced here as figures 10.8 and 10.9), which many readers might make sense of without special instruction.

Whyte explains that politicians must choose how to spend the limited influence they have with other parts of the city's political apparatus. In the case of "fixing a pinch": "A man is to be prosecuted by one of the assistant district attorneys. He speaks to a ward politician. If he has made connections at such a level in the hierarchy, the politician speaks directly to the district attorney, and the district attorney tells his assistant to drop the case. Otherwise it is frequently possible to secure results without taking the case up to the district attorney. His subordinates are susceptible to certain sorts of political pressure" (247), As the picture shows, this is relatively simple. The corner boy, having been arrested (1), talks to a corner boy leader (2), who talks to a politician (3), who talks to the captain (4), who talks to the arresting officer (5), and the case is dropped.

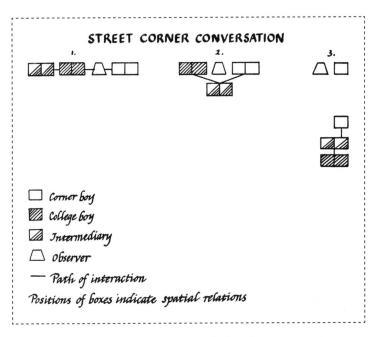

10.7 William Foote Whyte, *Street Corner Society* (1943), p. 95: Street Corner Conversation.

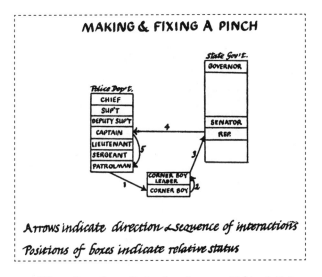

10.8 Whyte, *Street Corner Society* (1943), p. 250: Making & Fixing a Pinch.

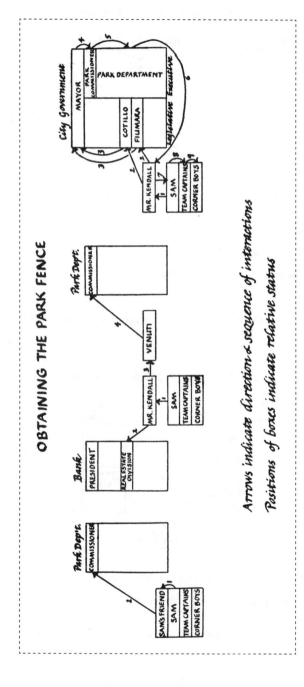

OBTAINING THE PARK FENCE

Arrows indicate direction & sequence of interactions

Positions of boxes indicate relative status

10.9 Whyte, *Street Corner Society* (1943), p. 251: Obtaining the Park Fence.

When Sam Franco organized a corner boy softball league, the local park wasn't available for league play because earlier games had led to broken windows in a nearby building. The league needed a wire fence to contain the balls and prevent window breaking. How to get it? The book spends three full pages detailing the various possible routes and explaining the one that finally worked. Sam approached Mr. Kendall, a social worker at the neighborhood settlement house he had met through Doc, a corner boy leader and Whyte's good friend. Kendall first tried Venuti, a local politician whose connections were not strong enough to get the fence, and then went to Alderman Angelo Fiamura: "Angelo Fiamura was not interested in acting for Mr. Kendall until he realized that the social worker was part of a well-knit organization, which in this case included Sam Franco, sixteen corner boy leaders, and all their followers. Then he and Andy Cotillo acted upon the mayor. Cotillo was in the mayor's office, and Fiamura had made his connections through Cotillo. Both men were in a position to exert pressure upon the top point in this legislative hierarchy, and, when they did, the course of action initiated by Sam Franco was brought to a successful conclusion" (250). All this, as well as the failed attempts, is summarized in the figure.

Someone once told me that "word people" and "picture people" are two different breeds, but I don't believe it. The people whose studies I've discussed here made both words and pictures work for them. The combination produces, I'm convinced, increased understanding. But it is uncommon. Like Tukey's statistical innovations—box-and-whisker diagrams, for instance—they require users to work a little harder. Data don't appear in simple formulaic patterns that users can inspect quickly. Users have to put some effort into extracting the meaning.

I said earlier that I was proselytizing in this chapter. I'd like to see more people use devices like these, create formats that say exactly what they want to say rather than forcing their ideas into standard packages. It's not too much to hope for.

11

Visual Sociology, Documentary Photography, and Photojournalism

Representations of society get made and used in social organizations, and we understand them best when we put them into that context. This chapter demonstrates that idea in the specific case of photography, showing how the same object, in this case the same photograph, can have a different meaning in a different organizational context, and going into the nature of those contexts in detail.

Three Kinds of Photography

People who want to use photographic materials for social science purposes—to do what is sometimes called visual sociology—often get confused. The pictures visual sociologists make so resemble those made by others, who claim to be doing documentary photography or photojournalism, that they wonder whether they are doing anything distinctive. They try to clear up the confusion by looking for essential differences, the defining features of each genre, as if it were a problem of getting the definitions right.

The labels of these genres do not refer to Platonic essences whose meaning we can discover by profound thought and analysis, but rather are just what people have found it useful to make them mean. We can learn what people have been able to do using documentary photography or photojournalism as a cover, but we can't find out what the terms *really* mean. Their meaning arises in the organizations they are used in, out of the joint action of all the people involved in those organizations, and so it varies from time to time and place to place. Just as paintings get their meaning in a world of painters, collectors, critics, and curators, so photographs get their meaning from the way the people involved with them understand them, use them, and thereby attribute meaning to them (see Becker 1982).

Visual sociology, documentary photography, and photojournalism, then, are whatever they have come to mean, or been made to mean, in their daily use in worlds of photographic work, social constructions pure and simple. In this they resemble all the other ways of reporting what we know, or think we have found out, about the societies we live in—all the ways discussed in this book. We can raise at least two kinds of questions about this activity of naming and attributing meaning.

ORGANIZATIONAL : People who name classes of activity, as they have named these forms of picture making, don't do that just to make things convenient for themselves and others by creating some shorthand tags. They almost always mean to accomplish other purposes as well: drawing boundaries around the activities, saying where they belong organizationally, establishing who is in charge, who is responsible for what, and who is entitled to what.

So we want to ask, of these different ways of talking about photography, who uses these terms? What are they trying to claim for the work so described? How do they thus mean to locate that work in some work organization? Conversely, what kind of work and which people do they mean to exclude? In short, what are they trying to accomplish by talking this way?

HISTORICAL : Where did these terms come from? What have they been used for in the past? How does their past use create a present context, and how does that historically based context constrain what can be said and done now? "Documentary photography" was one kind of activity around the turn of the twentieth century, when great waves of social reform swept the United States and photographers had a ready audience for images exposing evil and plenty of sponsors to pay them to create those images. "Visual sociology," if we can talk about such a thing in that era, consisted of much the same kind of images, but published in the *American Journal of Sociology*. Neither term means now what it did then. The great social reform organizations have changed in character, their use of photographs now subsidiary to a host of other techniques, and sociology has become more "scientific" and less open to reports in anything but words and numbers. The meaning of photojournalism has changed from simple illustration of news stories to a conception of photography as a coordinate semi-independent way of conveying information (Hagaman 1996, 3–12). The three terms, then, have varying histories and present uses. Each is tied to and gets its meaning in a particular social context.

"Photojournalism" is what journalists do, producing images as part of the work of getting out daily newspapers and weekly news-magazines (probably mostly daily newspapers now, since the death in the early 1970s of the big illustrated news magazines like *Look*). What is photojournalism commonly supposed to be? Unbiased. Factual. Complete. Attention-getting, storytelling, courageous. Our image of the photojournalist, insofar as it is based on historical figures, consists of one part Weegee, sleeping in his car, typing his stories on the typewriter stored in its trunk, smoking cigars, chasing car wrecks and fires, and photographing criminals for a New York tabloid; he said of his work, "Murders and fires, my two best sellers, my bread and butter" (Weegee 1945, 11). A second part is Robert Capa, rushing into the midst of a battle to get a close-up shot of death and destruction (his watchword was "If your pictures aren't good enough, you aren't close enough"—quoted in Capa 1968) for the news magazines. The final part of the stereotype is Margaret Bourke-White in aviator's gear, camera in one hand, helmet in the other, standing in front of an airplane wing with the engine and propeller to her side, flying around the world producing classic photoessays in the *Life* style (Callahan 1972, 24). Contemporary versions of the stereotype appear in Hollywood films: Nick Nolte standing on the hood of a tank as it lumbers into battle through enemy fire, making images of war as he risks his life.

The reality is less heroic. Photojournalism is whatever it can be, given the nature of the journalism business. As that business changed, as the age of *Life* and *Look* faded, as the nature of the daily newspaper changed in the face of competition from radio, television, and eventually the Internet, the photographs journalists made changed too.

Photojournalism is not what it was in the days of Weegee or the first picture magazines in Germany (K. Becker, 1985). Today's photojournalists are literate and college educated; they can write and so are no longer simply illustrators of stories reporters tell. They have a coherent ideology, based on the concept of the storytelling image (Hagaman 1996). Nevertheless, contemporary photojournalism is, like its earlier versions, constrained by available space and by the prejudices, blind spots, and preconceived story lines of photographers' editorial superiors (Ericson, Baranek, and Chan 1987). Most importantly, readers do not expect to do any work deciphering ambiguities and complexities in the photographs that appear in their daily newspaper or newsmagazine. Such photographs must, therefore, be instantly readable and interpretable (Hagaman 1993, 8–12).

Photojournalism is constrained, too, by the way editors hand out photographic assignments. Except for sports photographers, who sometimes become specialized in that area, photojournalists, unlike reporters, never develop a "beat," an area of a city's life they cover continuously and know so well that they develop a serious analysis and understanding of it. Since the photographs they make inevitably reflect their understanding of the events and social phenomena they are photographing, that job-enforced ignorance means that the resulting images will almost necessarily be based on a superficial understanding. Heroic legends describe the few photographers—W. Eugene Smith, Henri Cartier-Bresson—who were brave enough or independent enough to overcome these obstacles. But the legends serve only to hearten those whose work still reflects those constraints. (A number of social scientists have studied the organization of newsgathering. See, for instance, Epstein 1973; Hall 1973; Molotch and Lester 1974; Schudson 1978; Tuchman 1978; Ericson, Baranek, and Chan 1987; and a reflective photojournalist, Hagaman 1996.)

Documentary photography was tied, historically, to both exploration and social reform. Some early documentarians worked, literally, "documenting" features of the natural landscape, as did Timothy O'Sullivan, who accompanied the U.S. Geological Exploration of the Fortieth Parallel in 1867–69 and the surveys of the southwestern United States led by Lieutenant George M. Wheeler, during which he made his now famous images of the Canyon de Chelle (Horan 1966, 151–214, 237–312). Others documented unfamiliar ways of life, as in John Thompson's photographs of street life in London (Newhall 1964, 139), Eugène Atget's massive survey of Parisian people and scenes (see the four-volume collection by Szarkowski and Hambourg 1983), or August Sander's monumental study of German social types (Sander, Sander and Keller 1986). The latter two projects were so large that they were, in a deep sense, impractical, that is, not tied to any immediate practical use.

Others worked, like Lewis Hine (Gutman 1967), for the great social surveys of the early part of the century or, like Jacob Riis ([1901] 1971), for muckraking newspapers. Their work was intended and used to expose evil and promote change. Their images were, perhaps, something like those journalists made but were less tied to illustrating a newspaper story and thus had more space to breathe in. A classic example is Hine's image "Leo, 48 inches high, 8 years old, picks up bobbins at fifteen cents a day," in which a young boy stands next to the machines that have, we almost surely conclude, stunted his growth.

What is documentary "supposed to do"? In the reformist version, it's supposed to dig deep, get at what Robert E. Park (a sociologist who had worked as a journalist for daily papers in Minneapolis, Denver, Detroit, Chicago and New York) called the Big News, be "concerned" about society, play an active role in social change, be socially responsible, worry about its effects on the society in which its work is distributed. Photographers like Hine saw their work, and it has often been seen since, as having an immediate effect on citizens and legislators. A photographically chauvinistic view of history often attributes the passage of laws banning child labor directly to Hine's work.

In its alternative version, documentary was not supposed to be anything in particular, since the work was not made for anyone in particular who could have enforced any requirements. Sander, who hoped to sell his work by subscription, described it variously as depicting the "existing social order" and as "a physiognomical time exposure of German man" (Sander, Sander, and Keller 1986, 23–24). Atget, more like an archetypal naive artist, did not describe his work at all but simply made it and sold the prints to whoever would buy them. Today, we see this work as having an exploratory, investigative character, more like social science. Contemporary documentary photographers, whose work converges more consciously with social science, have become aware, like anthropologists, that they have to worry about, and justify, their relations to the people they photograph.

Visual sociology is almost completely a creature of professional sociology, an academic discipline, and a poor relation of visual anthropology, which has a cozier connection to its parent discipline; in the anthropological tradition, which required investigators going to far-off places to gather skulls, linguistic texts, and archaeological materials, making photographs was just one more fieldwork obligation (Collier and Collier 1986). Since visual imagery has not been conventional in sociology since its beginnings, when it was more tied to social reform, most sociologists do not accept that obligation; they see few legitimate uses for visual materials, other than as "teaching aids." It is as though using photographs and films in a research report constituted pandering to the low tastes of the public or trying to persuade readers to accept shaky conclusions by using illegitimate "rhetorical" means (a version of the accusation of being "insidious"). Using visual materials seems "unscientific," probably because "science" in sociology came to be defined as objective and neutral, just the opposite of the crusading spirit that animated the early muckraking work, itself integrally tied to photography (Stasz 1979).

The definition of visual materials as unscientific is odd, since the natural sciences routinely use visual materials as evidence. Contemporary biology, physics, and astronomy are unthinkable without photographic evidence. In social science, only history and anthropology, the least "scientific" disciplines, use photographs. Economics and political science, the most "scientific," don't. Sociology, mimicking the supposed scientific character of the latter fields, doesn't. As a result, the few active visual sociologists are people who learned photography elsewhere and brought it to their academic work.

What are visual sociologists "supposed to do"? I guess they are supposed to do what they would have to do to compel the attention and respect of their discipline. What would they have to accomplish to convince other sociologists that their work is in some sense integral to the sociological enterprise? But it's not only a matter of convincing their professional colleagues. They must also convince themselves that what they are doing is "really sociology," not just making "pretty" or "interesting" pictures. To do that, they would have to show that their visual work furthers the enterprise of sociology, however the mission of the discipline is defined. Since sociologists differ on what sociology should be, the mission of visual sociology is similarly confused. At a minimum, it should help to answer questions raised in the discipline in a way acceptable to one or more disciplinary factions.

It might also add something now missing. Are there topics for which photography would be a particularly good research method? The publications of the International Visual Sociology Association and its members give examples of what might be done (see its home page, IVSA 2006).

I've made these distinctions, but the boundaries between the three activities are increasingly blurred, as the situations in which people work and the purposes for which they make photographs increasingly blend two or more genres.

Context

Like all cultural objects, photographs get meaning from their context. Even paintings or sculptures, which seem to exist in isolation, hanging on the wall of a museum, get their meaning from a context made up of what has been written about them, either in the label hanging beside them or elsewhere, other visual objects, physically present or just present in viewers' awareness, and discussions going on around them and around the subject the works are about. If we think there is no context, that only means that the maker of the work has cleverly taken advantage of our willingness to provide the context for ourselves.

As opposed to much contemporary photography made in the name of art, the three photographic genres I'm discussing insist on giving a lot of explicit social context for the photographs they present. This isn't the place to consider the fluidity of definitions of photographic art. But my last statement should be qualified to recognize that the world of art photography has frequently incorporated into its photographic canon work made for reasons quite different from those of self-conscious art, including work made as journalism or documentary. The extreme case is Weegee, the photojournalist whose work now rests in many museum collections. Contemporary art photographs often show us something that might well have been the subject of a documentary photograph (poor kids standing on a slummy street, for instance). But they seldom provide any more context than date and place; they withhold the minimal social data we ordinarily use to orient ourselves to others and leave viewers to interpret the images as best they can from the clues of clothing, stance, demeanor and household furnishings they contain. What might seem to be artistic mystery is usually only ignorance created by the photographer's refusal to give users basic information.

Documentary, photojournalism, and visual sociology routinely provide at least a minimally sufficient background to make the images intelligible. Some works in the documentary tradition, often influenced by the photographer's exposure to social science, provide a great deal of text, sometimes in the words of the people involved (e.g., Danny Lyon's *Bikeriders* (1968) or Susan Meisalas's *Carnival Strippers* (1976), both done as independent projects). The text may be no more than an adequate caption, in the style of Lewis Hine or Dorothea Lange, or as in Jack Delano's portrait of a railroad worker, made in Chicago for the Farm Security Administration, whose caption reads, "Frank Williams, working on the car repair tracks at an Illinois Central Railroad yard. Mr. Williams has eight children, two of whom are in the U.S. Army. Chicago. November, 1942" (Reid and Viskochil 1989, 192). Photographic books often contain extensive introductions and essays setting the social and historical stage for the images.

But things aren't that simple: leaving the context implicit does not make a photograph art, and a full context doesn't automatically make it documentary, social science, or photojournalism. Not all good documentary works provide such context. Robert Frank's *The Americans* (to which I will devote more attention below) gives no more textual support to the images than most art photographs do, but it is not vulnerable to the above criticism. Why not? Because the images themselves, sequenced, repetitive, variations on a set of themes, provide their own context and teach viewers what they need to know in order to arrive, by their own reasoning, at some conclusions about what they are looking at. (As we've seen, Walker Evans used similar devices to lead people to create context for themselves.)

In short, context gives images meaning. If the work doesn't provide context in one of the ways I've just discussed, viewers will often do the work, providing context from their own resources.

A Practical Demonstration

Let's pursue this line of thought by looking at images that exemplify each of the three genres and seeing how they might be interpreted as one of the others. That will show us what organizational context and the associated work users are ready to do contribute to the meaning of a photographic representation. Let's take photographs of each type to be what they weren't made as—take a documentary photograph, for instance, as a news photograph or a work of visual sociology. What happens when we read images in ways unconventional in the organizations they're made for, ways their makers didn't intend or, at least, different from the way they are conventionally read?

READING A DOCUMENTARY PICTURE AS VISUAL SOCI-OLOGY OR PHOTOJOURNALISM : In Robert Frank's "En route from New York to Washington, Club Car," an image from his book *The Americans* (Frank [1959] 1969, 25), three men sit in a railroad club car. Two large men with their backs to us are near enough to the camera to be slightly out of focus. They wear tweed jackets, have dark slick hair, lean toward each other, and occupy half the frame. Between them, in focus, we see a black-suited third man's bald head and, behind him, the bar, above which shine many small star-shaped lights. His face is jowly, his forehead lined, he isn't looking at either of the others. He seems serious, even somber.

Frank made this picture, as he made all the pictures in *The Americans*, with a documentary intent, as part of a larger project designed to describe American society. He explained his intentions in his application for the Guggenheim fellowship that made the project possible:

What I have in mind, then, is observation and record of what one naturalized American finds to see in the United States that signifies the kind of civilization born here and spreading elsewhere. Incidentally, it is fair to assume that when an observant American travels abroad his eye will see freshly; and that the reverse may be true when a European eye looks at the United States. I speak of the things that are there, anywhere and everywhere—easily found, not easily selected and interpreted. A small catalog comes to the mind's eye: a town at night, a parking lot, a supermarket, a highway, the man who owns the three cars and the man who owns none, the farmer and his children, a new house and a warped clapboard house, the dictation of taste, the dream of grandeur, advertising, neon lights, the faces of the leaders and the faces of the followers, gas tanks and post offices and backyards. (Tucker and Brookman 1986, 20)

In another place, he explained his project this way:

With these photographs, I have attempted to show a cross-section of the American population. My effort was to express it simply and without confusion. The view is personal and, therefore, various facets of American life and society have been ignored. . . .

I have been frequently accused of deliberately twisting subject matter to my point of view. Above all, I know that life for a photographer cannot be a matter of indifference. Opinion often consists of a kind of criticism. But criticism can come out of love. It is important to see what is invisible to others. Perhaps the look of hope or the look of sadness. Also, it is always the instantaneous reactions to oneself that produces a photograph. (reprinted from *U.S. Camera Annual 1958*, U.S. Camera Publishing Corp., New York, 1967, 115, in Tucker and Brookman, 1986, 31)

Seen in this context, we can understand "En Route to Washington, Club Car" as a statement about American politics. These large and physically imposing men are the kind who, we learn from Frank elsewhere in the book, occupy positions of political power and inhabit such places as the club cars of trains going between New York, the country's financial center, and Washington, its political center. What makes the image documentary, and gives it its full meaning, is its place in a sequence of images. It says nothing explicit about American politics. But we understand its political statement by learning, from their use elsewhere in the book, the meaning of the image's details. We learn that a big man is a powerful man (as in "Bar—Gallup, New Mexico," in which a large man in jeans and a cowboy hat dominates a crowded bar) and that a well-dressed big man is a rich and powerful man ("Hotel lobby—Miami Beach," where a large middle-aged man is accompanied by a woman wearing what seems to be an expensive fur). We learn that politicians are big, thus powerful, men ("City fathers—Hoboken, New Jersey," in which a group of such men fill a political platform). We see these big, well-dressed men on the train between these two power centers. The stars in the lights above the bar recall the stars on American flags and their use and misuse in political and everyday settings, documented in other photographs in the book; they suggest that we are looking at the powerful at work in some unspecified way, probably one that won't do us any good. The image functions as part of Frank's analysis—implicit, but nonetheless clear—of how the U.S. political system works.

If the analysis were made explicit, its complexity might well qualify it as a work of visual sociology. We would probably, in that case, want to know more about what we were seeing. Who are these people? What are they actually doing? But more important, we would want to know more clearly what Frank was telling us about the nature of U.S. politics. We would want to replace the nuance of the photographic treatment of U.S. society, as many commentators have in fact done (cf. Brumfeld 1980; Cook 1982, 1986), with an explicit statement about the nature of that society, its class and political structure, its age grading, its sexual stratification, and its use of such major symbols as the flag, the cross, and the automobile. Such an explicit statement of cultural patterns and social structure would make the image speak to the kind of abstract questions about the organization of society that sociologists care about.

Even then, it's not likely that many sociologists would accept Frank's book as a work of scientific sociology. They would assume, correctly, that photographs are easily manipulated; the sophisticated ones would know that you need not alter the actual image, just frame the elements properly and wait for an opportune moment. They would worry, properly, about using one image as a surrogate for a larger universe of similar situations. They would be justifiably unsure that the images have the meaning I am imputing to them. They would not, however, take the next step, which would be to see that every form of social science data has exactly these problems and that no method solves them very well.

If it were set on the front page of a daily newspaper, we might read the same photograph as a news photograph. But the people in it are not named, and newspapers seldom print photographs of anonymous people. Quite the contrary: photojournalists are trained, until it is instinctive for them, to get names and other relevant information about the people they photograph (a student in a course in photojournalism will be warned that a misspelled name in the caption will automatically lead to failure in the course). To function as a news photograph, the image would require a quite different caption from the one Frank gave it. For instance: "Senator John Jones of Rhode Island discusses campaign strategy with two assistants." But even then it's unlikely that the picture would appear in the daily newspaper, because it is grainy and not in sharp focus, and the two staff aides have their backs to us. The editor would send the photographer back for a more sharply focused image of such a routine event, one that was less grainy and showed us the faces of all three men.

In fact, many conventional photographers and critics complained about Frank's work just as this imagined editor would have. The editors of *Popular Photography*, for instance, didn't like Frank's book. These comments appeared in volume 46, number 5 (May 1960): "Frank has managed to express, through the recalcitrant medium of photography, an intense personal vision, and that's nothing to carp at. But as to the nature of that vision I found its purity too often marred by spite, bitterness, and narrow prejudices just as so many of the prints are flawed by meaningless blur, grain, muddy exposure, drunken horizons, and general sloppiness. As a photographer, Frank shows contempt for any standards of quality or discipline in technique" (Arthur Goldsmith, quoted in Tucker and Brookman 1986, 36–37). And another critic said, "It seems as if he merely points the camera in the direction he wishes to shoot and doesn't worry about exposure, composition, and lesser considerations. If you dig out-of-focus pictures, intense and unnecessary grain, converging verticals, a total absence of normal composition, and a relaxed, snapshot quality, then Robert Frank is for you. If you don't, you may find *The Americans* one of the most irritating photo books to make the scene" (James M. Zanutto, quoted in Tucker and Brookman 1986, 37).

If, however, a photojournalist had made the picture during an exposé of political corruption, an editor might well excuse such "technical" flaws because of the importance of what was revealed. In this case, the caption might read "James McGillicuddy, Boston political boss, talking with Senator John Jones of Rhode Island, chairman of the Senate Armed Forces Committee, and Harry Thompson, CEO of a major defense contracting firm." The editor might make this the basis of a strong editorial, and the senator, like so many politicians accused of wrongdoing, might want to deny he was ever there and insist that it was two other guys.

In fact, at least one of Frank's photographs (made at the 1956 Democratic Party convention in Chicago) might well, in the proper context, have appeared in a daily newspaper or newsmagazine as "news." The caption ("Convention hall—Chicago") characteristically names no one. Here we see the crowded floor of a political convention. Again, two men have their backs to us. On either side of them, two men face us. One, wearing dark glasses, looks suave and calm. The other, jowly, looks down worriedly. The faces of these two politicians were, at the time, recognizable, and their names might have given the picture "news value." The troubled-looking gentleman was a sociologist (from whom I once took a class at the University of Chicago, which is why I recognized him) who had left academia for politics: Joseph Lohman, a well-known criminologist who became, successively, sheriff of Cook County, Illinois, and Illinois secretary of state, made an unsuccessful try for the Democratic gubernatorial nomination in the state and then left politics to become dean of the School of Criminology at the University of California–Berkeley. At the time of the photograph he was still active in Illinois politics and was seen as a "good government" type in the Adlai Stevenson tradition. He is talking, I believe, to Carmine DeSapio, a major New York City political figure in the old-fashioned party boss tradition. In the context of that convention, the image of their conversation might, by indicating an unlikely and therefore interesting potential political alliance, have been "news."

READING A SOCIOLOGICAL PICTURE AS JOURNALISM AND AS DOCUMENTARY : Douglas Harper did his study of tramps as a work of sociology; the original dissertation relegated the photographs he had made to a "volume 2," where they had no captions. But the book he developed from the dissertation, *Good Company* (1981), contained a large number of photographs, not as illustrations, the way photographs appear in sociology textbooks, but as elements integral to the sociological investigation and therefore to a reader's sociological understanding. They contain, and express, ideas that are sociological in their origin and use and thus may not be as transparent to an immediate reading as other photographs. Take his photograph ("jungle; Wenatchee," n.p.) of Carl, a tramp Harper met during his fieldwork, shaving. Harper points out that this image, seen in context, stands as evidence that refutes a common notion (one that another image in this series—"Boston skid row," which shows a bum who needs a shave—might seem to support) that these men routinely don't take care of themselves and don't share conventional standards of decorum. As he says, when we see these men with a two-day growth of beard, we should realize that means they shaved two days ago.

What makes Harper's images visual sociology is not their content alone but their context. They appear surrounded by a sociological text, although an unconventional one, which explains their meaning to us. One part of the text recounts how Carl taught Harper hobo culture. A second part describes, in analytic sociological language, that culture, the characteristic forms of social organization hobos are involved in, and the conditions under which such adaptations grow up and persist. The text, both the narrative of Harper's training in how to live on the road and the later explicit sociological analysis, gives the pictures added substance, sociological meaning, and evidentiary value.

Try reading these same images as photojournalism. Imagine them as illustrations for a newspaper's series on the topic "homelessness." Read in that context, they would get their meaning, as photojournal-

11.1 Douglas Harper, *Good Company* (1981), unpaginated: Jungle; Wenatchee.

istic images typically do, from the stock of easily available stereotypes that daily newspaper readers carry with them. We probably would never see the man shaving, because, for one thing, it's unlikely that any working photojournalist would want, or be able, to spend the months on the road that allowed Harper the ease of access and, more important, the background of knowledge that gave him the image's meaning. As famous a photojournalist as W. Eugene Smith, at the height of his career, still had to fight with *Life* magazine repeatedly to be able to spend as much as three weeks in one place for a photoessay.

In addition, an editor would probably say to the photographer who brought such pictures in, "These don't say 'homeless' to me." Why don't they? Because editors know, or think they know, in advance of any investigation, what their story line is going to be. Whatever a story says about "the problem" of homelessness must be congruent with what readers already know and believe. An appropriate photograph relies, for its instant readability, on readers' having that knowledge. For the editor, and therefore for the photographer, *what* "homelessness" is has already been decided; they are not trying to discover things about it they didn't already know. Their problem is technical:

11.2 Harper, *Good Company* (1981), unpaginated:
Boston Skid Row.

how to get the image that best tells the already selected story (see
Hagaman 1993, 1996).

Can we read Harper's photographs as documentary? Yes, we could
see them, in Hine's classic phrase, as showing us what needs to be
changed or, perhaps, the other half of Hine's famous remark, what
needs to be appreciated. We might, in an appropriate setting of text
and other photographs, see them as part of the effort of an aroused
group of professionals to straighten out the lives of these men who
wandered the country. Or we might, nearer to Harper's own intention, want to celebrate the independence and way of life of these men,
in the appreciative way David Matza described the Chicago School of

sociology doing, appreciating forms of deviance conventional citizens ordinarily condemned (Matza 1969). This celebratory mode of reading shares much with the common anthropological injunction to respect the people you study.

READING A JOURNALISTIC PICTURE AS VISUAL SOCI- OLOGY AND AS DOCUMENTARY : Consider this picture. (I have never been able to find the image I describe here, but have found others sufficiently similar as not to mar the argument. I've taken the liberty of describing the "perfect" image I remember.) We see a helicopter on a lawn, in the garden of what looks like the White House in Washington, DC. A carpet runs from the building to the helicopter. A man, head down, shoulders hunched, walks along the carpet to the plane while, on either side, people stand weeping. People who were not reading the paper in 1974 may not know what it shows us, but the image was instantly recognizable to anyone reading a newspaper anywhere in the world then. It is Richard Nixon leaving the White House, having just resigned the presidency of the United States, his boast that he was not a crook belied by the continuing exposure of "what he knew and when he knew it." In its day, it was a classic news photograph.

Shortly after its publication, it suffered the fate of all news photographs. In a short time they are no longer news and have "only historical" value. Their news value depends on context, on the event's being contemporary, "now." In fact, the pathos and emotional impact of the Nixon image required every viewer who picked up the paper and saw it to furnish that context, to know the second they saw the picture exactly what they were looking at. The image summed up a story they had followed for months in the papers and on television, the gradual and seemingly inevitable downfall of a powerful political leader, toppled by his own lies and paranoia, finally defeated by a combination of political and journalistic attacks.

Years later the image has no such connotations. It records an event that people who did not read newspapers and magazines at the time may have read or heard about. But it is not news, not the end point of a story whose denouement was, until then, unknown and in doubt. It has to be something other than news. What else could it be?

In the proper context, news photographs of continuing interest become documentary, as Erich Salomon's photographs, made between the two world wars, of such phenomena as the Versailles Peace Conference, have become documentary (Salomon 1967). The politicians Salomon photographed—such luminaries of the time as Gustav Streseman and Aristide Briand—are no longer news. But we might combine the Nixon image—no longer news to us—with Salomon's photographs to create a generalized document of aspects of the political process. Others, more historically minded, might embed the Nixon image in a larger consideration of the Watergate events.

Could the Nixon image be part of a sociological analysis? An analyst might be concerned, as many have been, with the way the print media deal with the generic phenomenon of political scandal, how they use the devices of photographic representation to indicate the political downgrading of a disgraced leader (Molotch and Lester 1974). A good sociological analysis of this problem would require comparisons of photographs of Nixon at various stages of his career. Nixon would be an excellent subject for such an analysis because his career and reputation fluctuated widely in a relatively short time and the photographic representations could be expected to vary correspondingly.

Other analysts of political behavior might concern themselves with the public rituals of societies, with the use of quasi-regal paraphernalia and events to create a sort of monarchical regime within a political democracy. Photographs of Nixon, in such a research, would be surrounded by other photographs of similar rituals and by texts that revealed other devices aimed at the same result.

Summing Up

Representations don't have fixed meanings whose further ramifications analysts can then interpret. They live in social contexts and are truth or fiction, document or imaginative construction, depending on what the ultimate users make of them. The experiment here shows how the same image can have quite different meanings, as it is used in different settings by different kinds of people.

12

Drama and Multivocality
Shaw, Churchill, and Shawn

Do we want to include the voices and viewpoints of some or all of the participants in our representations of the social situations we study? Many sociologists think that to give a coherent and believable account of social life, we must deal with the meanings actors give to objects, to other people, and to their own and others' activities. To speak of meanings is to speak of voices, because meanings arise in interaction, and interaction consists in some large part of talk, the voices of real people talking to each other.

Not everyone thinks this. A skeptic might say that we needn't hear any voices at all. It doesn't matter what people say, it's what they do and have done that matters. The puppets of social forces beyond their control, people don't know the reasons for their own actions. Hidden powers manipulate them. We've arrived at the famous dilemma of agency and structure. Can people act of their own volition or not? If they can't, then meanings don't matter. Whatever they think and whatever meaning they give to other people and to things, they have no choice and must do what the larger forces make them do.

Analysts who talk this way, however, invariably sneak the voices of the people they are talking about back in, attributing all kinds of meanings and interpretations to those whose actions they propose to explain. Their own omniscient analytic voices represent all the others whose activity they claim to analyze. Bruno Latour describes this as a "spokesman" effect: someone else tells you what the people whose actions you want to understand have in mind (Latour 1987, 70–74). This omniscient explainer—the voice of the voiceover in the documentary film, the voice of the social scientist who "interprets" the results of a survey—tells you what it all means, what those people who answered the survey's questions must have had in mind. This authoritative voice speaks in the standard classical journal article, in the section where the analyst "discusses" the findings.

The authoritative voice gets its authority, its power to persuade, from the assumption its speakers and listeners accept: that behind the voice lies scientifically (or otherwise) verified knowledge. James Clifford explains how anthropology, first conceived as a scholarly putting-together of what "men on the spot" (missionaries, traders, explorers) had recorded, became a science made by trained scientists who gathered material (which, in their hands, became "evidence") in a scientific way and used it to verify carefully drawn scientific hypotheses (Clifford 1988). As anthropologists do this—according to this account—they preserve a scientific neutrality. But they combine it with a claim to intimate firsthand knowledge. So the final justification for our belief in the results announced by the one voice of the researcher is the combination of a generalizing, systematic scientific neutrality and a detailed knowledge that could come only from having been there, seen it all firsthand, and recorded it in your field notes. (To be sure, the "having been there" can get considerably watered down or become highly metaphorical, when "there" turns out to be, in the case of survey or demographic research, the office in which someone ran the survey results through a computer.)

Clifford traces these two claims in the specifics of the anthropological prose of Bronislaw Malinowski and others: the alternation between passages of generalizing "objective" prose and the stirring accounts of personal experience ("Our party, sailing from the North . . ."), the first testifying to the science, the second to the personal involvement. Classic anthropological reports simultaneously told the story of the peoples studied and of the anthropologist's participation in their lives, which made the study possible and believable.

Mikhail Bakhtin insisted on the necessity of including more than the authoritative authorial voice (which he identified with the epic form and a stable hierarchical society). He proposed the ideas of multivocality and dialogical prose (and, so far as I know, invented the terms as well). He developed these notions to say something he thought it important to say about novels—he wanted to praise Dickens for allowing so many voices of so many kinds of people to speak in his books—but the idea can be moved onto new terrain without harming it any.

Here's how Bakhtin, in *The Dialogic Imagination* (1981), explains the idea: "A word, discourse, language or culture undergoes 'dialogization' when it becomes relativized, de-privileged, aware of competing definitions for the same things. Undialogized language is authoritative or absolute" (427). In a world where meanings shift, depending on who's talking and on the speaker's social situation and position, a work of literature that claims to increase our understanding of that world can't speak in one clear authoritative voice, because there is no way to pick out the one voice that has the whole truth. A work of literature that wants to be accurate will have to include those different voices, which say the words with different meanings. It will contain talk between people who see things differently. So it will take the form of a dialogue, be "dialogical."

A simple idea. How do we apply it to the problem of representing society? Society is made up of a variety of groups, each giving its own meanings to things and people and events. (In the limiting case, the group is just one person, whom no one else agrees with about what things mean. We usually treat such people as crazy.) A group's members, defining things similarly, can act together to do things based on that common definition. If they don't share similar meanings, their attempts at collective action flounder. I don't have anything mystical in mind here. If we want to build a house, we will do a lot better if we have a vocabulary of terms we all understand in the same way. If my dentist asks the assistant for a "Hollenbeck," my teeth stand a better chance if the dentist and assistant both think that word stands for the same instrument.

If we want to represent the activities of some small segment of society adequately, we can't just focus on the people immediately involved. Every activity, however small, consists of people acting together, and in principle we want to represent the variety of people engaged in that activity. So we should look at their connections to other groups and organizations. If we want to understand a hospital, we can't just observe and talk to nurses and doctors. To understand what they're doing and why, we should also talk to and observe administrators, patients, technicians, practical nurses, janitors, cooks, suppliers, insurance companies, people who work in the laundry, and all the other individuals and organizations, including especially the patients, whose activity contributes to the hospital's opening its doors every morning. And having seen and heard all that, we will want to make sure that each group "speaks" in our representation, that its meanings, present and accounted for, contribute their piece of the puzzle's solution. Otherwise, we will give an inadequate account of what we want to explain. To be blunt, though the job of sociology is to understand and then communicate our understanding, we won't understand a thing that goes on in our data, our reports will misconstrue the findings, our predictions will be a mile off, and we will be continually surprised by what happens.

If there were a unity or consensus among the people we study, if we were sure that one spokesman really did speak for all of them, so that we could say or assume that they all really think and believe the same thing and act in the same ways—that would simplify the job. We wouldn't need to bother with all those voices. One would do. But that's just what Bakhtin complained about. A good listen to any social phenomenon brings us a Babel of differing voices. If we want to do the representational job accurately, we have to hear and report all those voices.

I'm not making the conventionally sentimental plea to "give voice" to people who would otherwise not be heard because it's the morally right thing to do. Nor do I suggest that those otherwise unheard other voices have some "truth" (maybe "The Truth") that the people who usually get heard, with or without our help, don't have access to or won't tell even if they know it. This is a more hardheaded argument. We can't get our self-appointed job of accurate description done unless we listen to everyone. Each person and group knows one thing better than anyone else, and that's what they think and have done and will do. They might not tell us the truth about that, but that's a general problem. If anyone knows what they think, they do. (And yes, I think the idea of "false consciousness" grossly misrepresents reality.) If we don't incorporate what people of all kinds know into our description of an organization, we will necessarily leave many important things out of our analysis and get many things wrong.

Accepting this line of argument creates some difficult problems for anyone who wants to describe social life. Does every voice really have to be represented? That's a lot of voices, even in the simplest situation. It's easy to show—it's one of the things I did in Art Worlds (Becker 1982)—that an enormous number of people are involved in even the simplest activity. They may not all be in the room at the same time, they may never meet face to face, they may not know the others exist, but it doesn't take a complicated analysis to see that things could not come off as they have if all those people didn't do their part. I insisted in Art Worlds, for instance, that if you don't have people running the parking lot, the opera will be different, because it will affect how easy it is for people to attend, thus who and how many attend, thus the sources and amount of revenue earned, thus how much can be spent on a production, and thus who can be hired and what can be bought.

But we usually don't think we need to have the voice of the parking-lot attendants represented when we write about the opera. Philippe Urfalino settled for representing a major development in the history of the Paris Opéra by quoting four voices, the four men who most affected the development of the new building in which it was housed and the policies that went with that (Urfalino 1990). It would be easy to make a good argument that that isn't enough people, that there ought to be more voices than that. Urfalino acknowledges the problem, adding that these four are not particularly well known as important figures in the story but insisting that they were crucial actors in the major technical and political decisions and operations that led to the project's successful completion (7–17). It's easy to see that including these four is a major step in the right direction. Insisting on including every voice is just to insist that we could always include more voices with profit, not to complain about anything's being less than perfect. (We can compare it with Latour's 1996 account of a failed project to build a new and innovative subway system in Paris, which takes account of many more people and organizations in explaining how the project failed because, in the end, none of the very many actors involved loved the new subway enough to make it happen.)

We may not need every voice, but we need more than a few, and certainly more than the voice of the omniscient author or researcher, if we want to tell a complete and convincing story. But we have no algorithm for deciding how many voices to include or how to choose them. We've had some conventional solutions to the problem for a long time. We can, for instance, let the people who run organizations speak for everyone else who participates in them. The organizing principle of the idea of hierarchy proposes that, in any hierarchical organization, those in the top echelons know more about it, understand it better, and can speak more authoritatively about it than those beneath them (see Becker 1967 for further discussion of the "hierarchy of credibility"). We needn't believe this, but people who analyze society often succumb to that danger and participate in and accept the hierarchies they study. When they do, just because they become well-socialized participants in the organization, they accept this theory about the distribution of knowledge. Then they only have to get the word from authorities at the top and their job is done.

Some sociologists who study medicine have thought that, after all, doctors know more about disease and health than sociologists do, so we shouldn't question their knowledge. The voices of the people whom doctors diagnose, or of disinterested observers, needn't be heard. Thomas Scheff (1974, 1975) and Walter Gove (1970, 1975) argued, for instance, over whether the people psychiatrists labeled as mentally ill really differed in any significant way from other people they hadn't so labeled. Gove thought they did, that doctors knew more about mental illness than anyone else, so the people doctors said were crazy really were crazy. Scheff thought that being truly crazy wasn't a necessary condition for acquiring the label. Others study the legal profession and think that lawyers, especially those who speak for the profession, after all know most about it. It's become a thorny issue for social scientists who study the workings of science, because scientists get angry when sociologists and other "relativists" treat their hard-won knowledge as socially contingent (see the discussion in Hacking 1999).

That's the easy solution to the dilemma of how many voices a research report should include. Ask the authorities—the professionals in charge, the CEO of a corporation, the officials of the law enforcement system—and they'll tell you what you need to know.

No one, of course, any longer thinks you can study industrial workers by asking their bosses what they think and do. So they interview workers or send them questionnaires directly. But they accept a sneakier form of the hierarchy of credibility. They ask the questions the bosses think should be asked, investigate the problems the bosses think should be investigated, incorporate the variables the bosses think should be incorporated—and leave out what the bosses don't think is necessary. Thus, sociologists of education persistently look for the causes of educational "failures" in students rather than in teachers, let alone administrators or school organizations.

Some social scientists long ago decided to find out what others involved in these processes thought and did, and to let their interests and questions also inform our research plans and activities. The study of so-called deviant activities blossomed when investigators started listening to and incorporating the meanings and ideas and theories of those labeled as deviant, as well as those of the people who did the labeling. This has become more or less institutionalized under the heading of "taking the point of view of" the subordinates in an organization or any of the other participants.

Suppose we decide to incorporate all these other voices. How do we do it? Social scientists have been debating about this (Clifford and Marcus 1986; Clifford 1988), but the practitioners of other ways of telling about society have been there before us and have paid far more attention to the problem. Bakhtin (1981) focused on the novel, the way novels incorporated all sorts of voices in order to be interesting, how they created characters from everywhere in the society, and let them talk and talk and talk. Dickens brought the whole society to life: bureaucrats and pickpockets and lawyers and schoolmasters and . . . . you name it. Bakhtin's key terms—*dialogue, dialogical, heteroglossia*— give names to this feature of novelistic practice that almost automatically makes room for the voices of many people.

George Bernard Shaw:
Two Sides of an Argument

As we saw earlier, analyses of society in whatever medium typically identify the good guys and bad guys. The plots often revolve around wickedness punished and virtue rewarded; in the ironic versions, wickedness goes unpunished and virtue unrewarded, but sophisticated viewers (and unsophisticated, too) often deplore this outcome. Many of the most effective organizational analyses (like Erving Goffman's study of mental hospitals and other total institutions, explored in the next chapter) don't make this judgment easy. They explain the circumstances and thinking of the bad guys, as well as the good guys, in such detail as to make it clear why they did the things they did, which makes it difficult to condemn them on simplistic moral grounds.

Playwrights solve the problem by putting several characters on stage, speaking in recognizably different voices. (Even the sole character in such monologues as Samuel Beckett's *Krapp's Last Tape* and *Happy Days* [Beckett 1960, 1961] talks to others, and we get to know the others through their unspoken half of the conversation.) Using a dramatic form, the author has to let everyone make themselves understood; otherwise there's no dramatic conflict and you're boring your audience. As David Mamet says somewhere I have never been able to find (which is why there is no reference here), every character enters a scene wanting something, and what they do in the scene reflects their attempts to get what they want. It follows that if the audience isn't aware of what those characters want, the scene won't make sense to them. George Bernard Shaw used the dramatic form to create lively intellectual discussions of serious social and sociological problems. In *Major Barbara*, Mr. Undershaft, the armaments manufacturer, and his daughter Barbara, the Salvation Army officer, discuss the morality of war. Major characters incarnate and speak for opposing points of view.

Shaw used this device masterfully in *Mrs. Warren's Profession*, his exploration of prostitution and the moral arguments surrounding it.

In this play about Vivie Warren, a young woman just graduated from Cambridge in mathematics, and her mother, who lives abroad and whose source for the money she has paid for Vivie's upkeep has never been explained, Shaw intends to argue a point:

> Mrs. Warren's Profession was written in 1894 to draw attention to the truth that prostitution is caused, not by female depravity and male licentiousness, but simply by underpaying, undervaluing, and overworking women so shamefully that the poorest of them are forced to resort to prostitution to keep body and soul together. Indeed all attractive unpropertied women lose money by being infallibly virtuous or contracting marriages that are not more or less venal. If on the large social scale we get what we call virtue it is simply because we are paying more for it. No normal woman would be a professional prostitute if she could better herself by being respectable, nor marry for money if she could afford to marry for love.
>
> Also I desired to expose the fact that prostitution is not only carried on without organization by individual enterprise in the lodgings of solitary women, each her own mistress as well as every customer's mistress, but organized and exploited as a big international commerce for the profit of capitalists like any other commerce, and very lucrative to great city estates, including Church estates, through the rents of the houses in which it is practiced. (Shaw [1925] 1946, 181)

He makes his points by letting the mother and daughter, each of whom has a case to make, argue with each other. Their arguments get their force partly from the drama of their relationship, in which the secret of Mrs. Warren's business has finally come into the open. Having two major characters make the best case they can for opposing arguments guarantees that the analysis, and therefore the audience, will not accept one side of the debate unthinkingly.

Mrs. Warren's profession, we quickly learn, is owning and managing a chain of brothels in major European cities. Vivie, who has hardly ever seen her mother, knows nothing of this but is, naturally, very curious. When her mother visits, on the occasion of her graduation, Vivie pushes for more information and, though it is never quite said openly, soon realizes that her mother's business is to own and manage houses of prostitution and that she has made a good thing out of it, paying for many luxuries, including Vivie's education. Mrs. Warren makes the pro-prostitution argument by telling how Liz, her sister who had preceded her in the trade and done well, persuaded her to join the business. The sister has retired and is a lady in good society in Winchester. Mrs. Warren knows the much worse fate of her half-sisters, who did not go into her line of work: "They were the respectable ones. Well, what did they get by their respectability? I'll tell you. One of them worked in a whitelead factory twelve hours a day for nine shillings a week until she died of lead poisoning. She only expected to get her hands a little paralyzed; but she died. The other was always held up to us as a model because she married a Government laborer in the Deptford victualling yard, and kept his room and the three children neat and tidy on eighteen shillings a week—until he took to drink. That was worth being respectable for, wasn't it?" (Shaw [1925] 1946, 247).

She gets a job in a bar, where her sister, who had disappeared when she was still a child, meets her by acccident:

> When she saw I'd grown up good-looking she said to me across the bar "What are you doing there, you little fool? Wearing out your health and your appearance for other people's profit!" Liz was saving money then to take a house for herself in Brussels; and she thought we two could save faster than one. . . . The house in Brussels was real high class: a much better place for a woman to be than the factory where Aunt Jane got poisoned. None of our girls were ever treated as I was treated in the scullery of that temperance place, or at the Waterloo bar, or at home. Would you have had me stay in them and become a worn out old drudge before I was forty? (248)

Vivie, impressed by these arguments, makes the conventional moral case that this kind of work is degrading; these familiar arguments aren't presented at length, but you feel their presence in the few things Vivie says. She thinks that there must be a better way to earn a living, one in which her mother's evident business acumen and capacity for hard work would have paid off just as well, but Mrs. Warren won't have it. This was the only business where she and Liz could use their good looks as capital. She agrees with Vivie that there are some tough times with unruly customers but says that, of course, you "have to take the rough with the smooth, just like a nurse in a hospital or anywhere else."

When Vivie asks her mother, in a to-be-expected rhetorical move, if she isn't ashamed of what she does, Mrs. Warren says, "Well, of course, dearie, it's only good manners to be ashamed of it: it's expected from a woman." She adds: "If people arrange the world that way for women, there's no good pretending it's arranged the other way. No: I never was a bit ashamed really. I consider I had a right to be proud of how we managed everything so respectably, and never had a word against us, and how the girls were so well taken care of. Some of them did very well; one of them married an ambassador" (251).

Vivie soon has her own temptation, the other version of women's being bought and sold Shaw mentioned. Sir George Crofts, an older man who is her mother's partner in the brothel business (though Vivie doesn't know that he put up the capital to get it started), asks her to marry him and explains that it will be worth a lot of money to her. She refuses, and out of spite he reveals his role in the business. He tells her further that her mother's announcement that she had wound up the business was just a convenient lie. Vivie now finally understands that the brothels have financed her easy way of life all along. Crofts makes clear the system of interconnected relations that involves practically everyone in the society, the conventionally good as well as the conventionally bad, including her:

> You wouldn't cut the Archbishop of Canterbury because the Ecclesiastical Commissioners have publicans and sinners among their tenants. Do you remember your Crofts scholarship at Newnham? Well, that was founded by my brother the M.P. He gets his 22 per cent out of a factory with 600 girls in it, and not one of them getting enough to live on. How d'ye suppose they manage when they have no family to fall back on? Ask your mother. And do you expect me to turn my back on 35 per cent when all the rest are pocketing what they can, like sensible men? No such fool! If you're going to pick and choose your acquaintance on moral principles, you'd better clear out of this country, unless you want to cut yourself out of all decent society. (265)

Both women have good reasons for their positions, and the arguments are all the more compelling for the emotion that lies behind them and that is dramatically justified by the situation. Vivie, of course, has learned a lesson; that's what the play is about. She tells her mother:

I don't object to Crofts more than to any other coarsely built man of his class. To tell you the truth, I rather admire him for being strong-minded enough to enjoy himself in his own way and make plenty of money instead of living the usual shooting, hunting, dining-out, tailoring, loafing life of his set merely because all the rest do it. And I'm perfectly aware that if I'd been in the same circumstances as my Aunt Liz, I'd have done exactly what she did. I don't think I'm more prejudiced or straitlaced than you: I think I'm less. I'm certain I'm less sentimental. I know very well that fashionable morality is all a pretence, and that if I took your money and devoted the rest of my life to spending it fashionably, I might be as worthless and vicious as the silliest woman could possibly want to be without having a word said to me about it. But I don't want to be worthless. (283)

Not to be preachy about it, but social scientists have systematically avoided any drama in their presentations and have paid the price in the difficulty of representing multiple points of view.

Caryl Churchill: Many Voices Tell a Story

Caryl Churchill's play *Mad Forest* (1996) deals with events in Romania in December 1989, when a spontaneous popular revolt overthrew Nicolae Ceausescu, the head of the government, and eventually executed him and his wife Elena. In early March 1990, Churchill and director Mark Wing-Davey went to Bucharest for four days; they returned at the end of that month with a team of theater professionals and ten acting students. They interviewed people, worked with students at the Caragiale Institute of Theatre and Cinema, and "met with many other people." That is, they did some sort of sociological investigation. Then they wrote the play, rehearsed it, and on June 13, 1990, gave the first performance.

The first and third acts of the play deal with the marriage of Lucia, a schoolteacher who is the daughter of an electrician and a tram driver, and Radu, an art student, the son of an architect and a teacher—a middle-class boy marrying a working-class girl. Though this story and its resolution are interesting and important, I'm only going to talk about act 2 (29–43; all the quotes that follow are from these pages).

In act 2, the eleven actors appear (in the production I saw at the Berkeley Repertory Theater) sitting on the stage in chairs, side by side, facing front. The stage directions say, "None of the characters in this section are the characters in the play that began in part I. They are all Romanians speaking to us in English with Romanian accents. Each behaves as if the others are not there and each is the only one telling us what happened."

They speak in short declarative sentences, the speeches ranging from one line to perhaps 150 words, everyone describing what they saw and heard and knew and did on December 21, the day of the revolt, when crowds gathered in the public square, and afterward, as the revolt gathered momentum. None of them has an overview of the entire event; they only know what they did, what happened in their immediate vicinity. But as each tells what he or she knows, the audience gets a more comprehensive idea of the whole event. (This resembles the method attributed to S. L. A. Marshall, the military historian, who gathered information on battlefield behavior in group interviews, in which each participant in a unit told what he had seen and done [Chambers 2003]). No voice is particularly important. None of them represent a distinctive political point of view, though they do represent distinctive social positions—differing as they do in age, gender, family relationships, occupations, class, and so on—and possibilities. Between them, the many voices present a rounded and comprehensive view of what happened.

The eleven participants in the events of the revolt describe something sociologists have long been interested in, under the term "elementary collective behavior" (Blumer 1951), the study of crowds, mobs, and similar forms of unorganized collective action. The actors give the best description I have ever read of behavior in such a situation, through the buildup of homely details. The speakers identify themselves in their first speech and then describe what they were doing on That Day. The act begins with people's first awareness that something unusual was going on:

GIRL STUDENT. My name's Natalie Moraru, I'm a student. On the 21st of December I had a row with my mother at breakfast about something trivial and I went out in a rage. There was nothing unusual, some old men talking, a few plainclothes policemen, they think they're clever but everyone knows who they are because of their squashed faces.

TRANSLATOR. I'm Dimitru Constantinescu, I work as a translator in a translation agency. On the 21st we were listening to the radio in the office to hear Ceausescu's speech. It was frightfully predictable. People had been brought in from factories and institutes on buses and he wanted their approval for putting down what he called the hooligans in Timisoara. Then suddenly we heard boos and the radio went dead. So we knew something had happened. We were awfully startled. Everyone was shaking.

Some don't notice anything at first:

DOCTOR. My name is Ileana Chirița. I'm a student doctor, I come to this hospital from school, we must get six months' practical. The 21 was a normal day on duty, I didn't know anything.

But soon a crowd begins to form:

BULLDOZER DRIVER. I leave work to get my son from school and I don't go back to work, I go to the Palace Square.

STUDENT 1. There were two camps, army and people, but nobody shooting. Some workers from the People's Palace come with construction material to make barricades. More and more people come, we are pushed together.

Some people go home and try to ignore what is evidently going on, but others want to be there:

STUDENT 1. There are vans bringing drink and I tell people not to drink because Securitate wants to get us drunk so we look bad. In the evening we tried to make a barricade in Rosetti Place. We set fire to a truck.

SECURITATE. There are barricades and cars burning in my district, I report it. Later the army shoot the people and drive tanks in them. I go off duty.

And the story continues, always in this flat reportorial style, recounting further developments: the growing awareness of the "troubles," larger and larger crowds, rumors spreading ("We heard on the radio the General in charge of the Army had killed himself and been announced a traitor"). The soldiers join the crowds ("Then I saw there were flowers in the guns"), the state security breaks down ("And when I looked again the police had vanished"), and "There were no words in Romanian or English for how happy I was."

But there is a countermovement: *terroristi* start shooting, people bring out their guns, young people prepare to die to keep the movement going. They find guns in an undefended gun factory. People die. Then:

STUDENT 1. On the 25 we hear about the trial and their deaths [the Ceausescus]. It is announced that people must return their weapons so we go to the factory and give back our guns. Of the 28 who had guns only 4 are alive.

People come to terms with the new circumstances of their lives:

SECURITATE. When I heard about the execution of the 25 I came at night with my father to the authorities to certify what I was doing during the event. I was detained three days by the army, then told to remain at home. I will say one thing. Until noon on the 22 we were law and order. We were brought up in this idea. I will never agree with unorder. Everyone looks at me like I did something wrong. It was the way the law was then and the way they all accepted it.

The first night of the seminar, I handed out copies of the script. Eleven of the twenty-five copies had a different character's lines highlighted. If the part you got thus represented a character, you read the lines aloud when the time came. The students complained that they weren't actors, and I said it didn't matter, invoking David Mamet's mantra "Don't act, just read the lines." After further complaints that they weren't actors, they agreed to do it. It was true, they weren't actors, and that didn't make any difference at all. They read the parts and the dramatic result was extraordinary; everyone was silent, unmistakably moved, when we finished the short act. Try this experiment yourself and see how compellingly the spare theatrical experience conveys an episode that social scientists have trouble describing half so well.

Wallace Shawn: The Missing Voice

Shaw gives you two voices, arguing with each other. Churchill gives you many voices, none more important than the others, piecing together a complex activity. Wallace Shawn deliberately gives you one voice, and it's the wrong one.

We are so accustomed to fictional accounts' adopting a moral point of view that an author who doesn't do it disconcerts audiences and critics. The playwright Wallace Shawn has done this more than once and created a fair amount of discomfort every time. In his play *Aunt Dan and Lemon* (Shawn 1985), a young, sickly, naive woman (nicknamed Lemon) tells the story of her worldly, sophisticated Aunt Danielle, a U.S. expatriate in England, who, as the play proceeds, reveals herself (in her words and actions) as reprehensible — a sympathizer with all the worst features and actions of the U.S. and European social and political establishments, an apologist for (to begin with, but it gets worse) the likes of Henry Kissinger and Neville Chamberlain. These revelations proceed slowly, so it's really only toward the end that you grasp that Aunt Dan was a thoroughgoing Nazi sympathizer and that Lemon has adopted all her aunt's worst opinions as her own, and is proud of them and proud of herself for having the courage to think such things. It's not only that Aunt Dan revered Kissinger. She admired politicians who had the nerve to do what they thought was necessary, even though it would seem to weaker people to lack compassion or even to be immoral. She's shown to be immoral in a variety of ways that conventional people, left or right, would find repellent. Lemon doesn't follow her in all this, but she admires all of it.

Lemon's last speech, which I won't quote extensively (it's much longer than the excerpt below), gives us her frankest expression of admiration for what anyone who sees the play will almost surely find disgusting. She explains that for the Nazis to achieve the society of brothers they sought, they had to eliminate non-Germans and prevent interbreeding, just as in order to achieve the kind of European society they wanted to make in America, the early settlers had to kill the Indians, who were fighting them for every scrap of land. Then she says:

> We have to admit that we don't really care any more. And I think that that last admission is what really makes people go mad about the Nazis, because in our own society we have this kind of cult built up around what people call the feeling of "compassion." I remember my mother screaming all the time, "Compassion! Compassion! You have to have compassion for other people! You have to have compassion for other human beings!" And I must admit, there's something I find refreshing about the Nazis, which is partly why I enjoy reading about them every night, because they sort of had the nerve to say, "Well, what *is* this compassion? Because I don't really know what it is. So I want to know, really, what is it?" And they must have sort of asked each other, at some point, "Well say, Heinz, have *you* ever felt it?" "Well, no, Rolf, what about you?" And they all had to admit they really didn't know what the hell it was. And I find it sort of relaxing to read about those people, because I have to admit that I don't know either. I mean, I think I've felt it reading a novel, and I think I've felt it watching a film—"Oh, how sad, that child is sick! That mother is crying!"— but I can't ever remember feeling it in life. . . . Because if there's one thing I've learned from Aunt Dan, I suppose you could say it was a kind of honesty. It's easy to say we should all be loving and sweet, but meanwhile we're enjoying a certain way of life—and we're actually *living*—due to the existence of certain other people who are willing to take the job of killing on their own backs, and it's not a bad thing every once in a while to admit that that's the way we're living, and even to give to those certain people a tiny, fractional crumb of thanks. You can be very sure that it's more than they expect, but I think they'd be grateful all the same. (Shawn 1985, 83–85)

What makes Shawn's work special is not that he portrays these villainous or ignorant types frankly and in detail but that nothing in the play, not a word, not a gesture, says that there is anything wrong with what they say and do. They articulate their own thoughts and actions fully, as though they were speaking to a sympathetic audience, as though a sympathetic playwright had overheard and written down these lovely conversations and soliloquies. No character in the play represents another point of view. No one challenges them in the name of reason or humanity. That voice is missing. Shawn doesn't portray a debate between characters who have different, but reasonable, approaches to some problem. There is no debate, because no one from the other side is there to speak. It's as though the only person you heard from in Shaw's play were Sir George Croft, the only character for whom it's hard to find a good word to say.

Theater audiences (audiences for every sort of fictional representation) expect the author to identify the Bad Guys for them. That's the conventional division of labor between users and makers in theater. Frank Rich, reviewing Shawn's play for the *New York Times*, commented, "The single-minded Mr. Shawn never supplies a character to challenge Lemon's articulate arguments. Instead, the audience is left to think up its own rebuttal—forcing us to wonder whether we could and would counter the spurious polemics of a clever fascist like Lemon in real life. I can't remember the last time I saw a play make an audience so uncomfortable, and I mean that as high praise" (Rich 1985).

No one in the audience has any trouble working out for themselves who the Bad Guys in *Aunt Dan and Lemon* are. You might try to excuse Lemon on the grounds of youth and ignorance, but you can't convince yourself; she's not that dumb, or shouldn't be. It wasn't an inability to distinguish Good Guys from Bad Guys that upset the people who saw and read the play. It was that Shawn had not said so himself, through the mouth of a character who transparently represented him, or by bringing the story to a satisfactory ending in which Dan got what was morally coming to her. (At the end Dan dies of some unspecified lingering disease, but you can't read that as dramatically appropriate punishment for her evil thoughts and ways; nice people die the same way.) And people reacted strongly to Shawn's refusal to say what they knew he agreed with. We're prepared for fictions to be complex, to present us with weighty and difficult choices, but not to ignore the responsibility of making a more or less explicit moral judgment. People want to hear that other voice.

This is the same expectation Erving Goffman violated in his analysis of mental hospitals, when he used carefully neutral scientific language to describe situations most readers would find distressing, as we'll see in the next chapter.

13

Goffman, Language, and the Comparative Strategy

These last four chapters of the book take a different tack, giving close readings of some classic works of social description and analysis, made in the light of the ideas presented earlier. The final three chapters deal with authors of fiction, while this one examines a sociological classic.

The Problem of Conventional Language

Erving Goffman's deservedly famous essay "On the Characteristics of Total Institutions" (Goffman 1961, 1–124) exemplifies the problematic relation, never simple and direct, between methods of presenting research and scholarship and the political content of the work. It exemplifies, in fact, Goffman's presentational solution to a problem that perpetually plagues social science writing and research: how to avoid the analytic flaws and failures that arise from our unthinking acceptance of the constraints of conventional thinking. It's a problem most clearly manifested in the near-universal partisanship of social science, the way research "takes sides," easily and too quickly identifies (as we have seen) the Good Guys and the Bad Guys, and distributes praise and blame when the real job at hand is to figure out how things work and present an accurate account of that understanding. Novelists and playwrights deal with this problem by letting multiple characters represent different points of view, typically but not invariably letting users know which voice is "right." Goffman's way of dealing with these problems in social science deserves close study.

When social scientists study something—a community, an organization, an ethnic group—they are never the first people to have arrived on the scene, never newcomers to an unpeopled landscape who can name its features as they like. Every topic they write about makes up part of the experience of many other kinds of people, all of whom have their own ways of talking about it, their own distinctive words for the objects and events and people involved in that area of social life. Those words are never neutral objective signifiers. Rather, they express the perspective and situation of the people who use them. The natives are already there, were there all along, and everything in that terrain has a name, more likely many names.

If we choose to name what we study with words the people involved already use, we acquire, with the words, the attitudes and perspectives the words imply. Since many kinds of people are involved in any social activity, choosing words from any of their vocabularies commits us to one or another of the perspectives in use by one or another of the groups already on the scene. Those perspectives invariably take much for granted, making assumptions about what social scientists might better treat as problematic.

When I studied marijuana smoking and smokers (Becker 1973), I deliberately avoided using the word *addiction* when I described the activity, even though many or most others writing about the topic spoke of "marijuana addicts." I thought the word contained a false assumption, and so I spoke of "marijuana use" instead. Many readers understood that minor linguistic variant to imply that the people who smoked marijuana were actually engaged in a harmless practice and therefore should not be harassed legally. They weren't wrong, of course. I did think that, and still do, but I didn't say it in my early writing on the topic.

What we call the things we study has consequences. Interested parties try to define what they deal with in ways that will advance their interests, accomplish what they want to accomplish. And they try to influence researchers to define what's studied in the ways they have decided are "right." Interested organizations and their members and employees used to argue incessantly, and probably still do (though I don't read about it anymore), about how many heroin addicts there

were in the United States or in New York City or in whatever juris-
diction was being discussed. That is a technical matter, a question of
making an accurate census of users, and, on the face of it, ought not
to have aroused a lot of heated argument. But it did. Why? Well, the
answer affected a lot of people's and organizations' budgets. If I run a
treatment center for addicts and am looking for funding for my operations, I'd like people with money to give away to think that there are
a lot of junkies out there in the city. Why? Because that would mean
that a lot of people need help of the kind my organization can give and
funders will be more likely to give me and my people money to do the
job than if they think there aren't very many addicts in need of our services. I want the problem to look "serious," and it won't unless the
number of potential clients for my operation is large.

But if I am an official of an urban police force or of a federal drug
enforcement agency, I might want to see that same number low. Why?
Well, if the number is high, if a lot of addicts are running around
loose, my bureaucratic and political enemies (and if I am such an official, I will have those enemies) could use it to show that my organization's efforts to stamp out drug use are not working, the taxpayers'
money spent on what we do will be wasted, and my organization and
I, as its responsible director, don't deserve support.

Deserve is the important word here, because it's a term of moral
judgment, not a conclusion verified by some scientific operation and
results. It's a conclusion about what ought to be and implies a set of
judgments about what's worthwhile, what's good, what's nice, what's
reprehensible—all that. Most social scientists have been trained to
distinguish between judgments about facts and what are called "value
judgments," judgments about what's good and bad, and warned especially not to let their ideas about what's wrong influence their conclusions about what exists. Whether we like it or not, we'd better be
ready to see the phenomenon and acknowledge its existence in our
analyses.

If I had made the analysis I just suggested about the implications of
the number of addicts a census discovered, I wouldn't have had to say
that if there aren't very many heroin addicts we need a smaller police
force to handle them. My readers would do that work for me, reach-

ing that conclusion without my saying it. And when I called the practice in question "marijuana use" instead of "marijuana addiction" and presented an analysis that didn't fit the standard stereotype of addiction, readers would do the work of deducing the judgments about good and bad that followed from that too. They recognized that it followed "logically" (and it did follow logically, if you shared the premises that my readers and I mostly shared), that marijuana users shouldn't be hassled because they smoked dope.

The language of drugs goes beyond calling the activity "use" or "addiction." People who use marijuana have a language for talking about it; that's an important part of what's meant by a "drug culture." They speak of "getting high" rather than being "intoxicated." They have many synonyms for marijuana, calling it, for instance, "grass." They might speak of the person they buy marijuana from as a "connection." Other people whose worlds also contain marijuana—physicians, lawyers, and police—will have other words for the same objects and activities, perhaps speaking of "cannabis" and "pushers." Users' language typically suggests that use is voluntary, pleasurable, and innocent. The languages of medicine and law typically suggest that use is involuntary, evil, and harmful.

How objects and activities are named almost always reflects relations of power. People in power call things what they want, and since they control many of the situations in which others participate, those other people have to adjust to that, perhaps using their own words in private but accepting in public what they cannot avoid. Whatever my friends and I think about "grass," marijuana is defined as a narcotic drug by people who can make that name, and the activities and prohibitions it implies, stick.

Social scientists have to decide, every time they do research, what to call the things they study. If they choose the terms decided on by the interested and powerful parties already involved in the situations they are studying, they accept all the presuppositions built into that language. If I choose the terms used by the people who "own" the territory, and therefore choose the perspectives associated with those terms, I let my analysis be shaped by conventional social arrangements and the distribution of power and privilege they create. The study of educational institutions, as I suggested earlier, has suffered from researchers' easy acceptance of the twin ideas, which no one in the education business questions, that teaching and learning are what goes on in places called schools and that if it isn't happening in a school, no matter what people are learning, it isn't education (see the discussion in Becker 1998, 143–45).

Accepting conventional definitions of what we study has both technical and moral consequences.

The technical consequence is that the class of phenomena I want to generalize about contains things that have in common only the moral attitudes toward them of powerful people and groups in the society and the actions that have been taken toward them in consequence. As a result, a researcher who uses a conventional definition has tremendous difficulty finding anything general to say about the phenomenon he studies, other than things associated with those moral attitudes. You can talk about the results of being thought about that way—that's what the labeling theory of deviance did (Becker 1963). But you can't find anything to say about how people get that way, underlying causes, or similar matters, because there is nothing related to those matters that all the cases in the class have in common. You can't make science if you can't find similar entities to generalize about (Cressey 1951).

The moral consequence of adopting existing language and perspectives toward what we study is that we accept, willingly or not, all the assumptions about right and wrong contained in those words and ideas. We accept, in the case of drugs, the idea that addicts are people who have lost control of themselves and therefore cannot help doing things that are inherently bad. We accept, in the case of schools, that they have the monopoly on teaching and learning that their language claims for them.

This was Goffman's problem as he began to write a book about the mental hospital he had studied. The existing language for discussing the people confined in such institutions embodied just one voice and one perspective, that of the people who had the power to confine others—the professional medical staff who ran the institutions, the legal professionals who assigned people to them, the families who had solved their problem by putting an unruly family member in such a place, the police for whom the people who had ended up in the hospital were what is sometimes called a public nuisance. How could Goffman avoid taking for granted such categories as "mental illness" and the perspectives associated with them? He had to avoid that, because accepting those categories and their entailed assumptions would get in the way of the comprehensive study he had in mind.

The Linguistic Solution

To make clear how Goffman found a workable solution to the problem of conventional categories and their associated moral judgments, I'll begin with a simple stylistic observation. No reader of Goffman's essay on total institutions can be unaware of the considerable disparity between the social reality he talks about and the way he talks about it. He describes and analyzes social practices that are quite common, whose existence and character are known to most adults, if not through their personal experience then through the experience of others they know and through secondhand accounts in the press, films, drama, and fiction. He relates and analyzes organized social practices of incarceration and degradation that repel and disgust many readers and arouse feelings of shame in us for living in a society where such things have happened and continue to happen. His detailed and comprehensive descriptions make it impossible to ignore the continued existence of these shameful organized, socially accepted activities and have on occasion instigated attempts at their reform (although Goffman was only one among many whose writing nourished the movement to reform mental hospitals).

The disparity I mentioned exists, first, in the language he uses to describe the actions institutional personnel take with respect to inmates. Despite the repellent nature of many of the activities he describes, he never uses judgmental language. He doesn't explicitly denounce the practices his descriptions make us want to denounce, nor do his adjectives and adverbs betray a negative assessment of them. He might just as well be describing an anthill or a beehive as a common form of social institution that treats some people (never forget, with the complicity of the rest of society, and that does mean us) in such a way that their lives resemble those of members of those insect societies: regimented in an inflexible and humiliating caste system without regard for their own feelings or wishes. His detailed account of what we might find in such places brings us to that sort of conclusion, though he never says anything like that himself. Here are some of the ways he uses language to avoid built-in judgments.

He uses the word *echelon* (instead of, for instance, *domination*) to denote the typical authority system of a total institution: "*any* member of the staff class has certain rights to discipline *any* member of the inmate class, thereby markedly increasing the probability of sanction" (42). The word is neutral. Since it is not commonly used for this purpose, it has no immediately negative connotations, of the kind a term like *domination* has. It simply denotes one way among many of organizing authority relations, just as Weber's distinction between charismatic, bureaucratic, and traditional forms of authority describes three other ways.

It's far easier to find examples of "echelon control" than of "domination." The former simply requires demonstration of an observable fact—who gives orders to whom—while the latter includes, scarcely beneath the surface, a judgment as to the moral suitability of the order-giving arrangement, which is always more arguable.

Some further examples of this kind of neutral language used by Goffman to refer to matters about which readers like us would probably have strong negative feelings:

"role dispossession," to explain how new recruits are prevented from being who they were in the world they previously inhabited

"trimming" and "programming," to describe how "the new arrival allows himself to be shaped and coded into an object that can be fed into the administrative machinery of the establishment, to be worked on smoothly by routine operations"

"identity kit," to indicate the paraphernalia people ordinarily have with which to indicate who they are but which is routinely denied to inmates in total institutions

"contaminative exposure," to indicate how inmates are humiliated and mortified in public "looping," to indicate how an inmate's attempts to fight mortification lead to more mortification

"privilege system," to indicate the way withholding ordinary rights transforms them into privileges that can be used to coerce conformity

"secondary adjustments," to refer to "practices that do not directly challenge staff but allow inmates to obtain forbidden satisfactions or to obtain permitted ones by forbidden means"

a variety of "personal adjustments," such as "situational withdrawal," which (he notes) psychiatrists might call "regression"

He also uses words that have negative overtones but uses them in a neutral way, so that they lose their negative charge. For instance, he talks of new recruits' being "mortified," but examples of this include the treatment of officer candidates in military organizations.

Goffman discusses the staff by treating what they do as a kind of work (thus showing himself the student of Everett C. Hughes he often claimed to be), to be seen as part of a series that includes many other kinds of work. He emphasizes that the work of a total institution's staff deals with people, rather than inanimate stuff, and notes the distinctive problems that creates. "The multiplicity of ways in which inmates must be considered ends in themselves, and the large number of inmates, forces upon the staff some of the classic dilemmas that must be faced by those who govern men. Since a total institution functions somewhat as a state, its staff suffers somewhat from the tribulations that beset governors" (77). Here too he uses the linguistic devices I have discussed, speaking "objectively" of staff work as dealing with "human objects" or "human material."

The Comparative Solution

The disparity I spoke of—between the social reality Goffman describes and the way he talks about it—also exists in the comparative procedure he uses to arrive at the ideal type of the total institution. He creates this type, readers of his book will remember, by comparing a variety of organizations found in modern societies that have an important distinguishing characteristic and abstracting from them their common features. He first defines the general class of "social establishments" as consisting of "places such as rooms, suites of rooms, buildings or plants in which activity of a particular kind regularly goes on," and he speaks of the difficulty of classifying members of this class. Nothing could be more "neutral" or "scientific." He then classifies establishments, roughly, by their relations to the lives of the individuals who participate in them. Some institutions will not accept people of certain kinds at all. Many institutions have a changing population of customers or workers. Others, like families, change their personnel less frequently. Some institutions house activities that their participants take seriously; others are for more frivolous activities.

This dispassionate sorting of social organizations in the essay's first paragraph—treating families, leisure-time activities, and workplaces as all equal, simply establishments that vary along one or more dimensions—warns us that Goffman isn't engaging in social-science-as-usual. Ordinary social science, unlike Goffman, typically uses as classificatory categories the words, and their associated judgments of moral and social worth, that are common in the organizations being analyzed (as in the case of educational research). The distinction, for instance, between "deviant" and "normal" activities contains just such judgments, common in the legal and therapeutic organizations that deal with the matters conventionally so classified. So do classifications of organizations and activities as "functional" or, more clearly, "dysfunctional." These are categories whose coiners fully intended them to be scientific and dispassionate. The judgmental character of social science categories is clearer yet in more politically and ethically engaged research and writing, which routinely use terms like *repressive* and *corrupt* to describe the phenomena they analyze.

Goffman is less neutral, more ironic, in his discussion of the ideas on which institutional staff base their actions toward inmates. He treats theories in social science and related areas as raw material, whose analysis will reveal the basic character of the institutions that use them, rather than as "science," as in his offhand discussion of psychiatric theorizing: "Mental hospitals stand out here because the staff pointedly establish themselves as specialists in the knowledge of human nature, who diagnose and prescribe on the basis of this intelligence. Hence in the standard psychiatric textbooks there are chapters on 'psychodynamics' and 'psychopathology' which provide charmingly explicit formulations of the 'nature' of human nature" (89). Needless to say, he explains that the purpose of these theories is to validate the methods used to accomplish the end of managing large numbers of people under the conditions of a total institution.

Having defined social establishments, Goffman immediately proposes yet another principle for their classification, one that will distinguish a group whose "members appear to have so much in common . . . that to learn about one of [them] we would be well advised to look at the others." He then isolates the defining characteristic of this class this way:

> Every institution captures something of the time and interest of its members and provides something of a world for them; in brief, every institution has encompassing tendencies. When we review the different institutions in our Western society, we find that some are encompassing to a degree discontinuously greater than the ones next in line. Their encompassing or total character is symbolized by the barrier to social intercourse with the outside and to departure that is often built right into the physical plant, such as locked doors, high walls, barbed wire, cliffs, water, forests, or moors. These establishments I am calling total institutions, and it is their general characteristics I want to explore. (4)

So: institutions take up varying amounts of the time and interest of the people who participate in them, from a little to a lot. Some take up so much of their participants' time and lives that they are "discontinuous" with others in this array. They are "total institutions." Goffman distinguishes among the institutions this single criterion isolates by whether people are confined in them because they can't take care of themselves, because they are a danger to others, or both, or whether they are so isolated in order to better accomplish some important work or as a retreat from the world for religious or similar purposes. His analysis will look for the other features that commonly accom-

pany such total control over the lives of the people in the organization, whom he soon starts calling "inmates," thus adopting for the
whole class (including nuns, priests, soldiers, and others not usually
thought of as incarcerated) the demeaning term typically used in
mental hospitals (and prisons).

Goffman's analytic tack emphasizes the disparity between the kind
of place he is talking about and the way he talks about it. Though he
will, through most of the essay, be discussing places about which we
routinely make strongly negative judgments—mental hospitals, concentration camps, prisons—he treats them as members of the same
class as organizations about which we usually make no such simple
negative judgments—military establishments, ships at sea, and religious retreats. This creates what seems to be a moral confusion at the
heart of his method, for he confronts us with a classification that com-
bines and treats as equivalent things that, as morally competent
members of our society, class, and profession, we "know" are morally
disparate. We may be antimilitarist, but few of us, probably, think of
army camps as concentration camps. We may have little sympathy for
organized religion yet not be quite ready to agree that monasteries or
convents are prisons.

The comparative method works by establishing, as we have seen, a
common dimension along which a variety of cases can be ranged. So
there is a dimension of how much of the person's time an establishment controls, and organizations vary widely in this respect. Some—
a tennis club you belong to, for instance—control very little, while
others—a family—control more. There is a general problem or question of how people's time is divided among the groups they participate
in, and the total institution takes its place as providing one of the
many possible resolutions of this question. The total institution no
longer stands out as aberrant—as though the social world were divided into institutions and practices that are "ordinary" or "normal"
and do not ask for an abnormal commitment from a person, and then
there were this strange one, completely different, which requires
total control. Instead of being different and strange, it is now just a
different reading on a dial, another of the possible positions on this
scale. This is not a trivial result.

An example. Goffman analyzes how three classes of total institutions give differing rationales for "assaults on the self": religious institutions say such assaults are good for people, assisting them to reach a goal they aspire to (for example, transcendence of the self); prisons and concentration camps do it for the sake of mortification itself; others excuse themselves on the grounds that it is necessary for some other important purpose to be achieved (e.g., military readiness or security). Then he says that in all three classes, these are rationales "generated by efforts to manage the daily activity of a large number of persons in a restricted space with a small expenditure of resources" (46–77).

Goffman avoids leaving us with the queasy feeling Wallace Shawn achieves for us in *Aunt Dan and Lemon*, because he does include the voices of other participants in the organization besides the mortified, humiliated lowest echelon. We learn what psychiatrists think, although Goffman usually indicates, as he does here, that what they have to say pretends to a scientific status it doesn't achieve. Note that his criticisms take a scientific form, pointing out how the ideas and practices of total institutions and their workers lack a solid basis in empirical research and result from the same kinds of everyday organizational pressures no matter what higher rationalizations staff provide. He let his comparisons imply his judgments.

Note that analysts can condemn contemporary institutions they disapprove of with a similar maneuver. Edgar Friedenberg compared U.S. high schools to prisons not just as an analytic device to understand them better but, more importantly, because he wanted to communicate his abhorrence of the violations of students' civil liberties he had observed in them (Friedenberg 1965).

The Technical and Moral Result

The avoidance of built-in judgment is not evidence of a moral confusion on Goffman's part. He was not a moral dope (to adapt Harold Garfinkel's famous description of the homunculus in most sociological theorizing as a "cultural dope"). Far from it. Any careful reader feels, beneath the cool, unemotional language of Goffman's essays in this volume, the beating heart of a passionate civil libertarian. By adopting a method that entailed both antiseptic "scientific" language and a nonjudgmental comparison of cases, Goffman found a solution to the problem of the assumptions built into conventional thinking. If you accept the conventional categorizations built into ordinary language and the ordinary way that institutions and practices are sorted out in conventional thought, if you unthinkingly refer to people who drink a lot of alcohol as alcoholics, if you refer to people who smoke marijuana as addicts, then you accept the ideas that those words more or less oblige you to accept, ideas built in to the words themselves and into the perspectives associated with them. If a person who smokes marijuana is an "addict," then that person will smoke it uncontrollably, will be a "slave" to the practice, will engage in crimes in order to pay for the drug, and so on. If you use these words to define the class you are studying, as I have suggested earlier, you will not find empirical regularities to make scientific generalizations about.

By using the neutral language he constructs to discuss total institutions, Goffman isolates a class of social objects that share well-defined characteristics, empirically observable and connected to one another in verifiable patterns. He can make science.

Other makers of representations who use similar tactics of ostensible neutrality, like conceptual artist Hans Haacke or playwright Wallace Shawn, do not worry about making science. But they do want what they have to say to be taken seriously as Goffman wanted his work to be taken, as saying something true about the world they depict.

Why do I speak so insistently of "making science"? It is not often appreciated to what degree Goffman was a serious empiricist, even perhaps what might be called (in some meaning of the term) a positivist. (In this he resembled, I might say in passing, Margaret Mead.) He believed that there was an empirical reality and was wary of anything that smacked of the supernormal, could not be verified empirically, or was overly speculative. I confess to sharing all those prejudices.

A personal reminiscence will give some flesh to that general remark. Sometime in the early 1960s, when he was teaching at the University of California in Berkeley, Goffman asked me to come to his seminar to hear a student, Marvin Scott, present his research on horse racing. This excellent research (Scott 1968) dealt with the way the social organization of what he called "the racing game" made it reasonable for some trainers, owners, and jockeys to want their horse to lose rather than win. That might seem counterintuitive, but the organization of horse racing created incentives for people to behave in ways that seemed on the surface irrational. However, in the course of his presentation, Scott suggested in passing that gamblers, including horse players, sometimes had "winning streaks" or "losing streaks." Goffman, who had been listening appreciatively until that point, interrupted to say that of course Scott meant that they *thought* they had such streaks of good or bad luck. But Scott said no, these were observable "facts." Goffman, unwilling to accept such apparently supernatural talk, persisted, appealing to the laws of probability to assure Scott that such "streaks" were natural occurrences in any long run of tries in such a game as blackjack or craps. (I suppose he had been boning up on these topics in preparation for his research in Las Vegas.) He finally exploded in anger at Scott's "unscientific" insistence on gamblers' luck as a natural phenomenon.

Goffman used his linguistic inventiveness to name things in ways that evaded conventional moral judgments and thereby made scientific work possible. Instead of pointing with scorn at the "inhuman practices" of mental hospitals or defending the doctors and staff who worked in them as honest professionals doing the best they could with a difficult job, he situated their activities in a context of organizational necessity they shared with workers in other organizations with widely varying degrees of moral repute. The resulting generalizations made possible a deeper understanding of these phenomena than either denunciation or defense ever had or could.

His generalizations about total institutions simultaneously made possible a far more serious moral evaluation of those practices, since the judgment was now based on a more than superficial understanding of what the moral choices actors had to make actually were. This deeper understanding leads, inevitably, to blaming organizations rather than individuals, and not even to blaming them for doing what they have to do under the circumstances in which they exist. It is never easy to assign blame for what a whole society, in all its parts, is ultimately responsible for. As Goffman explains:

> I have defined total institutions denotatively by listing them and then have tried to suggest some of their common characteristics. . . . The similarities obtrude so glaringly and persistently that we have a right to suspect that there are good functional reasons for these features being present and that it will be possible to fit these features together and grasp them by means of a functional explanation. When we have done this, I feel we will give less praise and blame to particular superintendents, commandants, wardens, and abbots, and tend more to understand the social problems and issues in total institutions by appealing to the underlying structural design common to them all. (123–24)

14

Jane Austen
The Novel as Social Analysis

Jane Austen's *Pride and Prejudice* opens with this well-known remark: "It is a truth universally acknowledged that a single man in possession of a good fortune must be in want of a wife."

Is it? Universally acknowledged? A truth? Really?

An exciting piece of news in the little English town of Meryton provokes Austen's vast generalization. People have just learned, as Mrs. Bennet excitedly reports to her not exactly like-minded husband, that the nearby estate of Netherfield Park has been let to Mr. Bingley, a wealthy and unmarried young gentleman.

Before we could agree with the generalization this news has provoked, we'd certainly want some definitions. Well, that's easy. We all know what a "single man" is: a man who isn't married, as Mr. Darcy, Bingley's similarly single friend, was not married—married in the formally legal way demonstrated by the possession of a marriage certificate that attested to the performance of an appropriate ceremony at an appropriate time and place and to the fact that the state had recognized this state of affairs and would therefore enforce its consequences and allow others to enforce its consequences. In other words, "married" in all its social and legal senses and significance. "A wife" would easily be connected to this definition, as the female party to such an arrangement.

Things might have been that easy in Jane Austen's England in 1813. But she doesn't let us think so for long, since she immediately introduces a great variety of marriages, not all of them as unproblematic as that definition might lead us to think. For instance, young Elizabeth Bennet's own parents certainly are formally married but don't, as a couple, have many of the other attributes we think a married couple ought to have. They don't much understand or agree with each other, as their discussion of Bingley's arrival makes clear. When Mr. Bennet asks if Mr. Bingley is married or single, Mrs. Bennet replies:

> "Oh! Single, my dear, to be sure! A single man of large fortune, four or five thousand a year. What a fine thing for our girls!" [The Bennets have five daughters of marriageable age.]
>
> "How so? how can it affect them?"
>
> "My dear Mr. Bennet," replied his wife, "how can you be so tiresome! You must know that I am thinking of his marrying one of them."
>
> "Is that his design in settling here?"
>
> "Design! nonsense, how can you talk so! But it is very likely that he *may* fall in love with one of them and therefore you must visit him as soon as he comes."
>
> "I see no occasion for that. You and the girls may go, or you may send them by themselves, which perhaps will be still better, for you are as handsome as any of them, Mr. Bingley might like you the best of the party." [I will not give page references, since readers are likely to have any of a variety of editions, but will give chapter numbers instead. This exchange is found in chapter 1.]

Mrs. Bennet may not hear Mr. Bennet's sarcasm, but we do. It seems clear, or at least likely, that Mr. Bennet, in a time and place where custom, family, and legal organization were different, would long ago have left someone who irritated him as much as Mrs. Bennet does. The narrator describes them like this: "Mr. Bennet was so odd a mixture of quick parts, sarcastic humor, reserve, and caprice, that the experience of three and twenty years had been insufficient to make his wife understand his character. *Her* mind was less difficult to develop. She was a woman of mean understanding, little information, and uncertain temper. When she was discontented she fancied herself nervous. The business of her life was to get her daughters married; its solace was visiting and news" (chap. 1).

Which reminds us that even our definition of marriage has some historical contingency to it. In Mr. Bennet's time and place, marriage was for life, at least for respectable people like him. It isn't so any more in the United States or Europe. At least no one can count on that, as the statistics on marriage and divorce show. And, more complicated, there are many more stages between singleness and marriedness than there used to be. In the world of *Pride and Prejudice*, there was a stage of being engaged, but otherwise you went from single to married with no intermediate stops at stations like "seeing each other" or "living together," which we now accept as standard possibilities.

What about the "good fortune" a single man might have? How much would that be? Austen lets us know that Bingley's fortune consists of "four or five thousand a year," or at least that is what Mrs. Bennet has heard and relays to her husband. We don't know what that amounts to today, in (as they say) constant dollars, but it sounds like a lot, and clearly it enables him to live very well. Better than Mr. Bennet, who has two thousand a year (two thousand pounds, we can suppose, though the referent of the expression isn't mentioned) and lives well enough, with all his daughters. But those daughters are in potential financial trouble since, eventually, the estate that produces that income will go to a distant male relation on whom "it had been entailed." In fact, "two thousand" is made to seem like a lot of money to us, not just "comfortable" but what we might consider "rich." This is just the beginning of Austen's nuanced and detailed analysis of class differences in the town, not just between rich and poor but also those within those larger groupings, so that even what might seem like an unimportant difference between Bingley's and Bennet's fortunes gets its full analytic weight.

And what does it mean to "be in want of a wife"? Not exactly what the words might seem to say. Mr. Bingley himself doesn't show a strong desire for a wife or give any sign that he moved to the area in order to find one, as Mr. Bennet has pointed out to his eager wife. No, it seems to mean that Mrs. Bennet thinks he needs a wife whether he thinks so or not, that it is his duty to find a wife and find her locally, and that this is the common view in the community, at least among the mothers of daughters of marriageable age. As Austen explains in the book's second sentence:

However little known the feelings or views of such a man may be on his first entering a neighborhood, this truth is so well fixed in the minds of the surrounding families that he is considered as the rightful property of some one or other of their daughters.

In two sentences, Austen has presented us with a well-constructed analysis of the marriage customs of a particular group of early-nineteenth-century English country gentry. (Richard McKeon describes her construction as a "narrated civility," which I take to be near to what I have in mind here [McKeon 1979, 522].) Since it appears at the very beginning of the book, we might think of this brief analysis as a hypothesis, as the "to be proved" that appears at the beginning of a mathematical proof, with the actual proof to follow. We're shortly also given some of the complications and warnings that might accompany such a hypothesis, implicitly or explicitly: that just because people are married we shouldn't think they are necessarily well matched or happy with the result, that's not what marriage is about, though many of the participants might wish it were so; that marriage in fact takes a great variety of forms depending on the circumstances of the parties involved; even that there are marriages that turn out not to be real ones, as Elizabeth's flighty younger sister Lydia finds out when she runs off with the soldier Wickham. Thus, finally, the book delivers on this early implicit promise to provide a more or less complete analysis of shared beliefs and practices about marriage among the well-to-do of that time and place, the motivations and ambitions these situations engender in people, and the kinds of marriages that result.

In what way, exactly, is Austen's hypothesis true? One answer to that could be what Austen says about it, that it is "universally acknowledged," meaning that everyone everywhere believes it. Now we have to recognize that Austen is not simply a reporter of fact. She's a novelist, and a good one, and one aspect of her skill is that she has created a narrator, a persona who tells the story, and who has some traits and skills of her own. Here we see the narrator skillfully deploying an ironic point of view, which makes this statement of fact about the marriage customs of the county sound like she might not completely believe it, at least not in the form in which it's asserted.

So we should specify exactly what Austen, the author, means us to believe, clear away the underbrush of detail about specific characters and the layers of irony about who believes what, and then decide what the hypothesis, which initially seemed so clear and unambiguous, "really means."

Without going into all the specifics of what Austen tells us about romance and marriage in this community—because her book doesn't present and demonstrate a single hypothesis but rather a complex web of connected observations—we might say that she has given us an account of its inhabitants' customs of courtship and marriage, as her characters enact them in a setting of law and custom that is heavily influenced by complex gradations of class and wealth. (To be compared, perhaps, with anthropological accounts of marriage customs in other kinds of societies.) These customs, we might further say, force women to marry in order to have any chance of a viable, happy life, as those things are assessed in that community by their parents, their peers, and themselves.

A variety of potential "marital careers" display themselves in the unfolding story. The career that most concerns readers is that of Elizabeth, Mr. Bennet's most intelligent and favorite daughter, who eventually does marry Bingley's friend Darcy, after the two overcome many misunderstandings and obstacles. But on the way to learning her eventual fate and how it comes about, we learn about many kinds of unhappy marriages. There is, first of all, Elizabeth's own parents' long-settled compromise. Neither makes the other very happy, but they have for many years accepted that they will make the best of it. Austen gives us a full description of this misalliance (chap. 42):

> Had Elizabeth's opinion been all drawn from her own family, she could not have formed a very pleasing picture of conjugal felicity or domestic comfort. Her father, captivated by youth and beauty, and that appearance of good humour which youth and beauty generally give, had married a woman whose weak understanding and illiberal mind had very early in their marriage put an end to all real affection for her. Respect, esteem, and confidence had vanished forever, and all his views of domestic happiness were overthrown. But Mr. Bennet was not of a disposition to seek comfort for the disappointment which

his own imprudence had brought on in any of those pleasures which too often console the unfortunate for their folly or their vice. He was fond of the country and of books; and from these tastes had arisen his principal enjoyments. To his wife he was very little otherwise indebted than as her ignorance and folly had contributed to his amusement. This is not the sort of happiness which a man would in general wish to owe to his wife; but where other powers of entertainment are wanting, the true philosopher will derive benefit from such as are given.

We learn, too, what Elizabeth, their daughter, has learned about the situations of marriage as a result:

> Elizabeth, however, had never been blind to the impropriety of her father's behaviour as a husband. She had always seen it with pain; but respecting his abilities, and grateful for his affectionate treatment of herself, she endeavoured to forget what she could not overlook, and to banish from her thoughts that continual breach of conjugal obligation and decorum which, in exposing his wife to the contempt of her own children, was so highly reprehensible. But she had never before felt so strongly the disadvantages which must attend the children of so unsuitable a marriage, nor ever been so fully aware of the evils arising from so ill-judged a direction of talents, talents which rightly used might at least have preserved the respectability of his daughters even if incapable of enlarging the mind of his wife.

Here's a more extended example of the detail of Austen's analysis of these marital situations and the calculations women make in accepting them. Her best friend, Charlotte Lucas, makes a compromise similar to that of Elizabeth's parents when she marries the unlikable clergyman Mr. Collins, the cousin on whom Mr. Bennet's estate is entailed: "Mr. Collins was not a sensible man, and the deficiency of nature had been but little assisted by education or society; the greatest part of his life having been spent under the guidance of an illiterate and miserly father; and though he belonged to one of the universities, he had merely kept the necessary terms, without forming at it any useful acquaintance. . . . [He was] altogether a mixture of pride and obsequiousness, self-importance and humility" (chap. 15).

Why would Charlotte marry such a man?

[Her] whole family in short were properly overjoyed on the occasion. The younger girls formed hopes of *coming out* a year or two sooner than they might otherwise have done; and the boys were relieved from their apprehension of Charlotte's dying an old maid. Charlotte herself was tolerably composed. She had gained her point, and had time to consider of it. Her reflections were in general satisfactory. Mr. Collins to be sure was neither sensible or agreeable; his society was irksome, and his attachment to her must be imaginary. But still he would be her husband. Without thinking highly either of men or of matrimony, marriage had always been her object; it was the only honourable provision for well-educated young women of small fortune, and however uncertain of giving happiness, must be their pleasantest preservative from want. This preservative she had now obtained; and at the age of twenty-seven, without having ever been handsome, she felt all the good luck of it. (chap. 22)

So she accepted living with this man, and the many small sacrifices that required, as Elizabeth sees when she visits her:

The chief of the time between breakfast and dinner was now passed by [Mr. Collins] either at work in the garden, or in reading and writing, and looking out of the window in his own book room, which fronted the road. The room in which the ladies sat was backwards [at the back of the house, with no view out]. Elizabeth at first had rather wondered that Charlotte should not prefer the dining parlour for common use; it was a better sized room and had a pleasanter aspect; but she soon saw that her friend had an excellent reason for what she did, for Mr. Collins would undoubtedly have been much less in his own apartment, had they sat in one equally lively; and she gave Charlotte credit for the arrangement. (chap. 30)

Austen makes clear that the situation of women like Charlotte—their total economic dependence on men, fathers or husbands, and the small number of men who could meet the strict requirements for a suitable husband—did not leave a rational person like Charlotte many possibilities or choices.

There are quasi-marriages of other kinds, as we see in the miserable fate of Elizabeth's younger, willful sister Lydia, who runs off, without being married, with an army officer, George Wickham. In fact, she says she doesn't care whether they are married or not, only that she knows they will be someday. The day comes more quickly than Wickham intends. He means to leave Lydia for the Continent, where he might find a richer woman to marry, one who could pay off his large gambling debts. But he does marry her, after all, even though Austen tells us it is clear he doesn't have much affection for her. Darcy tracks them down and forces the issue by proposing to pay all of Wickham's debts immediately if he marries Lydia. He realizes that he will not have a better offer, so they marry and go off to live in the North, where Lydia's infatuation eventually cools. They live, so far as we know, unhappily ever after, received by some of their relatives, rebuffed by others.

Some other couples provide models of a reasonably happy marriage, as for instance that of Elizabeth's Uncle and Aunt Gardiner (Gardiner is Mrs. Bennet's brother) and what we are given reason to think will come of the eventual marriage of Elizabeth and Darcy. "Mr. Gardner was a sensible, gentlemanlike man, greatly superior to his sister as well by nature as by education. The Netherfield ladies would have had difficulty in believing that a man who lived by trade, and within view of his own warehouses, could have been so well bred and agreeable. Mrs. Gardiner, who was several years younger than Mrs. Bennet and Mrs. Philips, was an amiable, intelligent, elegant woman, and a great favourite with all her nieces" (chap. 25). Throughout the book, the Gardiners are a great resource for the Bennet girls: a steady source of common sense, even wisdom; friends, as well as relations, who will listen to their troubles calmly, without making hasty moral judgments; ready to help in difficult situations, as Mr. Gardiner does when he assists Darcy in settling things with Wickham; and a constant model of a marriage between equals who love and respect one another.

Finally, we have some sense of the processes by which people arrive at one situation or another. The narrative is yet another way of presenting social facts as a series of steps (of the kind we saw graphically in Whyte's 1943 analysis of the way a political favor was granted in the Italian district of Boston). As we read the stories of the various couples' finally getting together, we see how contingent the process is, how many things can go wrong, how many misunderstandings can prevent a union, how many disapproving relatives can intervene. It seems a wonder that any of the characters manage to marry, but in the end the main ones all have: Elizabeth and Darcy, Bingley and Jane, Charlotte and Collins, Lydia and Wickham. *Pride and Prejudice* is, we might say finally, an ethnography of the local situation of mating and marriage, something like the one an anthropologist or sociologist or demographically minded historian might have produced with sufficient time and a large enough research grant.

Let's take it, provisionally, that the truth being alleged is the truth of the lengthy description I've just made and that we can take the description to be summed up in, but not exhausted by, the book's first sentence about a rich man's want of a wife. Is this truth indeed universally acknowledged? Well, not universally, because Mr. Bennet's questions soon enough show that he doesn't acknowledge it: when Mrs. Bennet explains that it is her intention that Mr. Bingley marry one of her daughters he wants to know if that is Mr. Bingley's "design in settling here." Which, of course, it clearly isn't. But that isn't what she means. His deliberate misunderstanding indicates that he doesn't share the universally acknowledged view. Presumably others don't either. We might guess that Mr. Bingley doesn't, though he probably hasn't thought about it much; and, almost certainly, neither does Mr. Darcy, who, as we soon learn, is as well fixed and "in want of a wife" as Mr. Bingley but who makes it clear that he does not want a wife at all. These instances embody Austen's ironic indications that we shouldn't take her hypothesis literally.

If we can't accept the hypothesis because it is universally acknowledged, because everyone knows it's true, because to doubt it would put us in the position of the foolish dissenter in Bruno Latour's account of a scientific laboratory, the dissenter who won't believe what everyone else believes and bases their practice as scientists on—if we can't believe it for that reason, what value should we give it? Is there some other reason to believe it?

And we do want to think that it is true or accurate, that a society something like this one with its marriage customs as portrayed did exist in small-town England in the early nineteenth century. This isn't an analysis based on ideal types, and it isn't a parable that exaggerates some features in order to make certain analytic possibilities apparent—it isn't the kind of analysis whose truth we just don't care about. But we do have reason to take Austen's analysis as a reasonably realistic account of a marriage system. Scientists, and intelligent people generally, take certain kinds of reasons into account in assessing factual statements about society. They will more likely accept an assertion if, for instance, it accords with the facts as they might independently ascertain them or with the facts as they have been ascertained by the person making the assertion, given that that person has exercised all the caution and care we expect an independent finder of fact to exercise (the kinds of precautions I summed up in discussing "reality aesthetics").

Readers of the novel would know or, at least in principle though perhaps not in fact, could know what those reasons were if we actually had any independently ascertainable facts to check the hypothesis against. But we don't have any facts like that. This isn't history— "Marriage Customs in English Country Towns in the Early Nineteenth Century, as Revealed in an Analysis of County Marriage Records," or something like that—and it isn't biography, where the marriages and the circumstances of the biographical subject and his or her relations would be laid out, based on the inspection of contemporary documents, both official records and such unofficial sources as letters, diaries, and newspaper accounts.

Pride and Prejudice is a novel, a fiction, so we can't make that sort of test, not just because the material isn't for some reason available but because no such material exists. Austen made the whole thing up: all the people and incidents, the marital careers and their outcomes. Which (remember John Hersey's worries) is all right for her to do, because the legend on a novelist's license says it's all made up. The more important question is whether she made up the larger truth these people and stories illustrate, the analytic story about marriage practices at this time, in this place.

A skeptical reader could certainly reasonably say that there's no obvious reason to believe any of this analytic story, since the facts that illustrate it were after all just made up. Austen could have made up anything, with just as much warrant, couldn't she? I don't think any reader of the book, or not many, believes that. On the contrary, most readers think they have learned something about those matters, about a style of life in which women were put in that position of having to marry, having to marry someone, anyone rather than no one, on pain of living a terrible second-class life as a governess or spinster or something equally degrading and unpleasant. Serious readers of Austen do not usually, further, think that what they have learned is inferior to a well-done historical account. Different, but not inferior. Maybe even, in some ways, superior.

Superior in this way: you can know more about the day-to-day details of the process of getting married, more about the ups and downs of a relationship, more about the moments when it seemed impossible and then how something happened to make it possible again, more about the shifts in people's sometimes volatile emotions and the way their interpretations of the other person involved change, as a result of all sorts of transient and not so transient influences of friends, relatives, and "the community" and its standards as those appear in small, subtle details of daily interaction. You learn about what a sociologist might call the contingencies of a marital career.

Why do readers believe they have learned all this? What in the text gives them such assurance?

First of all, the stories and their details have verisimilitude. They accord with our experience of life, with our (conventional, of course) ideas about how people behave, how they would behave in various circumstances. The stories "make sense": the sequences of events, the causal chains, seem like the kind of thing that could happen, that does happen, the kind of linking of events that is plausible. And we understand the characters' motivations, why they might do the kinds of things they do in the book. All these are ways of saying the same thing: we apply our general knowledge of the world to the story told here and see if it measures up or if, on the other hand, it requires us to accept something we hitherto had not known or believed. That means that the author has to give us an explanation of how something we didn't think likely actually happened, and that explanation has to meet the same general test of measuring up to our experience. That's a very conservative test, and much fiction makes sure to pass it by telling familiar stories that cater to our stereotypes and prejudices.

Other fiction, however, tells us things we think we know but manipulates our expectations so as to produce an outcome we had not anticipated, and that's when we think we have learned something we didn't know before. But, of course, that a story accords with what we already believe is not a very strong test of its truth. Something else is going on: a lot of reasoning that Austen herself doesn't do, not explicitly, anyway.

To arrive at the kind of conclusions they do arrive at, those readers have to do a lot of work: noting all the details, construing their meaning, relating them to one another and to materials contained in other books, putting them together informally into syllogisms, conclusions, and moral judgments. Austen does not provide neatly labeled conclusions to which she then attaches probative evidence. Instead, she tells a story. The story contains all sorts of factual details. An attentive reader absorbs those details and thinks about them, about how they are connected to each other. What is Elizabeth's situation? What will happen to her if she doesn't marry? Look at her friend Charlotte, married to the cloddish clergyman Collins. Wouldn't Charlotte be better off single? The reader performs an analysis, weighs evidence, assesses alternative understandings, and arrives at a conclusion. That takes work. From chapter to chapter, readers guess at what will happen now, who will pair up with whom, who will overcome this latest obstacle. It's never sure that the ending will be "happy." Readers look to the clues Austen gives them and assess likelihoods, develop expectations that may or may not be fulfilled. When attentive readers put that kind of work into something, they are likely to believe the results of their own analysis; their own labor and reasoning attest to the result's validity.

When we discussed *Pride and Prejudice* in the seminar, we demonstrated in our own talk how critical readers do work like this. One skeptical participant, alert to the possibility of methodological faults that a trained social scientist could uncover in Austen's analysis, questioned whether there was sufficient factual basis for the book's generalizations. Had we been told enough, one way or the other, on this or that point? In particular, did Austen, describing English marriage practices, give too rosy and optimistic a picture of married life among the gentry of the period? It might seem so because, after all their troubles, Elizabeth Bennet and Mr. Darcy overcome many obstacles, finally get together, and appear headed for a perfectly happy future. Does that make the marriage system, after all, seem to give women decent futures, though so much in the book indicates that things were not so rosy? Can contemporary women readers find flaws in a system that would have been acceptable to women of the period?

Another participant pointed out that, on the contrary, Austen gives readers a wealth of comparative data on which they can base a more comprehensive and nuanced analysis. Specifically, the large number of unhappy marriages she pictures in great and compelling detail, discussed earlier: Elizabeth's parents; her younger sister, who gets involved with a cad, ruining her own life and disgracing the family; her friend Charlotte, married to a silly clergyman; and so on. Not to mention Austen's careful attention to the exquisitely calculated differences of wealth and social position as these affect the chances and results of marriage at many points along the class scale. In short, Austen *does* give us sufficient data to allow for a more complex analysis than the original criticism suggested. It isn't exaggerating to say that Austen not only provides the data but provides the analysis too, to a reader alert enough to grasp it.

A long and complicated novel like *Pride and Prejudice*, just like Walker Evans's photographs, contains and presents so much information about such a variety of cases that attentive readers can use the book as a source for many and varied hypotheses, beyond the ones the book itself proposes. It has sufficient material for the sort of comparative analysis that led Goffman to the idea of total institutions. That's what it means to say that such a book is rich in possibilities for sociological analysis and thinking.

So novels can have, in addition to their qualities as literary works, qualities as social analyses. In *Pride and Prejudice*, Austen has described a situation not totally unlike the one described in *Deep South*: a small community, divided by class, families, and cliques, engaged in complex dramas of social mobility. There are many differences, but they are differences in detail (race is not an issue for Austen, nor does she spend any time on the economic and political underpinning of the activities she describes). *Deep South's* analysis of Natchez resembles Austen's analysis of Meryton, though it supports its conclusions by adding up many instances of similar kinds of events while Austen uses specific events, crucial in the lives of their protagonists, to come to similar conclusions, or to lead us to them. Realistic novels of social life often offer an alternative to a similar kind of sociological analysis, one that gives more detail of the processes involved, and more access to the day-to-day thinking of the people involved. This is one reason that many sociologists have used novels as sources of sociological insight (as in Coser 1972).

Oh, yes. Austen does, after all, prove her hypotheses. At the end of the novel, we see that Mr. Bingley, the eligible bachelor who provoked her generalization about single men, really was, after all, in need of a wife, as was his friend Mr. Darcy, though neither of them was aware of his need. And by finding and marrying their wives, they show that they have been, in fact, the rightful property of two of the daughters of local families. QED.

15

Georges Perec's Experiments in Social Description

Georges Perec, the French writer, experimented with a variety of literary forms, from more or less standard novels to crossword puzzles. He is probably best known in English-speaking countries for his massive "experimental" novel *Life: A User's Manual* (*La vie: mode d'emploi*, Perec 1987), a vast panorama of interlaced stories that you are encouraged, if not required, to read in any of a variety of possible orders and that therefore might now be seen as an early, noncomputer version of hypertext (see Joyce 1995). David Bellos's excellent biography tells you all about Perec (Bellos 1993).

Perec spoke of some of his writing as "sociological" in nature, immediately specifying that as a matter of "how to look at daily life" (1985, 10), and those who have written about him have sometimes taken that seriously. Several of his works can profitably be read as a kind of social description, a "telling about society," different from the organizational analysis typified by Jane Austen's novels, though still recognizably "literary." I will speak about three of those works: *Things* (*Les choses*, Perec 1965, English translation 1990), the early novel that made him famous; *I Remember* (*Je me souviens*, Perec 1978), a book, you could say, of reminiscence; and a late experiment in pure description, *Attempt at a Description of a Place in Paris* (*Tentative d'épuisement d'un lieu parisien*, Perec 1975). Perec, to jump to my conclusion, shows us the uses and limits of writing that approaches pure description, that includes more details than we are accustomed to (see also Becker 1998, 6–83). It is another solution to the problems of summarizing details and representing "lived experience," and it exemplifies still another way of pushing some of the representational work off onto users. These works aim to describe aspects of social life that are certainly social, but not organizational in the way studies of communities or marriage customs might be, and so are less familiar to social scientists.

Les choses

Les choses tells about a young couple, Jérôme and Sylvie, twenty-four and twenty-two respectively, who work part time as psychosociologists (which we eventually understand to mean market researchers), live beyond their scanty means in a hip Parisian neighborhood, yearn for something more and better though they aren't sure what that would be—and whose friends are just like them. There is a story of sorts. Things eventually happen to them, nothing very good. But the novel's interest is not in its plot nor in a profound exploration of individual character. Its chief interest lies in its account of the way of life and the social character of just such young people, of something that was true not only of Jérôme and Sylvie but of a whole generation of people like them (and what it means to be "like them" is, of course, an important, interesting, and difficult question).

To say that *Les choses* is a generalized account of a way of life would be misleading, for the book is nothing if not detailed. It is generalized in the style an old-fashioned work of ethnology that describes the way of life of an entire people without going into variations or changes that might pop up. It describes, in minute detail, the protagonists' clothing, the furnishings of their home, their work, what they saw when they went window shopping with their friends, what they ate at home and out, what they did in their leisure time, and (importantly) their aspirations and desires and dreams. The book in fact analyzes the social situation of these young people in a theoretically and historically interesting way. I won't go into that analysis here—many others have written about it extensively (e.g., Leenhardt and Józsa 1999)—but will rather devote myself to the way Perec gives us this analysis, the literary devices he uses, devices that offer an interesting comparison to what social scientists do.

As you read the book, you notice that Perec's choice of tenses—the imperfect and the conditional—is unusual for a narrative (unusual enough in English, perhaps even more so in French). As is well known, French offers a choice of three tenses for the description of past actions. The "simple past" is used in fiction or history but not in conversation. It describes specific actions undertaken at a particular time by specified people or things: "Mary opened the door. John did the dishes. The dog howled. The rain came down." Its equivalent in all other contexts, especially more formal spoken French, is the compound tense sometimes called the "perfect," also known in French as the *passé composé*. It is a compound tense, made up of an auxiliary verb (either "to be" or "to have") and a past participle. It translates into English in roughly the same way as the simple past, although it can be literally rendered with the use of auxiliary verbs in English so that it looks just like the French—"Mary has opened the door and John has done the dishes"—though that would give a different feeling to the narration than a simple past tense. The third version of the past is the imperfect, which denotes actions that took place over some period of time or are repeated, customary, or habitual. English being as flexible as it is, this can be rendered in the same words as the more definite forms, often with an additional phrase to indicate the repeated or routine nature of the act: "John washed the dishes every night. The dog always howled when he did them."

French fiction usually tells stories in the definite past or the *passé composé*, reserving the imperfect for things that, as I said, take place over a period of time or are repeated, and for special grammatical situations, as when one action takes place while another longer action continues ("the dog barked at a noise outside while John read his book," the dog's barking put in the definite past and John's reading in the imperfect).

Perec tells much of the story of *Les choses* in the imperfect tense. He also often uses the conditional tense, usually understood to refer to things that could or would occur, given certain other conditions, occasionally (especially in fiction) to indicate a kind of make-believe or distance from specific reality. One common use of the conditional in English is as a classy way of denoting habitual or repeated, or at least common, actions: "Jean would go to the corner newsstand every morning to get a paper. Marie would wear her heavy black coat in colder weather. The cat would stretch out in the sun on a warm afternoon." The language of, say, the famous first chapter of *Les choses*, written entirely in the conditional, recalls this sort of meaning to me. For a French reader, it perhaps suggests that the apartment being described is not a specific apartment, real or imagined, but a kind of imaginary, make-believe, and therefore generalized place. To me, it suggests that this was the kind of place many people would live in. The result, either way the tense is taken, is similar.

This little lesson in French grammar is necessary for an understanding of what Perec does sociologically in *Les choses*. Using the imperfect and the conditional to recount the past turns most actions and events into things that were "usually" done, things that happened not just once but often, that were repeated often, that came to be a matter of course, things that went beyond the "this happened" of everyday life—things, that is, that made up a routine and, in some sense, fundamental part of the way of life of the people in the book. They didn't just go window-shopping on a particular night during which a specific conversation took place, which in turn led to a specific consequence. No. They went window-shopping in the evening often, and that repeated activity reinforced their longing for things they couldn't afford. And that longing, which was not momentary but long lasting, led them to spend money they didn't have and had no prospect of getting. And that had predictable consequences too. Here's a sample:

> What was probably the most serious thing was that they were cruelly lacking in ease—not material, objective ease, but easiness, or a certain kind of relaxedness. They tended to be on edge, tense, avid, almost jealous. Their love of well-being, of higher living standards, came out most often as an idiotic kind of sermonising, when they would hold forth, they and their friends, on the sheer genius of a pipe or a low table; they would turn them into *objets d'art*, into museum pieces. They would become passionate about a suitcase—one of those tiny, astonishingly flat cases in slightly grainy leather you could see on display around Madeleine and which seem the quintessence of the alleged pleasures of lightning visits to New York or to London. They

would cross all of Paris to see an armchair they'd been told was just perfect. And since they knew their classics they would sometimes even hesitate to put on some new garment, as it seemed so important to them, for it to look its best, that it should first have been worn three times. But the slightly ritualised gestures they would make to show their approval at a tailor's, or a milliner's, or a bootmaker's shop window display only managed, most often, to make them look slightly silly. (Perec 1990, 31)

So a story is told, finally. But it is enveloped in, buried in, a cloud of things that happened routinely, repeatedly, that were the way of life of Jérôme and Sylvie. And the way of their friends' lives. Because all these descriptions insist that these two (who are the focus of the book) aren't the only ones who dream these dreams, have these apartments, buy these tchotchkes, do these jobs. They belong to a social stratum for whom this is the way life is—young people who have, they think, prospects of something better. As Perec says, "In our day and in our part of the world, more and more people are neither rich nor poor. They dream of wealth and might get rich; it is here that their troubles begin" (57).

Because there are no specific events—no "John did this and Mary did that and then this happened"—the story feels amorphous, an atmosphere more than a narrative, an aura that surrounds you rather than a journey you make. In this it strongly resembles an ethnographic description of a culture, of a way of life, of shared understandings and routine activities undertaken in accord with them. It is just what an ethnography would give us. And Perec's ethnography is complete, covering material culture, kinship and other social relations, work and technology, beliefs and values, typical careers and lives, and all the other things ethnographers are enjoined to include in a "complete" description of a culture. The account of Sylvie and Jérôme eventually seems less the story of two people about whom we have learned a lot and for whom we have come to care than a sociologist's description of a typical career—something similar to the "career" of the breakup of a couple we get from Diane Vaughan (Vaughan 1986) or of the "career" of a musician I provided as part of the overall description of an occupational culture (Becker 1973, 101–20).

It's ethnography as generalized fiction, or generalized fiction as ethnography.

Les Choses makes use of another literary/ethnographic device: the detailed listing of objects and people, especially objects. The famous first paragraph of the book is a list:

> Your eye, first of all, would glide over the grey fitted carpeting, the narrow, long and high-ceilinged corridor. Its walls would be cupboards, in light-coloured wood, with fittings of gleaming brass. Three prints, depicting, respectively, the Derby winner Thunderbird, a paddle-steamer named *Ville-de-Montereau*, and a Stephenson locomotive, would lead to a leather curtain hanging on thick, black, grainy wooden rings which would slide back at the merest touch. There, the carpet would give way to an almost yellow woodblock floor, partly covered by three faded rugs. (Perec 1990, 21)

A list without explicit, formal analysis of its contents is a potent representational device, used much more by artists than by social scientists. I'll consider it in connection with two further works of Perec that can also be thought of as a sort of representation of social life and in which it is more prominent (see Sontag 1982; Goody 1977, 74–111).

Je me souviens

I Remember (*Je me souviens*) is quite different from *Les choses*. Not a novel or story at all, it consists simply of 480 numbered paragraphs, each very short, sometimes just one line. Each one names something Perec remembers from his childhood, between 1946 and 1961, when he was between ten and twenty-five years old. He says he used a simple principle of selection: "to try to recover a memory that is almost forgotten, inessential, banal, common, if not to everyone, at least to a great many" (119, my translation). He says further: "These 'I remembers' are not exactly memories, above all not personal memories, but rather small bits of daily life, things which, in this or that year, everyone of the same age had seen, had experienced, had shared, and which had then disappeared, been forgotten; they were not worth being memorized, they did not merit being made part of History, nor to figure in the Memoirs of men of state, of mountain climbers, or of stars" (dust jacket).

Here are a few samples:

> (4) I remember Lester Young at the *Club Saint-Germain;* he wore a blue silk suit with a red silk lining.
>
> (10) I remember that a friend of my cousin Henri used to stay in his bathrobe all day when he was studying for his exams.
>
> (131) I remember the *Kon-Tiki* expedition.
>
> (143) I remember that I believed that the first bottles of Coca-Cola—the ones the American soldiers could have drunk during the war—contained benzedrine (I was very proud that I knew that that was the scientific name of "maxiton").

That's it. Four hundred eighty of those, ending with an unfinished (480), which simply says "I remember " and is followed by the cryptic note "to follow . . ." (and, on a later page still, another note that says, "At the request of the author, the publisher has left, following this work, some blank pages on which the reader can note the 'I remembers' which the reading of these will have, it is hoped, provoked"). The book also contains a complete index of names, places, and titles of movies, books, and musical pieces mentioned in the text. Again, its interest seems to lie in its evocation of a way of life.

No narrative in the novelistic sense here. The arrangement of the 480 reminiscences in *Je me souviens* may not be random (though there is no guarantee that it isn't), and there might be a progression from one to the next that would generate some kind of narrative tension, but I didn't find any. The only character is the young Perec, whose life is being recalled by an older Perec. But there is nothing personal in it, nothing "emotional," unless we count his pride in knowing the scientific name of *maxiton*. Nothing in the book conveys a sense of drama or suspense or wonder as to how it will all turn out. Nothing "happens," things are just there.

There's no beginning and no end and no story and no narrative and, certainly, no analysis. A lot of synthesis is left to the reader to do. As you read, you sense that you are being challenged to find a pattern. Perec will not tell you what it is, and it's not clear that there are any clues in the arrangement of the items.

Instead, the book's intention seems straightforwardly historical and ethnographic. Its distinctiveness shows up more clearly if we compare it to the work Perec modeled it on; he says, in a preliminary note, that "the title, the form, and, to a certain degree, the spirit of these texts are inspired by Joe Brainard's *I Remember* (Brainard 1975 [1995])". Some of the distinctive character of Perec's book becomes clear when we look at Brainard's.

Perec says that Brainard inspired him "to a certain degree," and that qualification is right. The title is certainly the same, and the format—short paragraphs of reminiscence—is similar. But the differences are substantial. Brainard's paragraphs connect to one another. One reminiscence of a schoolteacher is likely to be followed by several others. The "I remembers" are often real stories, small anecdotes with a beginning, middle, and end.

And the qualification is certainly necessary with respect to "the spirit" of the work. Brainard's book is true autobiographical reminiscence, full of stories of what happened to this young gay artist in his childhood, his early sexual experiences, the new life he found in New York, a social, sexual, and artistic world he could never have imagined in his hometown of Tulsa, Oklahoma. Brainard appears in the book as a major character. His sensibility dominates its pages. His memories are not isolated traces of things anyone could and would have seen. On the contrary, they are the story of what he personally saw and felt (even though many others might have had similar experiences), what he noticed that others would have missed, his own experiences of sexual experimentation with boys and girls, his own sexual fantasies and embarrassments. And not only what he did but the things he wanted to do but didn't have the nerve for. The short paragraphs don't just describe what happened, what was there, they also depict his reaction to what happened and was there. He remembers not only having an erection at the swimming pool but how embarrassed he was when it wouldn't go away. He tells of men he found attractive, of his masturbatory fantasies. The book is effusive, extravagant, overflowing.

There is a lot about art but almost nothing about politics. There is a lot about sex but not much about places. When you finish it, you know a lot about Brainard and the world of artists and writers he moved in, and something about the world of Christian-Sunday-school

Tulsa he grew up in. But not a lot about the general political and popular culture of the country, or his part of it, during the period he's writing about (and you don't have much sense of the period; none of the names are, say, those of generals or politicians, though there are plenty of movie stars).

Perec's book, though there are some similarities (both he and Brainard, in one of the few overlaps, remember the Kon-Tiki expedition), is very different. It tells no stories of sexual awakening or embarrassing moments. With few exceptions, it deals only with public places and people and events (and the exceptions, like the item about the man who stayed in his bathrobe all day when he studied for exams, though they are not public, are not very personal). Perec's reactions to things don't enter into it. The book does not list the new, exciting things a migrant to the Big City saw. Instead it lists ordinary everyday things that anyone who lived in Paris after World War II saw, or at least what any male of a certain age and class would have seen, noticed, and perhaps remembered in later years as part of the background of his ordinary life.

It lists what people who participated in the daily, public life of the city would have seen: the buses and the Metro, the places where you bought food, the movie houses and other places of entertainment, the sports figures a young man would have been interested in. If the someone involved was a little adventurous and on the lookout for cool things to do, as Perec was, he would also remember Lester Young, Duke Ellington, Sidney Bechet and other American jazz players (including lesser-known ones—I was surprised to see the name of Earl Bostic, an alto saxophonist who was never a major figure, though good enough). If he was interested in literature, he would remember the names of such well-known writers as Michel Butor and Alain Robbe-Grillet and where they were born. If he was that much of an intellectual, he would also remember political figures and causes: Caryl Chessman (the by-now obscure focus of an anti–capital punishment campaign in California) and Lee Harvey Oswald, among the Americans listed in the index. But none of these would have been memories peculiar to Perec. On the contrary, they would have been what everyone like him remembered or, perhaps better said, could be reminded of.

Even if these things and places and people were exciting, as they surely must have been to a young, intellectual, somewhat politically engaged French Jew who had escaped being sent to the camps, as so many like him had been; even if American jazz and rock and roll and black artistic activity came as a promise of another kind of life; even if May 1968 and Biafra and the other great political events occasionally mentioned remind the reader that there were exciting things going on—even with all that, the style is dry, unexcited, listing things and people and events but not commenting or reacting, just remembering. And remembering things that are surely trivial right along with those that aren't: Lester Young's blue silk suit and its red lining, the birthplace of the actress Claudia Cardinale, that Dr. Spock once ran for president of the United States. I mean, so what?

Well, so what indeed? It adds up. The whole is more than the parts. Lester Young plus Claudia Cardinale's birthplace plus the names of Disney's Seven Dwarves (like everyone else, Perec remembers some, though not all, of them) plus 1950s fashions (it was chic for a while to wear shoelaces instead of a tie around your neck) plus the French transcription of the Russian word for crayon—all that adds up to a very palpable sense of what people had in their heads, people like Perec, lots of people, and of what they saw and read and heard about and talked about.

There is, oddly enough in so short a book, a very complete index, which unassumingly encourages you not to read the book linearly but to skip around and read it in any old order, as Perec's readers were encouraged to read *Life: A User's Manual*. (Many of the entries, by the way, meant nothing at all to me, since I didn't know who the people were: "I remember Dario Moreno" may or may not mean a lot to a French person of Perec's generation, maybe to many other French people, maybe to some American readers, but it didn't mean a thing to me until I looked up the name on the Internet and found out he was a French film star of the 1950s and 1960s. It does, however, add to the sheer bulk of the memory bank invoked by the book.)

I have somewhat overdrawn the differences between Perec's and Brainard's books. These are substantial, but there is some overlap. Brainard includes many of the kinds of items Perec includes—movie stars, for example—but not all of them; politics is a notable absence. It's a little as though Perec had thrown away about 80 percent of what Brainard includes, pared the content down to just what was public and widely shared, and left out everything personal and emotional. It's a big difference. Brainard is campy and gossipy. His book portrays a culture by portraying a specific life and body of personal experience. You can figure out from that something about the occupational and artistic culture and social organization in which that life and experience could occur. Perec's book, spare, lean, depicts something more amorphous but no less real, the cultural background of everyday life against which the more specific understandings that make up culture operate. It's not part of French or American or jazz culture that Lester Young should wear a blue silk suit with a red silk lining, but it is a fact of all those ways of life that he did and that some people noted that and knew it as what was happening. It's not a crucial part of U.S. or French culture that Disney's Seven Dwarves had the names they did, but they did have them and most people knew (most of) them. And all that is part of the body of reference and detail that plays some part in what we call cultural life, though I don't think we have a good idea of what that part is.

Here's what Perec says about that: "[These memories] return, some years later, intact and minuscule, by chance or because you tried to remember them one night, with friends: it was something you'd learned in school, a champion, a singer or a starlet who had had a big success, a song that was on everyone's lips, a hold-up or a catastrophe that made one of the papers, a best seller, a scandal, a slogan, a fad, an expression, a piece of clothing or a way of wearing it, a gesture, or something even more insignificant, inessential, completely banal, miraculously torn out of its insignificance, found again for a moment, exciting for a few seconds an impalpable little nostalgia" (dust jacket of Perec 1978).

A social scientist might want to say that such shared moments of remembering make up the glue that holds a generation together and perhaps make it capable of some kind of collective action that would otherwise be unavailable to its members.

Tentative d'épuisement d'un lieu parisien

A third work, *Attempt at a Description of a Place in Paris* (Perec 1975), belongs to a larger unfinished body of such description that Perec intended to make of a dozen sites in Paris, visiting each one once a year, always in a different month, so that at the end of twelve years he would have a complete description of each place over the entire year. The descriptions in this small book are, like the entries in *Je me souviens*, quite ordinary: what's to be seen from the vantage points he occupies on the Place St. Sulpice, lists of the letters and numbers that appear on various signs and trucks, descriptions of the people he sees from his seat in the café, of the buses that go by, of the pigeon flock that periodically takes off from its perch on the gutter of the *mairie*. Here is a sample (my translation):

> In a magnificent ensemble, the pigeons fly around the Place [St. Sulpice] and return to roost on the gutters of the town hall.
> There are five cabs at the taxi stand.
> An 87 [bus] goes by. A 63 goes by.
> The bells of St. Sulpice begin to ring (for the hour, no doubt).
> Three children being taken to school. Another apple-green *deux-chevaux*.
> The pigeons fly around the place again.
> A 96 goes by, stops at the bus stop (St. Sulpice stop); Geneviève Serreau gets off and goes down the rue des Canettes; I call to her, rapping on the cafe window and she comes over to say hello to me.
> A 70 goes by. [And so on.]

The only narrative here is that of Perec the observer sitting on a *terrace* in Place St. Sulpice looking at what there is to see, and the fragmentary narratives of what he sees, the people walking, the buses moving, the pigeons flying.

It reminds me of James Agee's similarly detailed, although more focused, descriptions of material objects and events in *Let Us Now Praise Famous Men* (Agee and Evans [1941] 1988). It also reminds me of John Cage's composition for solo piano *4'33"*, in which a pianist, in full concert attire, comes on stage, sits at the piano, puts a stopwatch on the music rack and starts it, waits that length of time, gets up and leaves. Cage meant to make listeners aware of the sounds that occur when no official "music" is being played.

Perec describes the commonplace, the quotidian . . . . In fact, as I try to generalize what he's done in this little book, I find myself increasingly tongue-tied, as though there were no other way to represent it than just to repeat what he wrote and list what he has already described, and that isn't helpful.

As you read Perec's descriptions, you increasingly succumb to the feeling (at least I do, and I think others would and do as well) that this is important, though you can't say how. If we social scientists don't have ideas and theories about it, we ought to. A very large layer of such stuff—buses going by, people putting up umbrellas, pigeons flying, letters on the sides of trucks—surrounds us all the time. We become aware of it when something is "out of order," when the pigeon shits on our head, when someone puts up an umbrella and it isn't raining, when a bus appears going the wrong way down a one-way street. Sociological common sense tells us that just such events remind us of what we take for granted and rely on as the conditions under which we carry on our ordinary lives. When those conditions aren't satisfied, we know that "something is wrong," which is as fundamental a social and emotional belief as I can think of.

A further interest of this book is the running account of Perec's difficulties in keeping up the description, because it is not an even-handed systematic account of anything. Buses figure a lot in these pages, but they come and go. Sometimes there are long lists of which bus just passed and whether it was full or not. But then he gets tired of that and turns away from the street, or just stops mentioning buses for a while. He gets interested in the pigeons and what sets off their sudden collective departures from the *mairie* gutters. But that doesn't hold his attention for long either. In fact, the book is, in a way, a lesson in the impossibility of the kind of aimless description Perec aimed at, and so it's a lesson in how and why investigators have to focus their attention on something.

Is Perec a Sociologist?

No, Perec is not a sociologist, though you could make that case. He seems to have known something about the sociology business, the American version of which invaded France in the 1950s and 1960s. One of the funnier things in *Les choses* is its description of the little tricks of the sociological interview as it was then and usually still is practiced, e.g., the lengthy pause that lets the interviewee know the interviewer isn't yet satisfied, wants to know more.

But leave that aside. Perec wasn't a professional sociologist, but he must certainly have meant to describe French society or some layer of it at a particular historical moment. (As I noted earlier, he says that one of the four categories into which he divides his work is "sociological." He includes in this group the three texts considered in this chapter.) And he did that in the two ways I've delineated. To generalize those two ways, we might say that they are different versions of the same strategy: to characterize a culture and way of life, both the relevant beliefs and their coordinate activities, by the accumulation of formally unanalyzed detail. In *Les choses* he does it by telling a story as though it were a collection of things that routinely happened; in *Je me souviens* and *Tentative* he does it by simply accumulating details of the public facet of collective life, rigorously excluding everything that is private, personal, and emotional, leaving only the surface. But what a surface!

The sociology in these works does not come from telling a story whose narrative conveys a social analysis. None of these three works tells a story in a conventionally novelistic way. There's no sense of necessary progression, a narrative unfolding, deep analysis of individual character or feeling, or social structure and the imperatives of its unfolding.

We ("we" here referring to sociologists first but also to all the critics and cultural analysts who do this) often speak of literary works as having value as renderings of social life, as describing in novelistic detail particular people and events that can be taken as embodying some kind of truth about not just those people but people like them, and some sort of general truth about events like those. We can view *War and Peace* as telling us, through the specifics of the story and the characters, something about war as a social phenomenon. *Bleak House,* and the story of Jarndyce vs. Jarndyce it relates, can be supposed, not least because Dickens insisted that it did, to embody a "truth" about the British legal system of the day, its incompetence and venality and injustice. More subtly, the very structure of the narrative can embody the organizations and tensions of the society it describes and in which it was made. The Brazilian critic Antonio Candido excels in readings that make such features of a novel explicit (Candido 1995).

Neither of these is quite what I mean here. With Perec, you don't participate in the emotional life of the characters or identify with them. Nor do you get a serious analytic rendering of major social institutions, which is such a mainstay of realistic fiction. Perec is not a model for sociological thinking and writing in those more or less conventional ways.

These three works embody, instead, three different ways of using literary devices to talk about matters of interest to social scientists, three methods social scientists might use themselves in their own tellings about society. *Les choses* is the nearest to conventional social analysis. You leave the book with a strong sense of what life was like for a whole stratum of society, for people of a certain kind, a certain class, a certain age and marital condition. We can compare it to more or less standard social science ways of telling about these aspects of social life (compare it, for instance, to anthropologist Robert Redfield's account of "the little community as a typical biography" (Redfield 1956, 50–65). The other two books simply do something social scientists don't do very well, give accounts of mundane experience— what Perec refers to, in the introduction to the description of Place St. Sulpice, as "to describe what's left: what isn't usually noted down, what isn't noticed, what has no importance: what happens when nothing is happening, just the weather, people, cars, and clouds" (Perec 1975, 12, my translation; see also Becker 1998, 95–98). All three books, each in a different way, rely on detailed "raw description" as a fundamental device by which "reality" is given to the reader.

I don't mean, by treating these works as protoethnography, to say that they aren't primarily, after all, literary works, with the potential of all the other virtues such works can possess. But let's, for the moment, bracket that and think about them as the sociology Perec himself said they were. (An author's notions about his own work may not be, as people sometimes say, "privileged," but that doesn't mean we should ignore them.)

It's not obvious where this stuff "that's happening when nothing is happening" fits into a social scientist's grid of the subject matter of a social scientific discipline. But this strategy overlaps more than a little with what at least some kinds of social scientists set out to achieve: the description of what a group of people interacting and communicating under particular historical circumstances have produced as a body of shared knowledge, understanding, and practice—what is usually called culture. Further, it goes some way toward producing a representation of what is sometimes referred to as the "lived experience" of people, though that expression is so vague as to be vacuous. But if it means anything at all, it must refer at least to this kind of "what everyone knew and felt" in a particular historical and social juncture. The part Perec calls our attention to is the part that seems "unimportant," not worth remarking on, not (certainly) worth making theories about.

Social scientists insist on evidence for what is proposed to them as social description and analysis. They want, not unreasonably, to have things proved. Perec, unsurprisingly, never alludes to the question or problem of "proof." But it will certainly come to a reader's mind to ask whether life was really like that in Paris at that time for people like that. Would I see the same kind of things if I sat in the Café de la Mairie at Place St. Sulpice? Or is Perec just a nut, imagining things that never happened? Perec cops out on this question, in a note following the main text of *Je me souviens:* "When I evoke these memories of the postwar period, they refer, for me, to an epoch belonging to the realm of myth: which explains that a memory can be 'objectively' false: thus, in 'I remember' n° 101, I remember correctly the famous 'Musketeers' of tennis, but only two of the four names I mention (Borotra and Cochet) actually belonged to that group, Brugnon and Lacoste being replaced by Petra and Destremeau, who became champions later" (1978, 119).

But he gives the reader plenty of reason to think that it probably was just like that or pretty much like that. To begin with, the note I just quoted confesses to an error of fact that makes no difference at all to the accuracy of *Je me souviens* as an account of a culture. What is important, as a cultural fact, is that the names of tennis stars would be part of what a somewhat knowledgeable person wanted to know, part of what E. D. Hirsch, Joseph Kett, and James Trefil called "cultural literacy" (1987). Whether Perec got the names right is no more important than if he had gotten the names of Disney's Seven Dwarves right. But the confession shows readers that Perec cared about accuracy on such matters (though not, of course, enough to change the names to the correct ones!) and thus to establish his reliability.

Most of the things mentioned in the book, however, are matters of public record, warranted in the way that Hans Haacke's similar citations from the public record in his conceptual artworks are, so well known that most readers will not be learning anything they didn't know. Rather, the book reminds readers of what they already know and of how, taken together, what they know constitutes some kind of cultural and social whole. This whole, however, is not easily characterized. It doesn't have the kind of cohesion, at least not obviously, that social scientists like to ascribe to a culture, a similarity or interlocking or affinity of the parts to one another that might enable an observer to characterize the culture with one of those apt summary phrases social scientists so love, as we might say that a society is "industrializing" or is characterized by the "Puritan ethic" or is "Dionysian" or "Apollonian."

Les choses is a somewhat different case. When it came out (I am indebted to Jacques Leenhardt's "postface" to the French edition for the account of the French critical reaction) in 1965 and won the prestigious Prix Renaudot, it provoked a lengthy critical discussion as to whether it could be properly called a novel or was, in fact, sociology. Critics noted that there was no real characterization, no emotion, no espousing of values, none of the things that were routinely expected in novels in postwar France (and, of course, not just there or then). Instead, there was a description of a society coming to be dominated by material consumption, a society in which, exactly, *things* were coming to shape people's lives in a way and to a degree not known before. These details did add up in a way that allowed that sort of summary description. And some of the heated critical discussion of the book had to do with whether that description was true or not, the argument attesting to how seriously the novel was taken as a description of France at that time.

As in the other two works, there are plenty of details. But now it is not the accuracy of the details that is in question, it is their representativeness. Jérôme and Sylvie live in a way whose details French readers could recognize—they knew those rugs and lamps, and all the other stuff, material and immaterial, that the two surrounded themselves with. But is that all there is? Weren't there other things to be included? Couldn't we say something that would relieve the harshness of what readers and critics took to be the implied verdict on that way of life? This is a problem of representation that occurs in all sorts of projects, from photographic work that seems to be "one-sided" (see the repeated criticisms of Robert Frank's photographic book *The Americans* as "biased") to sociological reports whose subjects complain that there were other, nicer things that could have been added that would have given a different overall picture.

All these considerations, finally, leave us to wonder whether every kind of social description does not have two aspects: a desire to show and a desire to explain. Perhaps it is the tension between these two that holds every kind of social analysis in place.

16

Italo Calvino, Urbanologist

Perec's sociological experiments have a lot in common with conventional sociology. Though they are clearly literary works, they look more than a little like something a sociologist (an imaginative one) might have done. Jane Austen's novels, though they tell a story the way novels do, just as clearly mean to show us a way of life in the kind of detail and with the kind of generalized understanding we might find in an anthropological or sociological monograph. Not so with Italo Calvino, whose later works, so avant-garde in intention and execution, make no pretense to a faithful description of any social organization or situation, not even the background noise that Perec made his province. But he was up to something we should be interested in, especially in *Invisible Cities* (1974a).

Calvino's prose is justly famous. The accumulation of unexpected detail, the vivid and unexpected imagery, and the alliterative listing of objects, people, and their properties continually create unforeseen pleasures. It is not to ignore Calvino's literary achievements that I call attention to another aspect of his work.

Calvino belonged to the Parisian literary group OULIPO (Ouvroir de Littérature Potentielle), another of whose well-known members was Georges Perec. Perec, remember, thought that about a quarter of his work could be classified as "sociological," a description of social reality that contained, even if implicitly, social theories or, at least, the raw materials for such theories. Calvino's book on cities, with a little imagination, can be seen as a far more "theoretical" style of sociology. And we profit if we renounce quibbling about calling such weird stuff sociology and just see what it has to tell us. *Invisible Cities* shares the features of those representations I characterized earlier as not true but featuring analyses that are nevertheless worth attention. Specifically, it belongs to the subdivision of that genre I called parables, though the segments are much shorter than Antin's story of the air-starved country.

Invisible Cities is, on the surface, a series of conversations between an aging Kublai Khan and a young Marco Polo. Khan sees that his empire has grown so vast that it cannot be effectively governed, that it is "an endless, formless ruin," and only in Polo's accounts of his travels can he see "the tracery of a pattern so subtle it could escape the termites' gnawing." "Kublai Khan does not necessarily believe everything Marco Polo says when he describes the cities visited on his expeditions," but he listens attentively to the fifty-five short descriptions of cities. So do we.

Polo describes each city by focusing on some dominant characteristic of its geographical situation, its building arrangements, its social practices, or much more subtle matters, occasionally explicitly indicating the major consequence of that dominant trait. So he first describes Diomira: "The special quality of this city for the man who arrives there on a September evening, when the days are growing shorter and the multicolored lamps are lighted all at once at the doors of the food stalls and from a terrace a woman's voice cries ooh!, is that he feels envy toward those who now believe they have once before lived an evening identical to this and who think they were happy, that time" (1974a, 7).

The language is evocative, even erotic ("a woman's voice cries ooh!"), and there is pleasure enough in that. Perhaps we needn't add anything sociological. But the accumulation of fifty-five such descriptions leaves the reader feeling that there is something here beyond the layering of evocative images, that the book's title says it is about cities because Calvino wants to tell us something about cities. He said as much in a talk given to students at Columbia University but not included in the English-language version of the book and not easy to find (though it is presented as a preface to both the Italian and French editions, which is why I have translated the quotes that immediately follow from the French, even though there is somewhere an English original written by Calvino himself):

> No city is recognizable in *Invisible Cities*. All these cities are invented; I gave each one a woman's name. The book is composed of short chapters, each being the pretext for a reflection which applies to every city or to the idea of the city in general. . . . (Calvino 1974b, i)

> I don't think that the book evokes only an atemporal idea of *city*, but rather that there is developed here, sometimes implicitly, sometimes explicitly, a discussion of the modern city. Some urbanist friends of mine said that the book touched different aspects of their problematic, and that is not by chance since the background is the same. And the metropolis of "big numbers" does not appear only at the end of the book: even what seems to be the evocation of an archaic city makes sense only if you think and write about it keeping in mind the city of today. . . .

> What is important to my Marco Polo is to discover the secret reasons which have led people to live in cities, reasons which would be relevant even if there were [no contemporary urban crisis]. (v–vi)

What cities is he telling us about? For the most part, not real cities, not thinly disguised versions of Paris or London or New York, but in many cases cities that could not exist at all, not if we take the descriptions literally, though perhaps they could if they are seen as metaphors. But even so, some of the cities described do seem to resemble recognizable cities. Esmeralda, made up of both streets and canals, is easily taken as a semirealistic version of Venice, though the observations Polo makes about it are perhaps not what we would expect. (Real cities of the past and present are named in the later conversations of the two men, and even imaginary cities of literature and myth. So San Francisco and New Atlantis are evoked in their talk and in Khan's perusal of his fabulous atlas.)

Where are the cities located? Polo presumably travels all over the known world, but during his lifetime far fewer places were known or existed than in centuries to come. The cities are often identified as being on seacoasts or the edges of deserts and seem, from the descriptions of people and objects, to be mainly in Europe and parts of Asia, not, probably, in the Americas.

Calvino warns us to beware of names, but the names have a flavor: romantic, vaguely Mediterranean, vaguely old-fashioned, almost all ending in vowels that are, in English and the Romance languages, feminine in feel and grammar.

When are the cities located? Since Marco Polo is describing them to Kublai Khan, they presumably date from their era, the late thirteenth century. Much of the voluptuous detail of the descriptions of the cities is congruent with that. But some isn't, especially later in the book, where we read, disconcertingly, about garbage trucks and cars and airports and cranes and bulldozers and other contemporary machinery.

One clue to what Calvino wants to tell us about cities lies in the subdivisions of the book. The fifty-five descriptions consist of eleven groups of five cities each, under a variety of tantalizing headings: "Cities and memory," "Cities and desire," "Cities and signs," "Thin cities," "Trading cities," "Cities and eyes," "Cities and names," "Cities and the dead," "Cities and the sky," "Continuous cities," "Hidden cities." These are interleaved in a complicated numerical order whose meaning is not apparent and which I suspect is a typical OULIPO creation: a systematically arbitrary arrangement of the work's parts (but see the discussion in Calvino 1974b, ii–iii). Each names a heading under which things can be said about cities and surprising features called to our attention. Some features are mundane physical facts, some point to ways people respond to cities, some are fanciful "what ifs" that challenge our belief in some ordinarily unquestioned feature of social life.

Calvino means us, as he told the Columbia students in 1983, to think that these cities in some senses, but not others, transcend time. This idea appears explicitly from time to time in the conversations of Khan and Polo. For all the specific detail of Polo's descriptions, they do not embody or allude to a specific historical period or real place (in the way, say, that Max Weber's analysis of the Protestant ethic relates to a specific historical time and place) but rather describe "the tracery of a pattern so subtle it could escape the termites' gnawing."

We think that Calvino is, after all, telling us something important about cities because we can extract generalizations about urban life from his parables. Each calls our attention to something intrinsic to the organization of city life, some dimension along which cities, or people's responses to them, vary. These features will be found in all cities. They will not all have the same water distribution system, for instance, but they must all supply their people with clean water and dispose of dirty water (the description of Armilla [1974a, 49–50] focuses on this feature of urban organization). How they do it will be related in some intelligible way to other features of the city's life.

Making such generalizations is the normal work of urban sociology. We compare cities along such dimensions as population size and components, geographical structure, "problems," even such intangibles as "culture" and "tradition" (Molotch et al. 2000). We might say, not intending to demean his work by talking about it in this prosaic scientistic way, that Calvino adds some new variables to these standard operations, new dimensions along which cities can fruitfully be compared, even though sociologists have not done so in the past—or have not done so systematically. The new dimensions are embodied in the stories Polo tells Khan and in their discussions of them.

Calvino's Methods

Calvino explains the method of constructing his theory of city life in eighteen dialogues between the emperor and the traveler which explore theoretical and epistemological problems of social science by talking about the status of the descriptions of cities Polo is presenting to Khan. As we listen to the two argue, we see the advantages and disadvantages of each possibility, as well as the impossibility of definitively choosing among them. The dialogical format (see chapter 12) encourages this indeterminacy. We aren't reading a treatise that comes to a conclusion but rather a discussion in which alternatives are considered, weighed, tried out, rejected, surpassed, returned to. The dialogues explore but do not resolve the methodological problems of how to understand a city. The agreements and disagreements of Khan and Polo serve dramatic and characterological purposes as well as "scientific" ones. But they certainly are remarks on problems of method that continue to worry social scientists.

Khan and Polo recognize the empirical basis of knowledge. They are subtle about this. On the one hand, they know that our ideas shape our facts. We see what our ideas prepare us to see. On the other hand, you can't control facts by manipulating ideas; facts are recalcitrant and will not be just any damn thing we want them to be. So the specifics of the cities Polo describes are not just things he could invent to suit himself. They are what they are, and any general ideas we hold must be congruent with them. As Khan tells Polo: "From now on I shall describe the cities and you will tell me if they exist and are as I have conceived them" (Calvino 1974a, 43). Khan's descriptions will undergo an empirical test.

They discuss the connection between the specific case and the general rule, between the description of a specific city, real or imaginary, and some general proposition about how cities are organized and function, about their histories and eventual fate. This too is a standard and perennial problem of social science method.

They recognize that, as I have already noted, Polo's descriptions imply dimensions of urban life that must be accounted for in the description of any city. Here I go beyond what is explicit in the text of their talk. It may be useful to think of these as "problems" that cities have to solve. The city of Fedora, for instance, preserves its multiple possible futures as tiny crystal globes in a museum. This reminds us that every city has multiple possible futures to which it responds. Any specific city will have its own way of dealing with these potential futures: it might preserve its futures, suppress them, ignore or forget them. "Our futures" are present, one way or another, in all cities.

Each specific city description implies at least one such dimension, and the full set of Polo's descriptions implies a large number of such dimensions. Since there are many possible ways for a city to deal with each dimension, the number of potential combinations is enormous. It's a problem in combinatorial mathematics.

These analytic possibilities can be thought of in several ways. You can say that knowing this general set of dimensions, you know all you need to know. Every place is just a version of the general law. Khan says, "And yet I have constructed in my mind a model city from which all possible cities can be deduced. . . . It contains everything corresponding to the norm. Since the cities that exist diverge in varying degree from the norm, I need only foresee the exceptions to the norm and calculate the most probable combinations" (69).

Polo proposes an alternative: a model "made only of exceptions, exclusions, incongruities, contradictions. If such a city is the most improbable, by reducing the number of abnormal elements, we increase the probability that the city really exists. So I have only to subtract exceptions from my model, and in whatever direction I proceed, I will arrive at one of the cities which, always as an exception, exist. But I cannot force my operation beyond a certain limit: I would achieve cities too probable to be real" (69).

This makes understanding cities like chess; once you know the rules and laws, that's all you need. But, Khan worries, that's too abstract, leaves too much out; chess just leaves you with a piece of wood, a chessboard. Polo immediately points out that there is a lot to know about a piece of wood.

Or you can say that once you know one city well, that's all you need because the generalizations about all the other cities are contained in it. When Khan asks why Polo never mentions Venice, Polo says, "Every time I describe a city I am saying something about Venice. . . . To distinguish the other cities' qualities, I must speak of a first city that remains implicit. For me it is Venice" (86).

That is, we discover new dimensions of city life by comparing specific cities. When we look at multiple cases, the familiar case is the contrasting background that makes new features and dimensions visible. Conversely, trying to understand the unfamiliar and strange awakens you to aspects of the familiar until then unnoticed. This occurs when we compare different cities or, historically, one city's present and past. Such comparisons provide a rationale for investigating imaginary cases, what might have been but didn't come to pass: "dead branches of the past."

Here, briefly, are some other rules of analytic method found in the dialogues between Khan and Polo:

- "From the number of imaginable cities we must exclude those whose elements are assembled without a connecting thread, an inner rule, a perspective, a discourse" (43–44).

- "Cities . . . believe they are the work of the mind or of chance, but neither the one nor the other suffices to hold up their walls" (44). That is, neither is a sufficient explanation of anything.
- Every element of the whole is important. No whole exists without parts, no parts mean anything without reference to a whole.
- Memory is changeable, not trustworthy. And yet "the form of things can be discerned better at a distance," in time as well as in space (98).
- What is the best place to describe from? It's good to be at a distance to make conclusions.
- The aim of all descriptions of cities is to know how to live, to see what is coming and accept it and become part of it or, better, see what could make life better and make those things endure. Imagining cities lets you search for the perfection that would produce happiness, and that is a major goal of the work.

Calvino's Theory of Cities

The short descriptions of cities present ideas applicable beyond the particular place Polo is talking about. We learn, for instance, that Eutropia is made up of many cities, all but one of them empty, and that its inhabitants periodically tire of their life, their spouse, their work, and then move en masse to the next city, where they will have new mates, new houses, new jobs, new views from their windows, new friends, pastimes, and subjects of gossip. We learn further that in spite of all this moving, nothing changes, since although different people are doing them, the same jobs are being done and though new people are talking, the same things are being gossiped about. This suggests a sociological generalization: in every city there is a body of social practices—forms of marriage, work, and habitation—that don't change much, even though the people who perform them are continually replaced through the ordinary demographic processes of birth, death, immigration, and emigration. *Plus ça change.*

Each of Polo's descriptions suggests such a generalization. Many of the city accounts amplify, comment on, or suggest a change in a generalization embodied in a previous vignette. After reading about

Eutropia's unchanging structure and changing population, for example, we hear about Melania, whose life can be described as a collection of perpetual dialogues, themselves the specifics of such a body of practice: "The braggart soldier and the parasite coming from a door meet the young wastrel and the prostitute; or else the miserly father from his threshold utters his final warnings to the amorous daughter and is interrupted by the foolish servant who is taking a note to the procuress" (80). People die and are born, but the dialogues continue unchanged: "[The] population renews itself: the participants in the dialogues die one by one and meanwhile those who will take their places are born, some in one role, some in another. When one changes role or abandons the square forever or makes his first entrance into it, there is a series of changes, until all the roles have been reassigned; [but the same scenes continue to be played with the same characters] even if none of them keeps the same eyes and voice he had in the previous scene" (80). Which adds to the generalization evoked by Eutropia that these unvarying practices are embodied in traditional roles and scripts—another way of saying that cities have a characteristic culture.

The remarks on Calvino's theoretical findings about cities that follow are incomplete and cursory; they do not extract all the lessons of the book. Each city could serve as the basis of an extended commentary. I will mention a few ideas and illustrate Calvino's exposition of them at length.

To repeat, an actual or imagined city represents a particular position on one or more dimensions of variation. So there is a continuum whose poles are *just* and *unjust,* on which a just city like Berenice seems to occupy a single position. But—another sociological lesson for us—each city contains, besides its apparent distinguishing characteristic, its opposite: "In the seed of the city of the just, a malignant seed is hidden, in its turn: the certainty and pride of being in the right—and of being more just than many others who call themselves more just than the just. This seed ferments in bitterness, rivalry, resentment; and the natural desire of revenge on the unjust is colored by a yearning to be in their place and act as they do. Another unjust city, though different from the first, is digging out its space within the double sheath of the unjust and just Berenices" (162).

Though one characteristic seems dominant or the only one present, the other pole of the implied continuum is there too: Berenice contains an unjust city waiting to take the place of the just one, and that unjust city in turn contains a just city waiting to replace it:

> Having said this, I do not wish your eyes to catch a distorted image, so I must draw your attention to an intrinsic quality of this unjust city germinating inside the secret just city; and this is the possible awakening—as if in an excited opening of windows—of a later love for justice, not yet subjected to rules, capable of reassembling a city still more just than it was before it became the vessel of injustice. But if you peer deeper into this new germ of justice you can discern a tiny spot that is spreading like the mounting tendency to impose what is just through what is unjust, and perhaps this is the germ of an immense metropolis. . . . All the future Berenices are already present in this instant, wrapped one within the other, confined, crammed, inextricable. (162–63)

This suggests a dialectic: justice calls forth injustice, which then calls forth justice. There is, by extension, no X that does not imply the necessary existence of *non-X*, not just in logic but in reality. Calvino embodies this in the story of Moriana, which has a beautiful face but also an ugly obverse; the two can neither be separated from one another nor look at each other.

A city may occupy these opposing poles in a regular rhythm (changing from one to the other every six months, as a city that caters to tourists might change between "the season" and the rest of the year) or historically (changing from one form to the other slowly, over centuries), but they are always both there, even though one is hidden, dormant, or invisible. Calvino often uses a spatial metaphor for the relationship of the two: one form of the city is in the sky, while the other is on earth; one is on earth, the other is underground. Sometimes, as with Valdrada, he speaks of a city and its reflection and wonders which is more valuable, the reality or the reflection.

The stories caution us not to be too quick to judge which version is more admirable. Beersheba aims for the virtues of a celestial city, but the underground city, whose characteristics the people of Beersheba try to avoid, is really the perfect one: Beersheba is "a city which, only when it shits, is not miserly, calculating, greedy" (113).

These opposites may have quasi-causal relations. Changes in one cause changes in the other. The inhabitants of Thekla are continually building. When Polo asks what plan guides their activity, they tell him to wait until sunset: "Work stops at sunset. Darkness falls over the building site. The sky is filled with stars. 'There is the blueprint,' they say" (127).

Such plans don't necessarily produce the intended result, which suggests a general suspicion of planning. The people of Perinthia also used the heavens to guide their building, "following the astronomers' calculations precisely":

> In Perinthia's streets and square today you encounter cripples, dwarfs, hunchbacks, obese men, bearded women. But the worse cannot be seen; guttural howls are heard from cellars and lofts, where families hide children with three heads or six legs. . . .
>
> Perinthia's astronomers are faced with a difficult choice. Either they must admit that all their calculations were wrong and their figures unable to describe the heavens, or else they must reveal that the order of the gods is reflected exactly in the city of monsters. (145)

The causal arrow may run in a direction we don't expect. Like those of Thekla and Perinthia, Andria's arrangements reflect the arrangements in the heavens. But not because the city mimics the heavens. No, the inhabitants assure Polo, whenever they change the city, the stars change accordingly: "The astronomers, after each change takes place in Andria (a new statue, a river port, a toboggan slide), peer into their telescopes and report a nova's explosion, or a remote point in the firmament's change of color from orange to yellow, the expansion of a nebula, the bending of a spiral of the Milky Way" (151).

Many of the cities suggest ideas about the relation of structure to function. You can, as in Dorothea, deduce everything there is to know about the city from its spatial plan: "you can then work from these facts until you learn everything you wish about the city in the past, present, and future" (9). Yet a plan need not tie functions to places: "In every point of this city [Zoe] you can, in turn, sleep, make tools, cook, accumulate gold, disrobe, reign, sell, question oracles" (34). The structure may be a sort of empty shell: "This city [Zora] which cannot be expunged from the mind is like an armature, a honeycomb in whose cells each of us can place the things he wants to remember: names of famous men, virtues, numbers, vegetable and mineral classifications, dates of battles, constellations, parts of speech" (15).

Some cities are organized as networks. Some of the imaginary cities are no more than networks: nothing is left of Armilla but its system for distributing water (now inhabited by the beings who would most appreciate that, naiads). In Ersilia relationships are represented by strings running between places: "When the strings become so numerous that you can no longer pass among them, the inhabitants leave; the houses are dismantled; only the strings and their supports remain" (76). So a city can be understood fully as a network of relationships, of which there are many kinds. Zaira consists of "relationships between the measurements of its space and the events of its past: the height of a lamppost and the distance from the ground of the usurper's swaying feet . . . the height of that railing and the leap of the adulterer who climbed over it at dawn. . . . The city . . . does not tell its past, but contains it like the lines of a hand, written in the corners of streets, the gratings of windows, the banisters of the steps, the antennae of the lightning rods, the poles of the flags, every segment marked in turn with scratches, indentations, scrolls" (10–11).

Calvino describes other city structures in images of containment. The present city of Olinda contains the Olinda-yet-to-be, the city's historical future, in embryo, as a kind of kernel or seed in its center, which then grows out (an echo of Berenice). Or, like Fedora, the city's museum contains, in crystal globes, the miniature representations of the city it might have become but did not, which are the individual dreams of its various inhabitants. The world (by which we can understand our theories about the world) must have room in it for "the big stone Fedora and the little Fedoras in the glass globes. Not because they are equally real, but because all are only assumptions. The one contains what is accepted as necessary when it is not yet so; the others, what is imagined as possible and, a moment later, is possible no longer" (32).

Calvino offers us historical theories, tracing the regular paths along which a city might develop. In a recurring theme, cities grow larger and larger until they merge into one vast, continuous city without boundaries. In one form, the city is continuous, but there are airports here and there with different names. "If on arriving at Trude I had not read the city's name written in big letters, I would have thought I was landing at the same airport from which I had taken off. . . . 'You can resume your flight whenever you like,' they said to me, 'but you will arrive at another Trude, absolutely the same, detail by detail. The world is covered by a sole Trude which does not begin and does not end. Only the name of the airport changes'" (128).

In Cecilia, the city and the countryside have merged, and everyone looks in the merger for traces of one or the other they remember and prize. In Leonia, even less happily, the city and all the other cities around it generate so much garbage that they merge at their garbage heap margins and eventually have to be bulldozed and started anew (these are some of the places where Calvino exploits anachronism).

Polo and Calvino, finally, caution us that names are misleading. This contains the larger point, of considerable theoretical significance, that things people call by the same name are not necessarily the same. (All "schools" are not alike.) A name may persist, suggesting continuity, when in fact the name is the only similarity between the old and new cities. Names convey a lot of meaning, but the meaning they convey may have little or nothing to do with a place's reality. In a reflection set off by his experience of Pyrrha, Polo says, "My mind goes on containing a great number of cities I have never seen and will never see, names that bear with them a figure or a fragment or glimmer of an imagined figure. . . . [The imagined city is still there,] but I can no longer call it by a name, nor remember how I could ever have given it a name that means something entirely different" (92).

Names (by extension, conceptually defined categories) have meaning only from the perspective of the viewer, only from a certain place. So "Irene is a name for a city in the distance, and if you approach, it changes." (125). A good reminder for social scientists so enchanted by words that they mistake them for the real thing.

Literature as Social Theory

If Calvino were a social theorist in reality, not just in my playful recasting of him and his work, he would not talk about cities as he has in this book. He never mentions, not even once, Max Weber or Émile Durkheim or Karl Marx, let alone more contemporary social theorists. He does not refer to people who wrote specifically about cities: Georg Simmel, Ernest W. Burgess, Louis Wirth. He includes no statistics on population and its components, on the economic situations or educational attainments of inhabitants. Instead he provides, through his mouthpiece Marco Polo, fanciful, poetic descriptions of cities. The descriptions do not pretend to characterize real places. They rely heavily on details, images that evoke complex thoughts and feelings, images that present general ideas metaphorically. The dialogues make the preliminary point that it is much easier to understand specific facts—detailed descriptions of cities—than abstract talk about them.

We social scientists present our ideas about urban life differently. We know what we think we gain by our habitual mode of description: precision, systematicity, the power of abstraction to create logical classes about which generalizations can be made. What has Calvino gained that we lose by the more abstract descriptive choices we make? Can we learn from him how to say things about cities that we now perhaps know but have no way of incorporating into our explicit results?

Calvino occasionally speaks of cities as made from "desires and fears" and says that what is unintelligible becomes clear if you approach cities through them. He also remarks that descriptions "smuggle" in emotion and mood, and he warns that you have to get rid of these to see, from a distance, the "real forms." Which is a problem social science methods are exactly designed to solve. Of course, since Calvino does his best to communicate mood and emotion, this is one of the many rules whose opposite must also be honored.

He communicates the nuances of mood and emotion largely through the description of small details, as in the mention, in the description of Diomira, of how "from a terrace a woman's voice cries ooh!" or in the mention, in his account of Despina, of "a windjammer about to cast off, with the breeze already swelling the sails, not yet unfurled" (17). These details do more than set a mood or elicit an emotion; they also provide information that the attentive reader uses to construct an understanding of the nature of the city being talked about.

As a result, each short description is rich in analytic possibilities, far beyond those available in the typical social science analysis. The possibility of using mood and emotion, which I have not much explored here, is just one such potential enrichment. Each detail could be, for the right reader, the taking-off place for the analysis of an area of urban life. The woman crying ooh! will push some readers to consider the erotic aspects of urban life (as do many other parts of the book). The windjammer about to set sail might provoke an exploration of forms of travel, of the way the modes of transportation available in a city condition its possibilities and our views of it. Despina "displays one face to the traveler arriving overland and a different one to him who arrives by sea" (17). Because literary descriptions contain many details capable of such expansion (as did Walker Evans's photographs discussed earlier), they make possible comparisons that provide the analytic distance Khan and Polo sometimes want. Paradoxically, the close-up, detailed look leads to distance.

This stands in direct contrast to urbanologists' desire for clearly defined concepts that let them assign a city to this or that category, to say that this or that feature is dominant or characteristic, so as to produce a definitive analysis. The social scientist's unambiguous concepts produce unambiguous results. The literary description trades clarity and unidimensionality for the ability to make multiple analyses of the multiple possibilities contained in one story.

The analyses that most resemble this way of doing analytic business are the sort of rich ethnographies Geertz praised as "thick description" (Geertz 1974). People who use that method typically know that they are doing something right but have trouble specifying what kind of right thing they are doing. The comparison with Calvino's method gives us a more concrete idea of what that is.

Calvino (unlike Perec) never spoke of what he did as sociology (though his talk to the Columbia students suggests that perhaps he would not have denied the charge), but we can look to his work for clues to how to free ourselves from the tyranny of conventional forms. There is more to say than our forms let us say and more to think as well. Calvino is a source we can draw from.

Finally . . . .

I've tried hard not to preach or moralize and, give or take a few minor slips, think I've succeeded. That doesn't mean that I don't have any convictions. By way of a conclusion, here they are.

I'm convinced that there is no best way to tell a story about society. Many genres, many methods, many formats—they can all do the trick. Instead of ideal ways to do it, the world gives us possibilities among which we choose. Every way of telling about society does some of the job superbly but other parts not so well. You can't maximize everything. Grownups have already learned this, but a lot of us forget it and get very righteous when it comes to methods of telling the story.

That's not to say that no differences exist between ways of telling about society. Defenders of science will want to ask, whose map would you rather have: a trained cartographer's or one made by your friend who lives in the next county? To which I would have to reply: it depends. Depends on what I need the map for. If it's to get to my friend's house, I'd rather have his with all the local landmarks drawn in. For calculating urban statistics, the cartographer's. Specialized scientific representations are made for specialized scientific purposes, and most people, most of the time, don't have those purposes in mind. When people are doing science, they need all the apparatus of science, but for more homely, everyday uses they might not. So I'll agree that scientific representations are very good for the uses scientists and others put them to. But I'll insist that there are other purposes for which they may not be the best. Remember the young Englishman whose scientifically drawn map hadn't told him about the hill he had to climb to get to his motel. There's a lot of that.

I'm convinced, further, that everyone involved in the production and use of representations of society plays a part in the final product, and I'm especially convinced that the users of representations play a crucial role. No matter what the makers of representations do, if the users don't do their part, the story doesn't get told, or doesn't get told as the story the makers intended.

Representations contain varying amounts of detail and information. Some makers tailor their report to contain just what is necessary to make users accept the case they want to make. Others include a lot of other information a user might consider necessary, might make minimal or semiconscious use of or ignore altogether. Every user doesn't have to use everything, it's up to them. Imagine a dimension ranging from the carefully constructed argument of a scientific journal article, which gives users just enough to judge and accept what the maker proposes, to the more inclusive content of a well-constructed documentary photograph (like the photographs Walker Evans made to explore the differing ways of being a woman in the United States in the 1920s and 1930s).

Now imagine a second dimension. One pole consists of representations that allow, and often absolutely require, users to do a lot of interpretive work and give them material they can use to investigate a large number of ideas, even some the maker didn't have in mind at all. At the other pole, some representations, stingier in what they provide, do their best to restrict the user's interpretive possibilities to the one the maker had in mind.

The universe of representations of society contains innumerable possible ways of doing this work and dividing it between makers and users. I'm convinced that contemporary social science has crippled itself by imposing strict limits on the permissible ways of telling what researchers find out about the things they study. The formulaic nature of journal articles leaves no room for "extraneous" detail or multiple interpretive possibilities that other modes of presenting what we know allow, encourage, or even require. Academic books leave more room for authors and publishers willing to take some chances (though the risks involved don't amount to anything very great).

Makers working in other worlds of representation making, especially in the arts, have their own professional and organizational environments to deal with, which can be just as restrictive. Every such world has its "right ways" of doing things, and people who don't use them take a chance with their careers and reputations. Artists can be criticized for acting too much like social scientists—critics complained that Georges Perec was writing like a sociologist, that Hans Haacke's work was sociology rather than sculpture. And social scientists who use unusual methods or ways of telling get criticized for not being "scientific." For social scientists, the archaic ways referees and editors judge work submitted to them for publication makes it difficult for them to even use such "unusual" devices as Tukey's box-and-whisker diagrams, let alone use visual materials or formats that look like, heaven forbid, "art." The resulting conservatism weakens the social sciences and work in the arts equally. We have a bad case of "it was good enough for Grandpa and it's good enough for me."

This book testifies to the possibilities that we, as participants in collective enterprises devoted to exploring and telling about society, have been ignoring. I'm convinced we should stop ignoring them and start using, all of us in whatever fields we happen to be in, the resources that already exist.

Can it be done, despite the heavy hand of organizational constraint, most clearly embodied in the editorial practices of journals, the standards of judgment used by university tenure committees, the curators and critics and theater directors and film studios that sit around saying no? Of course it can. The works I've relied on as examples show that it can be done. That's what mathematicians call an existence proof. More simply, anything that has been done can be done. (See, also, the discussion here and there in Becker, Faulkner, and Kirshenblatt-Gimblett 2006.)

I've preached my sermon. Like every preacher, I hope the congregation listens, but I'm not too hopeful. It would be nice to be proved wrong.

References

Agee, James, and Walker Evans. [1941] 1988. *Let Us Now Praise Famous Men.* Boston: Houghton Mifflin.

Antin, David. 1976. *talking at the boundaries.* New York: New Directions.

———. 1984. *tuning.* New York: New Directions.

Bakhtin, M. M. 1981. *The Dialogic Imagination: Four Essays.* Austin: University of Texas Press.

Bartow, Arthur. 1988. *The Director's Voice: Twenty-one Interviews.* New York: Theatre Communications Group.

Bateson, Gregory, and Margaret Mead. 1942. *Balinese Character: A Photographic Analysis.* New York: New York Academy of Sciences.

Bazerman, Charles. 1988. *Shaping Written Knowledge: The Genre and the Activity of the Experimental Article in Science.* Madison: University of Wisconsin Press.

Becker, Howard S. 1967. "Whose Side Are We On?" *Social Problems* 14:239–47.

———. 1973. *Outsiders: Studies in the Sociology of Deviance.* New York: Free Press.

———. 1982. *Art Worlds.* Berkeley: University of California Press.

———. 1995. "Hypertext Fiction." In *Cultura e Economia,* edited by M. Lourdes Lima dos Santos. Lisbon: Edicões do Instituto de Ciencias Sociais.

———. 1998. *Tricks of the Trade: How to Think about Your Research While You're Doing It.* Chicago: University of Chicago Press.

———. 2002. "Visual Evidence: *A Seventh Man,* the Specified Generalization, and the Work of the Reader." *Visual Studies* 17:3–11.

Becker, Howard S., and Robert R. Faulkner. 2006a. "'Do You Know . . . ?' The Jazz Repertoire: An Overview." Manuscript.

———. 2006b. "The Jazz Repertoire." Manuscript.

Becker, Howard S., Robert R. Faulkner, and Barbara Kirshenblatt-Gimblett, eds. 2006. *Art from Start to Finish: Jazz, Painting, Writing, and Other Improvisations.* Chicago: University of Chicago Press.

Becker, Howard S., and Michal McCall. 1990. "Performance Science." *Social Problems* 37:117–132.

Becker, Howard S., Michal McCall, and Lori Morris. 1989. "Theatres and Communities: Three Scenes." *Social Problems* 36:93–112.

Becker, Howard S., and John Walton. 1975. "Social Science and the Work of Hans Haacke." In *Framing and Being Framed: Seven Works, 1970–75*, edited by Hans Haacke. Halifax: Press of the Nova Scotia College of Art and Design.

Becker, Karin E. 1985. "Forming a Profession: Ethical Implications of Photojournalistic Practice on German Picture Magazines, 1926–1933." *Studies in Visual Communication* 11:44–60.

Beckett, Samuel. 1960. *Krapp's Last Tape, and Other Dramatic Pieces*. New York: Grove.

———. 1961. *Happy Days: A Play in Two Acts*. New York: Grove.

Bellos, David. 1993. *Georges Perec: A Life in Words*. Boston: David R. Godine.

Beniger, James R., and Dorothy L. Robyn. 1978. "Quantitative Graphics in Statistics: A Brief History." *American Statistician* 32:1–11.

Berger, John, and Jean Mohr. [1975] 1982. *A Seventh Man*. London: Writers and Readers Publishing Cooperative.

Bertin, Jacques. 1981. *Graphics and Graphic Information Processing*. New York: Walter de Gruyter.

Best, Joel. 2001. *Damned Lies and Statistics: Untangling Numbers from the Media, Politicians, and Activists*. Berkeley: University of California Press.

Blauner, Bob. 1987. "Problems of Editing 'First-Person' Sociology." *Qualitative Sociology* 10:46–64.

Blumer, Herbert. 1951. "Collective Behavior." In *New Outline of the Principles of Sociology*, edited by A. M. Lee. New York: Barnes and Noble.

Borges, Jorge Luis. 1964. *Labyrinths: Selected Stories and Other Writings*. New York: New Directions.

Bourdieu, Pierre. 1990. *Photography: A Middle-Brow Art*. Stanford: Stanford University Press.

Brainard, Joe. [1975] 1995. *I Remember*. New York: Penguin.

Brassaï. 1976. *The Secret Paris of the '30s*. New York: Pantheon.

Brumfield, John. 1980. " 'The Americans' and the Americans." *Afterimage* 8:8–15.

Callahan, Sean, ed. 1972. *The Photographs of Margaret Bourke-White*. New York: New York Graphic Society.

Calvino, Italo. 1974a. *Invisible Cities*. New York: Harcourt Brace.

———. 1974b. *Les villes invisibles*. Paris: Éditions du Seuil.

Campbell, Donald T., and J. C. Stanley. 1963. *Experimental and Quasi-Experimental Designs for Research*. Chicago: Rand McNally.

Candido, Antonio. 1995. *Essays on Literature and Society*. Princeton: Princeton University Press.

Capa, Cornell, ed. 1968. *The Concerned Photographer*. New York: Grossman.

Carpenter, Edmund S. 1960. "The New Languages." In *Explorations in Communication*, edited by Edmund S. Carpenter and Marshall McLuhan, 162–79. Boston: Beacon.

Chalvon-Demersay, Sabine. 1994. *Mille scénarios: Une enquête sur l'imagination en temps de crise.* Paris: A.-M. Métailié.

Chambers, John Whiteclay, II. 2003. "S. L. A. Marshall's Men against Fire: New Evidence regarding Fire Ratios." *Parameters* 33:113–21.

Churchill, Caryl. 1996. *Mad Forest: A Play from Romania.* New York: Theatre Communications Group.

Citron, Michelle, dir. 1979. *Daughter Rite.* New York: Women Make Movies.

Clifford, James. 1988. "On Ethnographic Authority." In *The Predicament of Culture*, edited by James Clifford, 21–54. Cambridge, MA: Harvard University Press.

Clifford, James, and George E. Marcus, eds. 1986. *Writing Culture.* Berkeley: University of California Press.

Cohen, Patricia Cline. 1982. *A Calculating People : The Spread of Numeracy in Early America.* Chicago: University of Chicago Press.

Collier, John, and Malcolm Collier. 1986. *Visual Anthropology: Photography as a Research Method.* Albuquerque: University of New Mexico Press.

Conquergood, Dwight. 1992. "Ethnography, Rhetoric, and Performance." *Quarterly Journal of Speech* 78:1–23.

Cook, Jno. 1982. "Robert Frank's America." *Afterimage* 10:9–14.

———. 1986. "Robert Frank." *Aperture* 24:31–41.

Cook, Thomas D., and Donald T. Campbell. 1979. *Quasi-Experimentation: Design and Analysis Issues for Field Settings.* Chicago: Rand McNally College.

Coser, Lewis. 1972. *Sociology through Literature.* Englewood Cliffs, NJ: Prentice-Hall.

Cressey, Donald R. 1951. "Criminological Research and the Definition of Crimes." *American Journal of Sociology* 56:546–51.

Danto, Arthur. 1964. "The Artworld." *Journal of Philosophy* 61:571–84.

Davis, Allison, Burleigh B. Gardner, and Mary R. Gardner. 1941. *Deep South: A Social Anthropological Study of Caste and Class.* Chicago: University of Chicago Press.

Desrosières, Alain. 1993. *La politique des grands nombres: Histoire de la raison statistique.* Paris: Editions La Dècouverte.

DuBois, W. E. B. [1899] 1996. *The Philadelphia Negro: A Social Study.* Philadelphia: University of Pennsylvania Press.

Duneier, Mitchell. 2000. *Sidewalk.* New York: Farrar, Straus, and Giroux.

Ehrenberg, A. S. C. 1981. "The Problem of Numeracy." *American Statistician* 35:67–71.

Epstein, E. J. 1973. *News from Nowhere.* New York: Random House.

Ericson, Richard, Patricia M. Baranek, and Janet B. L. Chan. 1987. *Visualizing Deviance: A Study of News Organization*. Toronto: University of Toronto Press.

Evans, Walker. [1938] 1975. *American Photographs*. New York: East River.

Ferguson, Eugene S. 1977. "The Mind's Eye: Nonverbal Thought in Technology." *Science* 197:827–36.

Fienberg, Stephen E. 1979. "Graphical Methods in Statistics." *American Statistician* 33:165–78.

Frank, Robert. [1959] 1969. *The Americans*. New York: Aperture.

Freeman, Linton C. 2003. "Finding Social Groups: A Meta-Analysis of the Southern Women Data." In *Dynamic Social Network Modeling and Analysis*, edited by Breiger Ronald, Kathleen Carley, and Philippa Pattison, 39–97. Washington, DC: National Academies Press.

Friedenberg, Edgar Zodiag. 1965. *Coming of Age in America: Growth and Acquiescence*. New York: Random House.

Geertz, Clifford. 1974. *The Interpretation of Cultures*. New York: Basic Books.

———. 1983. *Local Knowledge: Further Essays in Interpretive Anthropology*. New York: Basic Books.

Gerth, Hans H., and C. Wright Mills. 1946. *From Max Weber: Essays in Sociology*. New York: Oxford University Press.

Gitlin, Todd. 1980. *The Whole World Is Watching*. Berkeley: University of California Press.

Goffman, Erving. 1961. *Asylums*. Garden City: Doubleday.

Goody, Jack. 1977. *The Domestication of the Savage Mind*. Cambridge: Cambridge University Press.

Gopnik, Adam. 2000. "Street Furniture: The Mapmakers Who Know Where You Live." *New Yorker*, November 6, 2005, 54–57.

———. 2005. "Homer's Wars: The Simple Epics of an American Artist." *New Yorker*, October 31, 2005, 66–73.

Gottschalk, Louis, Clyde Kluckhohn, and Robert C. Angell, eds. 1945. *The Use of Personal Documents in History, Anthropology, and Sociology*. New York: Social Science Research Council.

Gove, Walter R. 1970. "Societal Reaction as an Explanation of Mental Illness: An Evaluation." *American Sociological Review* 35:873–84.

———. 1975. "The Labelling Theory of Mental Illness: A Reply to Scheff." *American Sociological Review* 40:242–48.

Gusfield, Joseph R. 1976. "The Literary Rhetoric of Science: Comedy and Pathos in Drinking Driver Research." *American Sociological Review* 41:16–34.

———. 1981. *The Culture of Public Problems: Drinking-Driving and the Symbolic Order*. Chicago: University of Chicago Press.

Gutman, Judith Mara. 1967. *Lewis W. Hine and the American Social Conscience*. New York: Walker.

Haacke, Hans. 1975. *Framing and Being Framed: Seven Works, 1970–75*. Halifax: Press of the Nova Scotia College of Art and Design.

Hacking, Ian. 1999. *The Social Construction of What?* Cambridge, MA: Harvard University Press.

Hagaman, Dianne. 1993. "The Joy of Victory, the Agony of Defeat: Stereotypes in Newspaper Sports Feature Photographs." *Visual Sociology* 8:48–66.

———. 1996. *How I Learned Not to Be a Photojournalist*. Lexington: University Press of Kentucky.

Hall, Stuart. 1973. "The Determination of News Photographs." In *The Manufacture of News: A Reader*, edited by Stan Cohen and Jock Young. Beverly Hills, CA: Sage.

Harper, Douglas. 1981. *Good Company*. Chicago: University of Chicago Press.

Hartman, Charles O. 1991. *Jazz Text: Voice and Improvisation in Poetry, Jazz, and Song*. Princeton, NJ: Princeton University Press.

Herndon, James. 1968. *The Way It Spozed to Be*. New York: Bantam.

Hersey, John. 1980. "The Legend on the License." *Yale Review* 70:1–25.

Hirsch, E. D., Joseph F. Kett, and James S. Trefil. 1987. *Cultural Literacy: What Every American Needs to Know*. Boston: Houghton Mifflin.

Hochschild, Adam. 1997. "Mr. Kurtz, I Presume." *New Yorker* 63:40–47.

Holt, John. 1967. *How Children Learn*. New York: Pitman.

Horan, James. 1966. *Timothy O'Sullivan: America's Forgotten Photographer*. New York: Bonanza.

Hughes, Everett Cherrington. n.d. "Action Catholique and Nationalism: A Memorandum on Church and Society in French Canada." Memo.

———. 1943. *French Canada in Transition*. Chicago: University of Chicago Press.

———. 1984. *The Sociological Eye*. New Brunswick, NJ: Transaction.

IVSA (International Visual Sociology Association). 2006. http://sjmc.cla.umn.edu/faculty/schwartz/ivsa/ (accessed March 16, 2006).

Jencks, Christopher. 1980. "Heredity, Environment, and Public Policy Reconsidered." *American Sociological Review* 45:723–36.

Jones, Lee. 1996. "Hollywood Realities: *Hoop Dreams*." *Jump Cut* 40:8–14.

Joyce, Michael. 1995. *Of Two Minds: Hypertext Pedagogy and Poetics*. Ann Arbor: University of Michigan Press.

Kaiser, David. 2005. *Drawing Theories Apart: The Dispersion of Feynman Diagrams in Postwar Physics*. Chicago: University of Chicago Press.

Karaganis, Joe. Forthcoming. *Structures of Participation in Digital Culture*. Durham, NC: Duke University Press.

Kawin, Bruce F. 1992. *How Movies Work*. Berkeley: University of California Press.

Kemeny, John G., J. Laurie Snell, and Gerald L. Thompson. 1974. *Introduction to Finite Mathematics*. Englewood Cliffs, NJ: Prentice-Hall.

Kluckhohn, Clyde. 1945. "The Personal Document in Anthropological Science." In *The Use of Personal Documents in History, Anthropology, and Sociology*, edited by Louis Gotttschalk, Clyde Kluckhohn, and Robert C. Angell, 78–173. New York: Social Science Research Council.

Kraft, Eric. 1994. *What a Piece of Work I Am (A Confabulation)*. New York: Crown.

Kuhn, Thomas. 1970. *The Structure of Scientific Revolutions*. Chicago: University of Chicago Press.

Latour, Bruno. 1983. "Give Me A Laboratory and I Will Raise the World." In *Science Observed*, edited by Karin D. Knorr-Cetina and Michael Mulkay. Beverly Hills, CA: Sage.

———. 1986. "Visualization and Cognition: Thinking with Eyes and Hands." *Knowledge and Society* 6:1–40.

———. 1987. *Science in Action*. Cambridge, MA: Harvard University Press.

———. 1995. "The 'Pédofil' of Boa Vista: A Photo-Philosophical Montage." *Common Knowledge* 4:144–87.

———. 1996. *Aramis: or, The Love of Technology*. Cambridge, MA: Harvard University Press.

Latour, Bruno, and Françoise Bastide. 1986. "Writing Science—Fact and Fiction: The Analysis of the Process of Reality Construction through the Application of Socio-semiotic Methods to Scientific Texts." In *Mapping the Dynamics of Science and Technology: Sociology of Science in the Real World*, edited by Michel Callon, John Law, and Arie Rip, 51–66. London: Macmillan.

Latour, Bruno, and Steve Woolgar. 1979. *Laboratory Life: The Social Construction of Scientific Fact*. Beverly Hills, CA: Sage.

Leenhardt, Jacques, and Pierre Józsa. [1982] 1999. *Lire la lecture: Essai de sociologie de la lecture*. Paris: L'Harmattan.

Lieberson, Stanley. 1980. *A Piece of the Pie: Blacks and White Immigrants since 1880*. Berkeley: University of California Press.

———. 1985. *Making It Count*. Berkeley: University of California Press.

Lutz, Catherine A., and Jane L. Collins. 1993. *Reading "National Geographic."* Chicago: University of Chicago Press.

Lynch, Michael. 1991. "Pictures of Nothing? Visual Construals in Social Theory." *Sociological Theory* 9:1–21.

Lyon, Danny. 1968. *The Bikeriders*. New York: Macmillan.

Mamet, David. 1991. *On Directing Film*. New York: Penguin.

Matza, David. 1969. *Becoming Deviant*. Englewood Cliffs, NJ: Prentice-Hall.

McCloskey, Donald. 1985. *The Rhetoric of Economics*. Madison: University of Wisconsin Press.

———. 1990. *If You're So Smart: The Narrative of Economic Expertise*. Chicago: University of Chicago Press.

McGill, Lawrence T. 1990. "Doing Science by the Numbers: The Role of Tables and Other Representational Conventions in Scientific Articles." In *The Rhetoric of Social Research: Understood and Believed*, edited by Albert Hunter, 129–41. New Brunswick, NJ: Rutgers University Press.

McGilligan, Pat, ed. 1991. *Backstory 2: Interviews with Screenwriters of the 1940s and 1950s*. Berkeley: University of California Press.

McKeon, Richard. 1979. "*Pride and Prejudice*: Thought, Character, Argument, and Plot." *Critical Inquiry* 5:511–527.

McPhee, William. 1963. *Formal Theories of Mass Behavior*. Glencoe, IL: Free Press.

———. 1967. "When Culture Becomes a Business." In *Sociological Theories in Progress*, edited by Joseph Berger Jr., Morris Zelditch, and Bo Anderson, 227–243. New York: Houghton Mifflin.

Meisalas, Susan. 1976. *Carnival Strippers*. New York: Farrar, Straus, and Giroux.

Meyer, Leonard B. 1956. *Emotion and Meaning in Music*. Chicago: University of Chicago Press.

Molotch, Harvey. 1994. "Going Out." *Sociological Forum* 9:229–39.

Molotch, Harvey, William Freudenburg, and Krista E. Paulsen. 2000. "History Repeats Itself, but How? City Character, Urban Tradition, and the Accomplishment of Place." *American Sociological Review* 65:791–823.

Molotch, Harvey, and Marilyn Lester. 1974. "News as Purposive Behavior: On the Strategic Use of Routine Events, Accidents, and Scandals." *American Sociological Review* 39:101–12.

Monmonier, Mark. 1991. *How to Lie with Maps*. Chicago: University of Chicago Press.

———. 1993. *Mapping It Out: Expository Cartography for the Humanities and Social Sciences*. Chicago: University of Chicago Press.

Motte, Warren F. 1998. *Oulipo: A Primer of Potential Literature*. Normal, IL: Dalkey Archive Press.

Newhall, Beaumont. 1964. *The History of Photography*. New York: Museum of Modern Art.

Nova. 1983. "Papua New Guinea: Anthropology on Trial." Ambrose Video Publishing (United States), first aired November 1.

Ogburn, William F. 1947. "On Scientific Writing." *Amerian Journal of Sociology* 52:383–88.

Oudshoorn, Nelly, and T. J. Pinch. 2003. *How Users Matter: The Co-construction of Users and Technologies*. Cambridge, MA: MIT Press.

Paumgarten, Nick. 2006. "Getting Where?" *New Yorker*, January 9, 86–101.

Penley, Constance. 1997. *NASA/TREK: Popular Science and Sex in America*. New York: Verso.

Perec, Georges. 1965. *Les choses: Une histoire des années soixante*. Paris: Julliard.

———. 1975. *Tentative d'épuisement d'un lieu parisien.* Paris: Christian Bourgois Editeur.

———. 1978. *Je me souviens.* Paris: Hachette.

———. 1985. "Notes sur ce que je cherche." In *Penser/Classer,* 9–16. Paris: Hachette.

———. *Life: A User's Manual.* Boston: D. R. Godine.

———. 1990. *Things: A Story of the Sixties.* Boston: D. Godine.

Polya, George. 1954. *Mathematics and Plausible Reasoning.* Princeton, NJ: Princeton University Press.

Price, Richard. 1990. *Alabi's World.* Baltimore: Johns Hopkins University Press.

Price, Richard, and Sally Price. 1995. *Enigma Variations.* Cambridge, MA: Harvard University Press.

Ragin, Charles C. 1987. *The Comparative Method: Moving beyond Qualitative and Quantitative Strategies.* Berkeley: University of California Press.

———. 2000. *Fuzzy-Set Social Science.* Chicago: University of Chicago Press.

Ragin, Charles C., Susan Meyer, and Kriss Drass. 1984. "Assessing Discrimination: A Boolean Approach." *American Sociological Review* 49:221–34.

Reid, Robert L., and Larry A. Viskochil, eds. 1989. *Chicago and Downstate: Illinois as Seen by the Farm Security Administration Photographers, 1936–1943.* Chicago: Chicago Historical Society; Urbana: University of Illinois Press.

Rich, Frank. 1985. "Wallace Shawn's *Aunt Dan and Lemon.*" *New York Times,* October 29.

Riis, Jacob. [1901] 1971. *How the Other Half Lives.* New York: Dover.

Robinson, Arthur H., and Barbara Bartz Petchenik. 1976. *The Nature of Maps.* Chicago: University of Chicago Press.

Rosenthal, Alan. 1971. *The New Documentary in Action: A Casebook in Film Making.* Berkeley: University of California Press.

———, ed. 1988. *New Challenges for Documentary.* Berkeley: University of California Press.

Salomon, Erich. 1967. *Portrait of an Age.* New York: Collier.

Sander, August, Gunther Sander, and Ulrich Keller. 1986. *Citizens of the Twentieth Century : Portrait Photographs, 1892–1952.* Cambridge, MA: MIT Press.

Schafer, Dennis, and Larry Salvato. 1984. *Masters of Light: Conversations with Contemporary Cinemaphotographers.* Berkeley: University of California Press.

Scheff, Thomas J. 1974. "The Labelling Theory of Mental Illness." *American Sociological Review* 39:444–52.

———. 1975. Reply to Chauncey and Gove. *American Sociological Review* 40:252–56.

Schelling, Thomas C. 1978. *Micromotives and Macrobehavior.* New York: W. W. Norton.

Schudson, Michael. 1978. *Discovering the News*. New York: Basic Books.

Scott, Marvin B. 1968. *The Racing Game*. Chicago: Aldine.

Sebald, W. G. 2001. *Austerlitz*. New York: Random House.

Shapin, Steven. 1994. *A Social History of Truth: Civility and Science in Seventeenth-Century England*. Chicago: University of Chicago Press.

Shaw, George Bernard. [1925] 1946. *Mrs. Warren's Profession*. In *Plays Unpleasant*, edited by Dan B. Laurence, 181–286. New York: Penguin.

Shawn, Wallace. 1985. *Aunt Dan and Lemon*. New York: Grove Weidenfeld.

Siegel, Taggart. 1990. *The Heart Broken in Half*. San Francisco: AV/ITV Center, San Francisco State University.

Small, Mario. 2004. *Villa Victoria: The Transformation of Social Capital in a Boston Barrio*. Chicago: University of Chicago Press.

Smith, Anna Deveare. 2001. *Twilight*. Los Angeles: PBS.

———. 1994. *Twilight Los Angeles, 1992 on the Road*. New York: Anchor.

Smith, Barbara Herrnstein. 1968. *Poetic Closure: A Study of How Poems End*. Chicago: University of Chicago Press.

Snow, C. P. 1959. *The Search*. New York: Scribner.

Snyder, John P. 1993. *Flattening the Earth: Two Thousand Years of Map Projections*. Chicago: University of Chicago Press.

Sontag, Susan. 1982. "Writing Itself." *New Yorker*, April 26, 122–41.

Sperber, Murray. 1996. "Hollywood Dreams: *Hoop Dreams* (Steve James, 1994)." *Jump Cut* 40:3–7.

Stasz, Clarice. 1979. "The Early History of Visual Sociology." In *Images of Information: Still Photography in the Social Sciences*, edited by Jon Wagner, 119–36. Beverly Hills, CA: Sage.

Stryker, Roy Emerson, and Nancy Wood. 1973. *In This Proud Land: America 1935–1943 as Seen in the FSA Photographs*. Greenwich, CT: New York Graphic Society.

Szarkowski, John, and Maria Morris Hambourg. 1983. *The Work of Atget*. New York: Museum of Modern Art.

Trachtenberg, Alan. 1989. *Reading American Photographs: Images as History, Mathew Brady to Walker Evans*. New York: Hill and Wang.

Tuchman, Gaye. 1978. *Making News*. New York: Free Press.

Tucker, Anne Wilkes, and Philip Brookman, eds. 1986. *Robert Frank: New York to Nova Scotia*. Boston: Little, Brown.

Tufte, Edward R. 1983. *The Visual Display of Quantitative Information*. Cheshire, CT: Graphics.

———. 1990. *Envisioning Information*. Cheshire, CT: Graphics.

Tukey, John W. 1972. "Some Graphic and Semigraphic Displays." In *Statistical Papers in Honor of George W. Snedecor*, edited by T. A. Bancroft, 293–316. Ames: Iowa State University Press.

———. 1977. *Exploratory Data Analysis*. Reading, MA: Addison-Wesley.

Turner, Victor, and Edith Turner. 1982. "Performing Ethnography." *Drama Review* 26:33–50.

Urfalino, Philippe. 1990. *Quatre voix pour un opéra: Une histoire de l'Opéra Bastille racontée par M. Audon, F. Bloch-Laine, G. Charlet, M. Dittman*. Paris: Editions Metailie.

Van Maanen, John. 1988. *Tales of the Field: On Writing Ethnography*. Chicago: University of Chicago Press.

Vaughan, Diane. 1986. *Uncoupling: Turning Points in Intimate Relationships*. New York: Oxford University Press.

Wainer, Howard. 1981. Comment. *Journal of the American Statistical Association* 76:272–75.

Watkins, Susan Cotts. 1985. "The History of Graphics in Demography." *Studies in Visual Communication* 11:2–21.

Weber, Max. 1949. *The Methodology of the Social Sciences*. Translated by Edward A. Shils and Henry A. Finch. New York: Free Press.

Weegee. 1945. *Naked City*. New York: Essential Books.

Weisstein, Eric. "Markov Process." From *MathWorld*—A Wolfram Web Resource. http://mathworld.wolfram.com/MarkovProcess.html.

White, Harrison C. 1963. *An Anatomy of Kinship: Mathematical Models for Structures of Cumulated Roles*. Englewood Cliffs, NJ: Prentice-Hall.

Whyte, William Foote. [1943] 1981. *Street Corner Society: The Social Structure of an Italian Slum*. Chicago: University of Chicago Press.

Wilson, Carter. [1965] 1974. *Crazy February: Death and Life in the Mayan Highlands of Mexico*. Berkeley: University of California Press.

Wiseman, Frederick, dir. 1967. *Titicutt Follies*. Cambridge, MA: Zipporah Films.

Zwerin, Charlotte. 1971. "Salesman." In *The New Documentary in Action: A Casebook in Film Making*, edited by Alan Rosenthal, 86–91. Berkeley: University of California Press.

Index

Lyon, Danny, 38
Lyons, Nathan, 39

M
- - - - -

Mad Forest (Churchill), 215–19
"Main Street, Saratoga Springs" (Evans), 51
Major Barbara (Shaw), 211
makers of representations: arguments and files and, 26–28; attempt to be ostensibly morally neutral, 140; challenge in organizing their argument, 31; existence of a moral community of makers and users, 135–36; filmmaker's control over users, 30; inherent attempt to persuade the user, 138–39; interpretative work done by the maker of a table, 42; photographic arrangement (*see* photographic arrangement); presence of a moral pact between makers and users, 134–36; role in telling about society, 7; scientific article author's control over users, 30; statistical data presentation, 32–35; work of making divided among makers and users, 69
making representations: arrangement of elements, 24–25; division of labor, 69; interpretation by the user, 25–26; order of images and (*see* photographic arrangement); selection of what is to be included, 20–21; standard formats, 21–23; translation/mapping of sets of elements, 21–24; varieties of social organizations surrounding representations, 137–38
Malinowski, Bronislaw, 205

Mamet, David, 8, 75, 211
Mann, Thomas, 8
maps: adequacy of degree of accuracy, 113–14; inevitability of distortions, 94; limitations of, 103; motivations for specialty projections, 95–96; as representations of society, 2–4, 5; role in telling about society, 9; usefulness dependent on intended use, 2, 285; users' desire for a flat representation, 94–95
marriage: analysis of marriage customs by Austen, 241; Austen's novel's function as an ethnography of local mating and marriage practices, 246; marriage as people in Austen's time view it, 238–40; presentation of how marriage customs play out, 242; rules example (mathematical model), 159–60; types of unhappy marriages described by Austen, 242–43
Marshall, S. L. A., 216
mathematical models: applied to symphonic repertoires, 160–61; compared to parables and ideal types, 164; described, 150, 159; marriage rules example, 159–60; reliance on identities, 162–63; reliance on knowledgeable users, 65–66; role in telling about society, 9–10; usefulness from establishing what would happen if the model were accurate, 162; users' requirement that models are accurate, 165; utility from identifying the rules of a system, 160–61; value in, 166. *See also* science
McGill, Lawrence, 58–59, 73, 75
McPhee, William, 161
Mead, Margaret, 129–30